BARBER COLLECTIBLES

A PRICE GUIDE

©1996

By L-W Book Sales
P.O. Box 69
Gas City, IN. 46933

ISBN#: 0-89538-077-3

Copyright 1996
L-W Book Sales

All rights reserved. No part of this work may be reproduced or used in any forms or by any means - graphic, electronic, or mechanical, including photocopying or storage and retrieval systems - without written permission from the copyright holder.

Published by: L-W BOOK SALES
P.O. Box 69
Gas City, IN. 46933

Printed by IMAGE GRAPHICS, INC., Paducah, Kentucky

Please write for our free catalog.

TABLE OF CONTENTS

Atomizers	197,198
Barber Bottles	310-336
Barber Catalogs & Magazines	388-393
Barber Chair Introduction	6
Barber Chairs	7-146
Barber Jackets	217-220
Barbers' Signs & Poles Introduction	221
Barbers' Signs & Poles	222-242
Combination & Mug Cases	179-183
Combs	215,216
Commercial Bottles	337-344
Costumers & Coatracks	184-186
Cuspidors	199-201
Decorated Shaving Mugs	269-309
Hair Clippers	202-205
Hones	261,262
Introduction	5
Lather Brushes	213,214
Lavatories & Washstands	175-178
Neck & Hair Brushes	210-212
Photographs	379-387
Photos and Postcard Introduction	355
Photos, Postcards, & Advertising cards	355-378
Price Guide	394-399
Price Guide Information	4
Razor, Strops, & Hones Introduction	243
Razors	244-256
Shears	206-209
Shoeshine Chairs & Rests	187-191
Sterilizers	192-196
Sterling and Plated Shaving Sets	264-268
Strops	257-260
Title Page for Shaving Mugs, Barber Bottles, Urns, & Vases	263
Urns & Vases	345-354
Wall Fixtures with Mirrors	147-174

ACKNOWLEDGMENTS

Most of the items illustrated in this book have been reproduced from the original catalogs in the original colors. We have tried to portray the correct date on each page, but a few dates have been estimated at (plus and/or minus) five years. The photographs and picture postcards were impossible to date precisely but we have attempted to place them in the correct era.

As you will see, this book is the most complete book on barbershop collectibles ever printed. We wish to thank the following people for their generous contributions to this book:

Gary Felton, Upland, Indiana and Fred Richards, Marion, Indiana

We would especially like to thank
Don and Mary Perkins
2317 N. Kessler Blvd., Indianapolis, IN 46222
317-638-4519

Without access to Don's catalogs, this book could not have been published. Don is one of the largest and most well-known barberiana collectors in the U.S. If you would like to correspond with him he would welcome your calls and letters.

So to Don, Gary, and Fred
A Big THANK YOU!!!!

PRICE GUIDE INFORMATION

All of the prices indicated within this book are very dependent upon the condition of the item involved. The following will provide brief guidelines to determine the appropriate condition of any piece noted within this guide.

All *mint* mugs and barber bottles must be bright and unfaded with absolutely no chips or cracks. Any condition less than mint will bring much less money to the seller. Occupational mugs are the most desirable among the selection of barber mugs. Silver and sterling mugs were gifts and were not generally available at barbershops.

All razors must have full blades with no nicks to be classified as *mint*. *Mint* razors must also be free of any rust or corrosion. Razor strops must be clean and pliable with no apparent cuts in the leather.

All pottery urns, vases, mugs, and other items formed from clayware could very well be worth much more if made by a well-known collectible pottery. Again, no cracks or chips- otherwise the value will be decreased significantly or will be practically undesirable.

All commercial bottles must be full and unopened to be considered *mint*. Empty bottles in similar condition which are clean and bear full labels are *near mint* and will bring *near mint* prices.

The current values as listed in this book are intended to be used as a guide only. They are not intended to set prices, which will vary from one region of the country to another. Auction prices and dealer prices often differ and are affected by condition as well as demand. Please note that the prices listed are the expressed opinion of the editor and this book is not an offer to buy or sell. Neither the author nor the publisher assume responsibility for any losses or gains that might be incurred as a result of consulting this guide.

INTRODUCTION

The age of convenience is upon us, yet it seems to spare us from many enjoyable social experiences as well as dismissing the time-consuming drudgery of generations past. The old courting ritual of a nice dinner and an evening at the cinema has been replaced by a drive to a fast-food service window after renting a videotape to take home. The Sunday family picnic brunch has been exchanged for a quick stop at the local gas station for a handful of munchies on the way home from church. No longer do the days of the barbershop entail in entertaining a throng of customers eager to bite on a new cigar while listening to the local chatter and getting his hair cut or his boots blackened. Today's barbershops are but small cubicles as compared to the eight-chair operations of the past. The boutiques and beauty salons which developed through the space age cater to women on the run, with as many or more chemicals as there is care and skill massaged into the scalp. Young men of modern day supporting their first facial growth now begin to groom themselves with the contraptions available at any drugstore, neglecting the notion to have a "professional" perform the duty. Long gone are the days when a traveler could learn where the necessities of life may be found around town by spending an hour in the local barbershop. Today, his handy grooming travel kit provides him with a clean face, yet he is still unaware of the best restaurants, stores, or taverns if that is his interest.

Alas, we have no singing quartet to croon an ode to the barbershop of the past, but collectors of today have found a place in their hearts and collections for barbershop furnishings and instruments, not to mention advertising, photographs, and anything else found in the common shop.

As good grooming developed into a preferred look for societies in civilizations long ago such as the Ancient Egyptians and Romans, styles have come, gone, returned, and changed throughout the regions and generations. The American barbershop had made it a focus to remain with whatever may be in vogue at the current time. The change in appearance and atmosphere of the barbershop throughout these active years reflected these styles and the necessity to upgrade practices in hygiene. Many antique items may be dated approximately as the instruments changed as well as the manner in which they were used. A mere photograph of an old time barbershop can fill an eager collector's eyes with envy as they gaze at the barber bottles standing side by side along suspended shelves, the plethora of shaving mugs about the room, and the razor-keen cutlery and accessories with which to whisk unbearable stubble from the faces of appreciative customers.

The task of today is discovering these old treasures, identifying them, and investigating its value, whether nostalgic or monetary. Obviously, by publishing this guide we can't ascertain nostalgic and sentimental values, but these are the forces which directly affect cash values of the current owner, whomever that may be. Thus, the values presented in this book may fluctuate depending on the region, circumstances, and disposition of the seller. Regardless, the search and discovery of barber artifacts is well worth the time and effort, and the venture will be made much easier with a copy of *Barbershop Collectibles* tucked under one arm.

BARBERS' CHAIRS INTRODUCTION

A barber chair is the essential fixture for rendering comfortable barber services to a customer. To meet the barber's needs, most were easily adjustable in height and position. Generally, barber chairs are spaced in a shop about 4 1/2 to 5 feet apart from center to center. As one patron would leave, another would soon take his place in the chair after it was briefly dusted and a clean tissue was affixed to the headrest (to prevent transmission of lice and the like).

HISTORICAL OUTLINE OF THE PROFESSIONAL BARBER

- Shaving as a regimen of hygeine began in Macedonia app. 400 BC; Egypt and Eastern countries began this tradition soon thereafter (Egypt already had combs, brushes, mirrors, and cosmetics at this time).

- Barbers rose to popularity in Greece app. 400 BC. In Rome, this occured during 296 BC according to ancient written records.

- The first organization of Barber/Surgeons was in France, 1094.

- The Journeyman Barber's Union was organized in 1887, with the first convention being held November 5th, 1887 at Buffalo, New York.

- First United States barber school founded by A.B. Moler in Chicago, Illinois, 1893.

- First of the United States to pass the barber license law was Minnesota in 1897.

- National Association of Barber Schools organized in 1927 in Cleveland, Ohio.

- Association of Master Barbers of America organized in 1924 in Chicago, Illinois; adopted Barber Code of Ethics in 1929 at convention in St. Paul, Minnesota.

ODD CUSTOMS AND SUPERSTITIONS ASSOCIATED WITH BARBERING

- Originally, only priests and medicine men would shave people due to the common superstition of being bewitched by someone who gathered the hair and utilized it in witchcraft.
- Native American Indians believed one could force his will over another if he possessed some of the victim's hair (thus, the tradition of scalping came about).
- Roman judges had Christians shaved bald before death during the years of persecution (as Jews and Christians believed of a connection between hair and the mortal soul).
- Royal messages during the Middle Ages throughout Europe would usually have three beard hairs of the King embedded within the wax on the seal.
- During the reign of Queen Elizabeth, citizens began to dye their hair in odd colors and cut their beards in a wild variety of shapes and lengths.
- Among early Jews, the beard was considered the symbol of manliness; to have it shaved or cut was considered an outrage.
- Pythagoras (Greek philosopher and mathematician) taught that the length of the hair was directly associated with the brain's inspiration and intellectual capacity.
- Alexander the Great ordered all soldiers in his forces to shave off their beards to prevent barbaric enemies from grabbing them during battle.
- Early devout Muslims saved any and all trimmed beard clippings to be buried with the owner upon his death.
- Peter the Great made shaving compulsory by imposing a stiff tax on all beards.

BARBER CHAIRS

J. Hambleton & Son, 1892 catalog page

BARBER CHAIRS

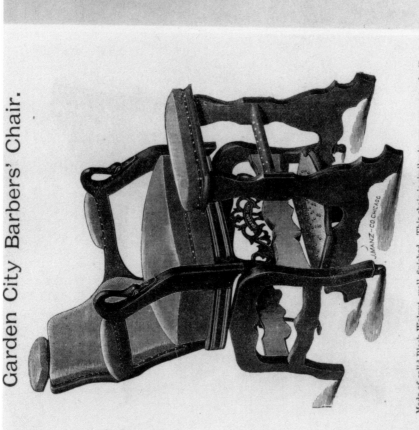

Eugene Berninghaus, 1882 catalog page.

KEYSTONE BARBERS' CHAIR.
Covered by Patents of Feb. 17th, 1880.

This chair is the prettiest, cheapest, strongest built and best chair for the money ever manufactured. So popular has this chair become that it has taxed our capacity to its utmost to keep pace with the demand for them. It is made of solid Black Walnut. The platform and cross-bar of the foot-stool are covered with sheet brass, studded with brass nails. The machinery for adjusting this chair is a new device, and is strong, simple and durable. Adjustable to every desirable position for shaving and hair cutting. The seat of the chair can be taken out.

PRICES:

Covered with Mohair Plush, Maroon, Green or Crimson, or with Moquette, . . . $30.00
Covered with Tapestry Brussels Carpet, . . . 25.00

Garden City Barbers' Chair.

Made of solid Black Walnut, well finished. This chair is similar in appearance to the No. 2; a prettier and more durable chair for the money is not made. It is adjustable to any desired position for shaving or hair cutting by the simplest device for that purpose ever invented. The platform of the foot-stool is covered with sheet brass.

PRICE:

Covered with Mohair Plush, Maroon, Crimson or Green, or with Moquette . . . $33.00
Covered with Tapestry Brussels Carpet . . . 28.00

BARBER CHAIRS

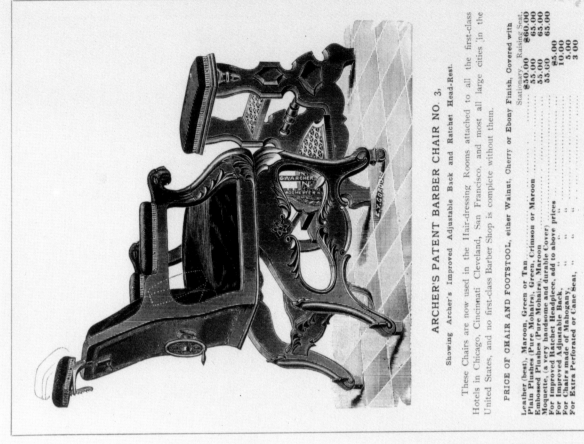

Archer Manufacturing Co., 1880 catalog page.

BARBER CHAIRS

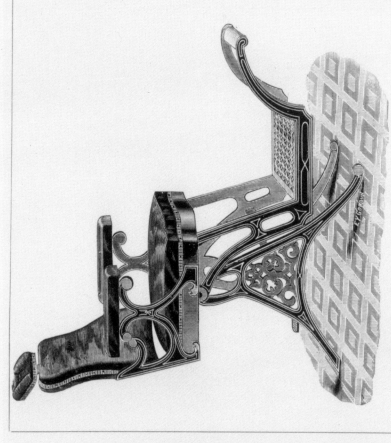

ARCHER'S PATENT ADJUSTABLE BARBER CHAIR, No. 5.
(Patented May 21, 1878.)

The above style Barber Chair is made of Iron, of beautiful design and tastily ornamented with gilding. It is adjusted to the position necessary for shaving by placing the foot on the treadle at the rear, which releases the segment and allows the seat and back to be tilted to any desired angle. As will be seen, the Chair and Foot-rest are combined, thereby making the seat a firm and strong chair. It has rollers under the front legs, to facilitate the moving of the chair about the room. It is the most handsome design, and withal the lowest priced Adjustable Barber Chair ever offered to the trade. It is well upholstered, with Steel Springs in the seat, and the best of materials, and covered with Plushes, Leather, &c., or the Seat and Back are made of cane seating, which makes it a very comfortable and cool chair for warm climates.

PRICES, EITHER WALNUT OR EBONY FINISH.

Seat and Back finished in Cane Seating	$22.00
Upholstered and Covered with Union Terries, Green or Crimson	24.00
" " " Best Tapestry Brussels Carpet, Green or Crimson	25.00
" " " Figured Plushes, Green or Crimson	25.00
" " " Leather (best), Maroon, Green or Tan	26.00
" " " Plain Plushes (Worsted), Green, Maroon or Clouded	26.00
" " " Plain Plushes (Pure Mohair), Green, Crimson or Maroon	30.00
" " " Moquette, (a handsome and durable cover)	~~36.00~~

Above Chairs fitted with an *Extra Cane* Seat and Back, which, by taking off the Upholstered Seat and Back, will fit in same place for summer use. Add to above prices for same, $7.00.

ARCHER'S PATENT ADJUSTABLE BARBER CHAIR, NO. 4.
Patented May 21, 1878.

The above illustrates our new style of Barber Chair. The Chair is made of Walnut or Maple finished as Ebony, finished in first-class style. The arms, back and seat are connected and securely fastened together by the tasty iron side arm, which is double Japanned and ornamented with gilt lines. The Footstool, as will be seen, is constructed in a similar manner, by tasty iron platform and step. The above connections are protected by Patent, issued May 21st, 1878. The above Chair is the most handsome and durable Chair for its price ever offered to the trade, the iron platform never wearing out and always looking clean and neat. This Chair is upholstered in a good and substantial manner. We can also supply it with Cane Seat and Back, making a very handsome and cool chair for warm climates.

PRICES, EITHER WALNUT OR EBONY FINISH.

Seat and Back finished in Cane	$22.00

UPHOLSTERED AND COVERED WITH

Union Terries, Green or Crimson	$26.00
Best Tapestry Brussels Carpet, Green or Crimson	27.00
Figured Plushes, Green or Crimson	27.00
Leather (best), Maroon, Green or any col'r	28.00
Plain Worsted Plushes, Green or Maroon	28.00
Clouded Worsted Plushes, Gr'n or Crim'n	28.00
Pl'n Mohair Pl'shs, Gr'n, Cr'son or M'roon	30.00
Embossed Mohair Plushes, Maroon	30.00
Moquette	~~30.00~~

Above Chair fitted with an *Extra Cane* Seat and Back, which, by taking off the upholstered seat and back, will fit in same place for summer use. Add to above price for same, $7.00.

BARBER CHAIRS

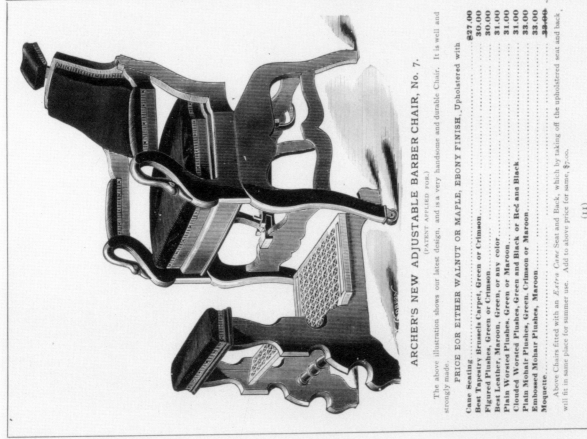

ARCHER'S PATENT ADJUSTABLE BARBER CHAIR, No. 6,
(with Open Arms.)

PRICE OF CHAIR AND FOOTSTOOL, either Walnut, Cherry or Ebony Finish. Covered with

	Stationary Seat.	Raising Seat.
Union Terries, Green or Crimson	$37.00	$47.00
Figured Plushes or Carpet, Green or Crimson	38.00	48.00
Leather (best), Maroon, Green or Tan	40.00	50.00
Plain Plushes (Worsted), Green or Maroon	40.00	50.00
Plain Plushes (Pure Mohair), Green, Crimson or Maroon	42.00	52.00
Moquette, (a very handsome and durable cover)	42.00	52.00
An Extra Patent Perforated or Cane Seat for Summer use	3.00	

Above Chairs fitted with an *Extra Cane* Seat and Back, which by taking off the upholstered Seat and back, will fit in same place for summer use. Add to above prices for same $8.00.

(10)

ARCHER'S NEW ADJUSTABLE BARBER CHAIR, No. 7.
(PATENT APPLIED FOR.)

The above illustration shows our latest design, and is a very handsome and durable Chair. It is well and strongly made.

PRICE FOR EITHER WALNUT OR MAPLE, EBONY FINISH. Upholstered with

Cane Seating	$27.00
Best Tapestry Brussels Carpet, Green or Crimson	27.00
Figured Plushes, Green or Crimson	30.00
Best Leather, Maroon, Green, or any color	31.00
Plain Worsted Plushes, Green or Maroon	31.00
Clouded Worsted Plushes, Green and Black or Red and Black	31.00
Plain Mohair Plushes, Green, Crimson or Maroon	33.00
Embossed Mohair Plushes, Maroon	33.00
Moquette	33.00

Above Chairs fitted with an *Extra Cane* Seat and Back, which by taking off the upholstered seat and back, will fit in same place for summer use. Add to above price for same, $7.00.

(11)

Archer Manufacturing Co., 1880 catalog page

BARBER CHAIRS

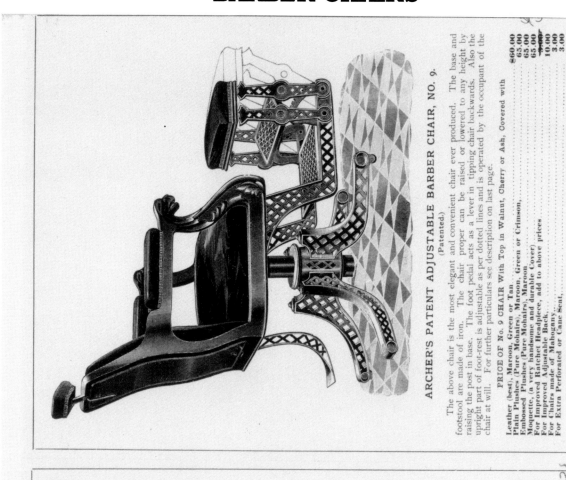

Archer Manufacturing Co., 1880 catalog page.

ARCHER'S PATENT ADJUSTABLE BARBER CHAIR, No. 8.
(PATENT APPLIED FOR.)

The above Chair is another of our late designs, and is an elegant Chair in every way. It is well made of Walnut or Maple, finished as Ebony or of any kind of wood desired.

PRICES OF EITHER WALNUT OR MAPLE, EBONY FINISH, Upholstered with

Cane Seating	$29.00
Best Tapestry Brussels Carpet	32.00
Figured Plushes, Green or Crimson	32.00
Best Leather, Maroon, Green or any color	33.00
Plain Worsted Plushes, Green or Maroon	33.00
Clouded Worsted Plushes, Green and Black or Red and Black	33.00
Plain Mohair Plushes, Green, Maroon or Crimson	35.00
Embossed Mohair Plushes, Maroon	35.00
Moquette	35.00

Above Chairs fitted with an *Extra Cane* Seat and Back, which by taking off the upholstered seat and back will fit in same place for summer use. Add to above price for same $7.00.

ARCHER'S PATENT ADJUSTABLE BARBER CHAIR, NO. 9.
(Patented)

The above chair is the most elegant and convenient chair ever produced. The base and footstool are made of iron. The chair proper can be raised or lowered to any height by raising the post in base. The foot pedal acts as a lever in tipping chair backwards. Also the upright part of foot-rest is adjustable as per dotted lines and is operated by the occupant of the chair at will. For further particulars see description on last page.

PRICE OF No. 9 CHAIR With Top in Walnut, Cherry or Ash, Covered with

Leather (best), Maroon, Green or Tan	$60.00
Plain Plushes (Pure Mohair), Maroon, Green or Crimson	65.00
Embossed Plushes (Pure Mohair), Maroon	65.00
Moquette, (a very handsome and durable Cover)	65.00
For Improved Ratchet Headpiece, add to above prices	10.00
For Improved Adjustable Back	
For Chairs made of Mahogany	3.00
For Extra Perforated or Cane Seat	3.00

The base and foot-rest of this chair can be attached to any style of top and will be sold separate or prices quoted with the top of any of our styles.

Price of Base and Footstool Complete, finished ready to attach top $22.00

BARBER CHAIRS

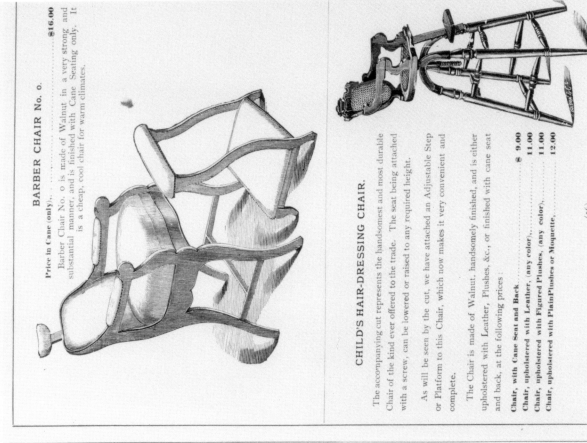

BARBER CHAIR No. 0.

Price in Cane (only), ... $16.00

Barber Chair No. 0 is made of Walnut in a very strong and substantial manner, and is finished with Cane Seating only. It is a cheap, cool chair for warm climates.

CHILD'S HAIR-DRESSING CHAIR.

The accompanying cut represents the handsomest and most durable Chair of the kind ever offered to the trade. The seat being attached with a screw, can be lowered or raised to any required height.

As will be seen by the cut, we have attached an Adjustable Step or Platform to this Chair, which now makes it very convenient and complete.

The Chair is made of Walnut, handsomely finished, and is either upholstered with Leather, Plushes, &c., or finished with cane seat and back, at the following prices:

Chair, with Cane Seat and Back .... $ 9.00
Chair, upholstered with Leather, (any color), ... 11.00
Chair, upholstered with Figured Plushes, (any color), ... 11.00
Chair, upholstered with Plain Plushes or Moquette, ... 12.00

ARCHER'S ADJUSTABLE BARBER CHAIR, NO. 10.

The above cut is inserted to show the Leg Rest turned up over the Seat. All who have seen this new Rest (for which patent is applied for) pronounce it as being not only tasty, but very convenient. When the Chair is not in use it can be thrown over the seat (as shown in cut) out of the way, leaving room to pass in front of the Chair and preventing any one occupying the Chair for other than business purposes. Also when sweeping or cleaning floor, moving the chair about, or in shipping chair this movement is very convenient.

The Leg Rest being attached to the upper part of Chair, goes with it and prevents the annoyance of the occupant shifting his position every time the chair is adjusted. This Leg Rest can be attached to any chair and will be sold separate at the following prices or be furnished with any of our Chairs in place of regular Stool without extra charge.

Price of Leg Rest covered with Carpet, Moquette or Plushes, any color to match Chairs, each $4.00

Archer Manufacturing Co., 1880 catalog page.

BARBER CHAIRS

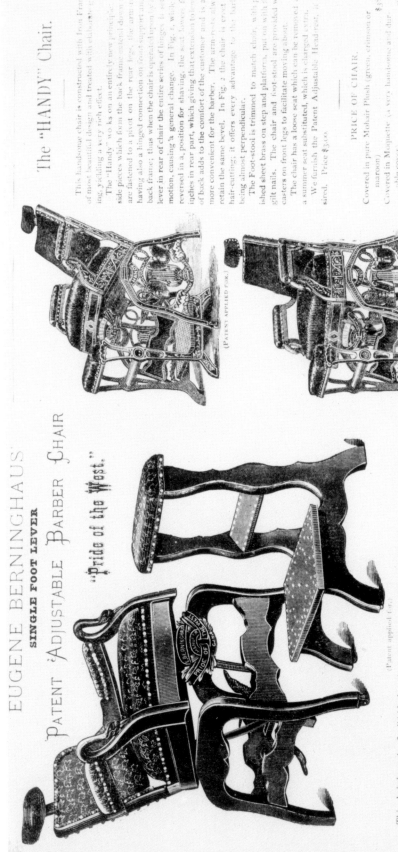

Eugene Berninghaus, 1882 catalog page.

BARBER CHAIRS

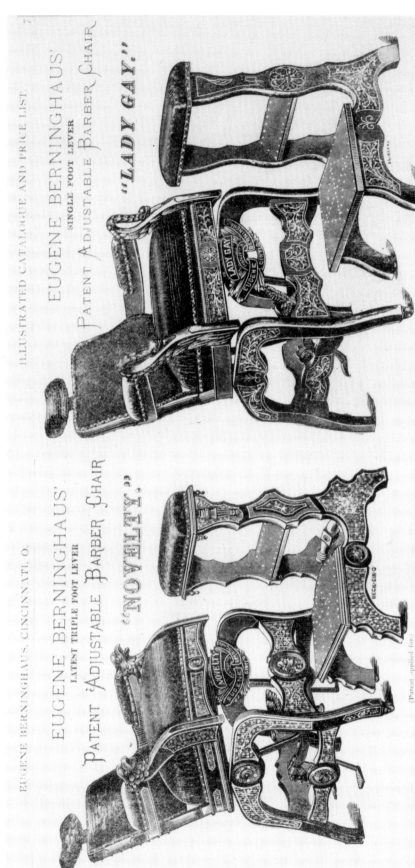

Eugene Berninghaus, 1882 catalog page

BARBER CHAIRS

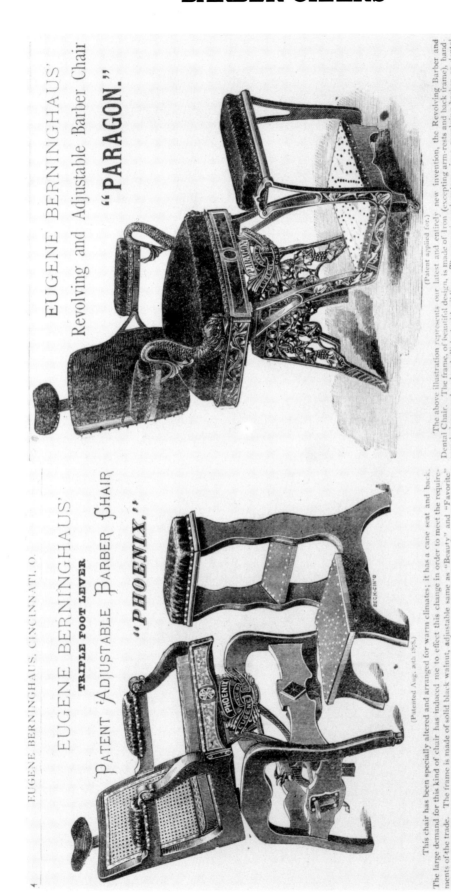

Eugene Berninghaus, 1882 catalog page.

BARBER CHAIRS

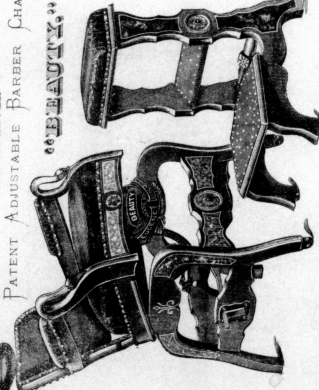

Eugene Berninghaus, 1882 catalog page.

BARBER CHAIRS

Eugene Berninghaus, 1882 catalog page.

Barbers' Chair, No. 12.

—The New Centennial Chair—

Is made of heavy black walnut, covered with the best Mohair Plush or Leather. In fact its the Smoothest Working Chair in existence.

Price. . . . $26.00

Barbers' Chair, No. 13.

Something New and a Great Saving to Barbers.

I have reversed the Ratchet Fixture so that instead of having to stoop to arrange the Chair from Hair Cutting to Shaving position, the operator can stand erect and with thumb and finger can change it instantaneously, so that with this chair after shaving a gentleman you can at once raise the back giving him great comfort while having his hair arranged. Having placed this fixture on the Centennial Chair, which is of heavy walnut, with panels deeply carved in front; back and side rails, legs elegantly moulded, with stool of solid walnut, moulded edges, both steps covered with brass, making it as complete and comfortable, and in fact as good a Barbers' Chair as ever manufactured.

PRICE:

In Good Mohair Plush or Real Leather . . . $22.00

New Patent Barbers' Chair, No. 14.

Don't pass this without paying Marked attention to the many advantages we claim for this chair. It always will be known as the **Geisse Patent Worm Wheel.** The shape is such that it reclines at an angle which makes it the most comfortable chair I have yet made ; the fixtures are highly ornamental and work with so much ease and smoothness that it would astonish the most experienced hair dresser.

We claim it to be the best Barber Chair ever placed before the hair dressing community.

PRICE:

Covered with the best Mohair Plush, Velvet, Carpet or Morocco . . . $24.00

BARBER CHAIRS

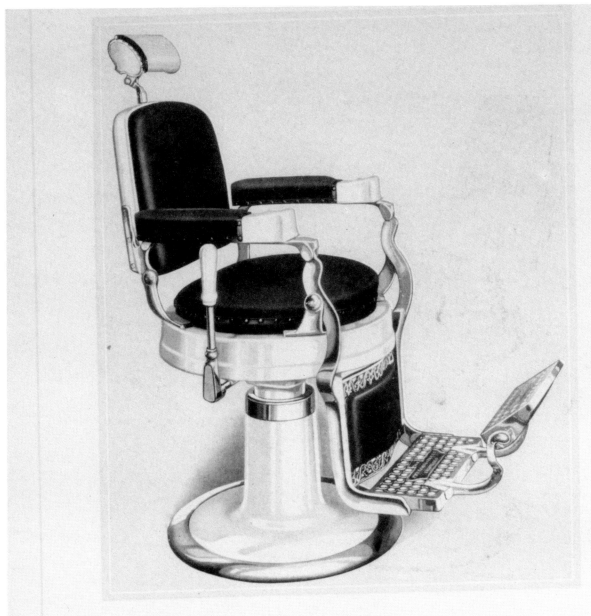

CHAIR No. 508-B

Hydraulic

Head-rest: Spring cushion. Rust-resisting polished metal. Hexagon slide.

Back: Square. Porcelain enameled rim. Leather cushion, spring construction.

Arms: Leather covered, with porcelain enameled arm caps.

Porcelain enameled arms optional.

Seat: Round. Porcelain enameled rim. Leather cushion, spring construction.

Base: Porcelain enameled, with nickeled collar.

Base ring: Solid brass, polished.

Other exposed metal parts: Nickel-plated.

Lever handle: Porcelain enameled.

Piston cover: Porcelain enameled.

Manicure attachments: In arm hinges.

Upholstering: Any color genuine leather. Black is standard.

PATENTED

Fred Dolle Inc., 1924 catalog page. (HERCULES patented chair.)

BARBER CHAIRS

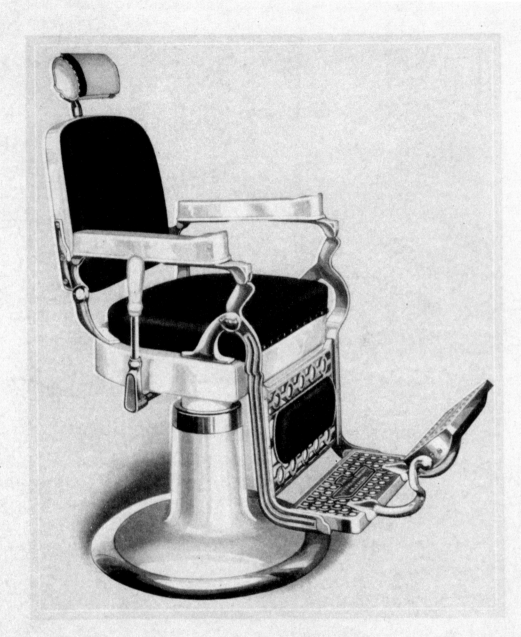

CHAIR No. 528-B

Hydraulic

Head-rest: Spring cushion. Rust-resisting polished metal. Hexagon slide.
Back: Square. Porcelain enameled rim. Leather cushion, spring construction.
Arms: Porcelain enameled.
Seat: Porcelain enameled rim. Leather cushion, spring construction.
Base: Porcelain enameled, with nickeled collar.

Base ring: Nickel-plated.
Other exposed metal parts: Nickel-plated.
Lever handle: Porcelain enameled.
Piston cover: Porcelain enameled.
Manicure attachments. In arm hinges.
Upholstering: Any color genuine leather. Black is standard.   PATENTED

Fred Dolle Inc., 1924 catalog page. (HERCULES patented chair.)

BARBER CHAIRS

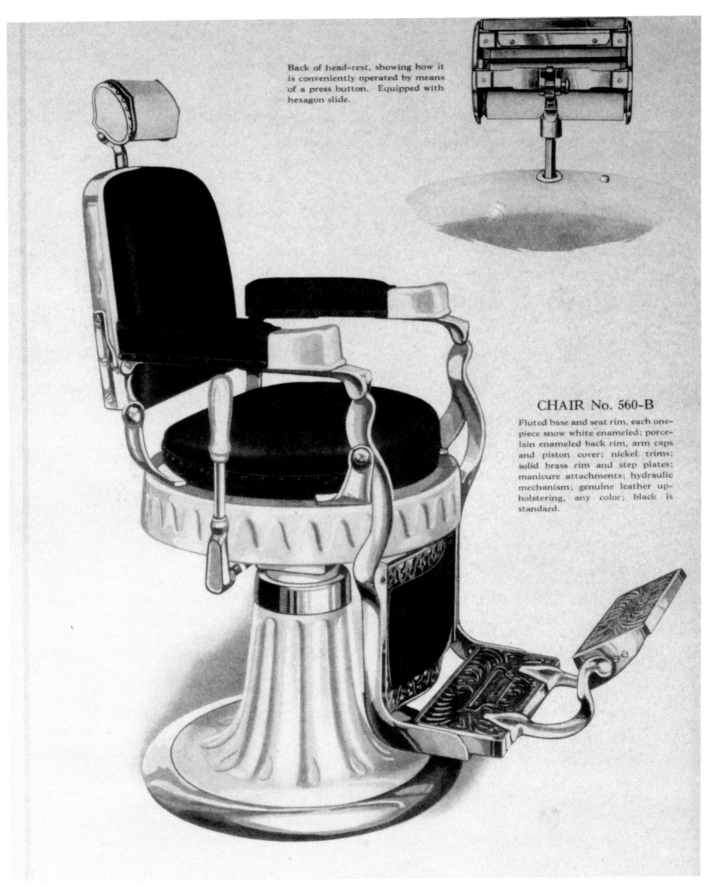

Back of head-rest, showing how it is conveniently operated by means of a press button. Equipped with hexagon slide.

CHAIR No. 560-B

Fluted base and seat rim, each one-piece snow white enameled; porcelain enameled back rim, arm caps and piston cover; nickel trims; solid brass rim and step plates; manicure attachments; hydraulic mechanism; genuine leather upholstering, any color; black is standard.

Fred Dolle Inc., 1924 catalog page. (HERCULES patented chair.)

BARBER CHAIRS

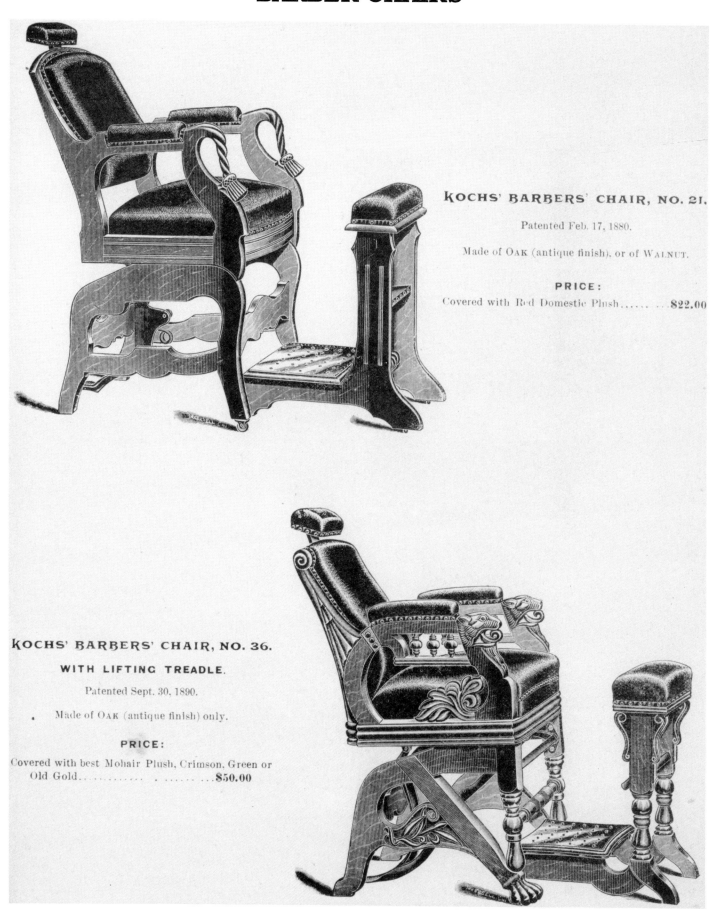

KOCHS' BARBERS' CHAIR, NO. 21.

Patented Feb. 17, 1880.

Made of OAK (antique finish), or of WALNUT.

PRICE:

Covered with Red Domestic Plush.............$22.00

KOCHS' BARBERS' CHAIR, NO. 36.

WITH LIFTING TREADLE.

Patented Sept. 30, 1890.

Made of OAK (antique finish) only.

PRICE:

Covered with best Mohair Plush, Crimson, Green or Old Gold.............$50.00

Theo. A. Kochs Co., 1897 catalog page.

BARBER CHAIRS
KOCHS' GRAND PRIZE HYDRAULIC BARBERS' CHAIR No. 2

RAISING AND LOWERING
REVOLVING AND RECLINING
SLIDING SEAT
STATIONARY ARMS

PATENTED
DECEMBER 8, 1891
JANUARY 11 - 1898
FEBRUARY 8, 1898
DECEMBER 3, 1901
APRIL 23 - 1908

Made of selected quarter-sawed oak. This chair is kept in stock in the golden finish, although we can also furnish it in English oak finish if desired. When ordering, please mention finish wanted. Upholstered with finest grain leather, green or maroon. Patent adjustable head-rest. Oxidized copper trimmings. The base is fitted with a solid cast-brass polished rim. The seat slides forward as the chair is reclined, the arms remaining stationary.

John Rieder & Co., 1912 catalog page.

BARBER CHAIRS
KOCHS' GRAND PRIZE HYDRAULIC BARBERS' CHAIR, No. 3

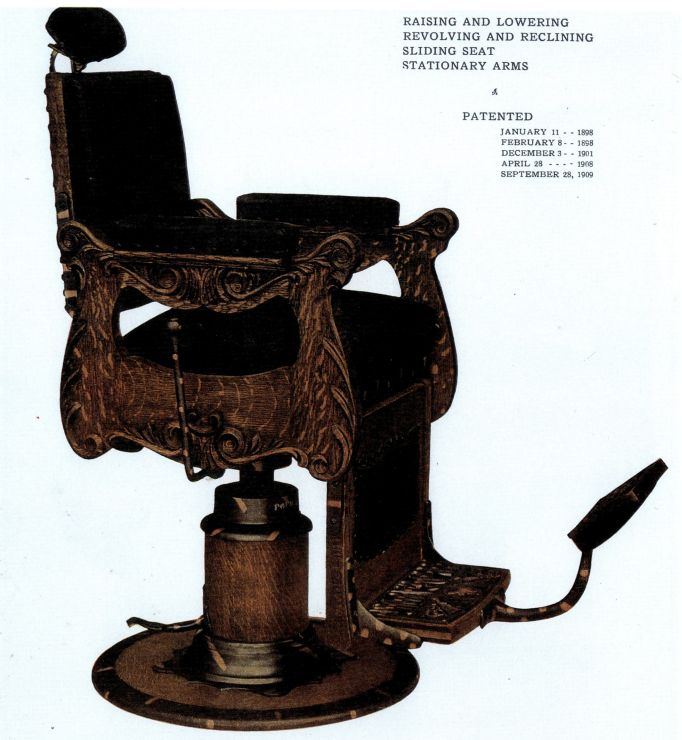

RAISING AND LOWERING
REVOLVING AND RECLINING
SLIDING SEAT
STATIONARY ARMS

PATENTED
JANUARY 11 - - 1898
FEBRUARY 8 - - 1898
DECEMBER 3 - - 1901
APRIL 28 - - - - 1908
SEPTEMBER 28, 1909

Made of quarter-sawed oak, golden finish. Upholstered with green or maroon leather. Oxidized copper finished trimmings. The improved adjustable head-rest is mounted on a steel stem which runs in a metal casing, insuring perfect rigidity. The base of this chair is fitted with a metal rim, oxidized copper finish, and is covered with quarter-sawed oak to match the chair. The seat of this chair slides forward as the chair is reclined, the arms remaining stationary. Equipped with foot-treadle hydraulic mechanism.

Price - - - - - - - - - - $57.50

John Rieder & Co., 1912 catalog page.

BARBER CHAIRS

Theo. A. Kochs Co., 1897 catalog page.

BARBER CHAIRS
KOCHS' GRAND PRIZE HYDRAULIC BARBERS' CHAIR, No. 6

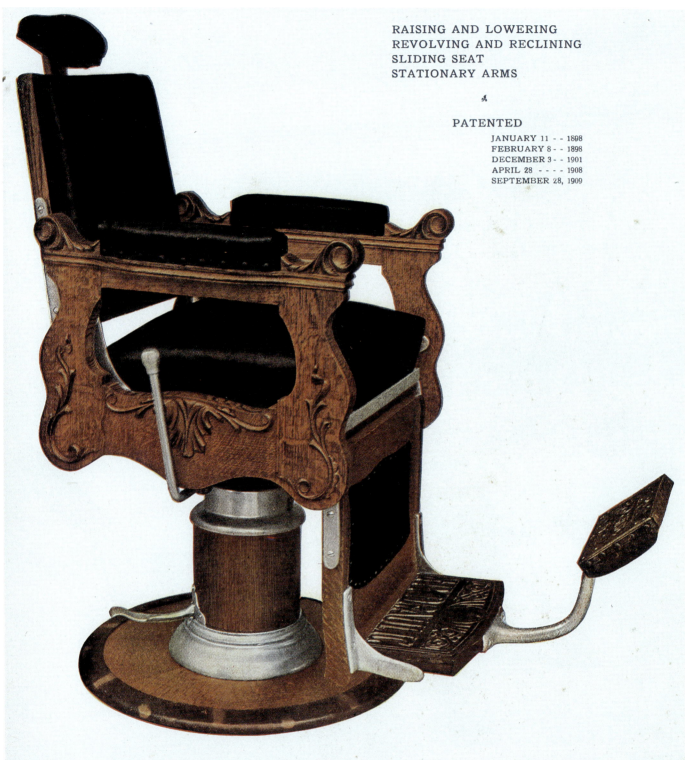

RAISING AND LOWERING
REVOLVING AND RECLINING
SLIDING SEAT
STATIONARY ARMS

PATENTED

JANUARY 11 - - 1898
FEBRUARY 8 - - 1898
DECEMBER 3 - - 1901
APRIL 28 - - - - 1908
SEPTEMBER 28, 1909

Made of quarter-sawed oak, golden finish. Upholstered with green or maroon leather. All metal trimmings highly nickel-plated, except rim upon base, which is oxidized copper finish. The base of this chair is overlaid with quarter-sawed oak. The seat of this chair slides forward as the chair is reclined, the arms remaining stationary. Equipped with foot-treadle hydraulic mechanism.

Price - - - - - - - - $52.50

John Rieder & Co., 1912 catalog page.

BARBER CHAIRS
KOCHS' GRAND PRIZE HYDRAULIC BARBERS' CHAIR, No. 10

REVOLVING AND RECLINING
SLIDING SEAT
STATIONARY ARMS

PATENTED
DECEMBER 8, 1891
JANUARY 11 - 1898
FEBRUARY 8, 1898
DECEMBER 3, 1901
APRIL 28 - 1908

Kept in stock in mahogany only and upholstered in Spanish hand-buffed leather. The crotch veneer used on the seat-frame inside and outside is of the choicest selection; it brings out to best advantage the exquisite coloring and figures on the smooth sides of the seat-frame. The base of the chair is covered with selected mahogany and is fitted with a heavy cast-brass rim. Nickel-plated trimmings. Brass heel-plate on leg-rest. The foot-board plate and foot-rest plate are also cast brass, nickel-plated. The stem of the improved adjustable head-rest is made of malleable iron, nickel-plated, and runs in a groove to hold it rigid.

John Rieder & Co., 1912 catalog page.

BARBER CHAIRS

KOCHS' COLUMBIA CHAIR, No. 12.

REVOLVING AND RECLINING.

PATENTED DEC. 8, 1891, AND JAN. 11, 1898.

Made of quarter-sawed Oak, golden finish. Upholstered with Mohair Plush, crimson, maroon or green, or with Maroon Leather; oxidized copper trimmings. Brass feet, oxidized.

PRICE, ... $35.00

Theo. A. Kochs & Son, 1899 catalog page.

BARBER CHAIRS

KOCHS' COLUMBIA CHAIR, No. 14.

REVOLVING AND RECLINING.

PATENTED DEC. 8, 1891, AND JAN. 11, 1898.

Made of quarter-sawed Oak, golden finish. Upholstered with Mohair Plush, crimson or green, or with Maroon Leather; nickel-plated trimmings. Brass feet.

PRICE, ... $32.00.

Theo. A. Kochs & Son, 1899 catalog page.

BARBER CHAIRS

KOCHS' COLUMBIA CHAIR, No. 15.
REVOLVING AND RECLINING.

PATENTED DEC. 8, 1891, AND JAN. 11, 1898.

Made of quarter-sawed Oak, golden finish. Upholstered with Mohair Plush, crimson, green or old gold, or with Maroon Leather; nickel-plated trimmings. Brass feet.

PRICE, ... $33.50

Theo. A. Kochs & Son, 1899 catalog page.

BARBER CHAIRS

KOCHS' COLUMBIA CHAIR, No. 16.

REVOLVING AND RECLINING.

PATENTED DEC. 8, 1891, AND JAN. 11, 1898.

Made of quarter-sawed Oak, golden finish. Upholstered with Mohair Plush, crimson or green; nickel-plated trimmings. Brass feet.

PRICE, . . . $30.00.

Theo. A. Kochs & Son, 1899 catalog page.

BARBER CHAIRS
KOCHS' COLUMBIA BARBERS' CHAIR, No. 17

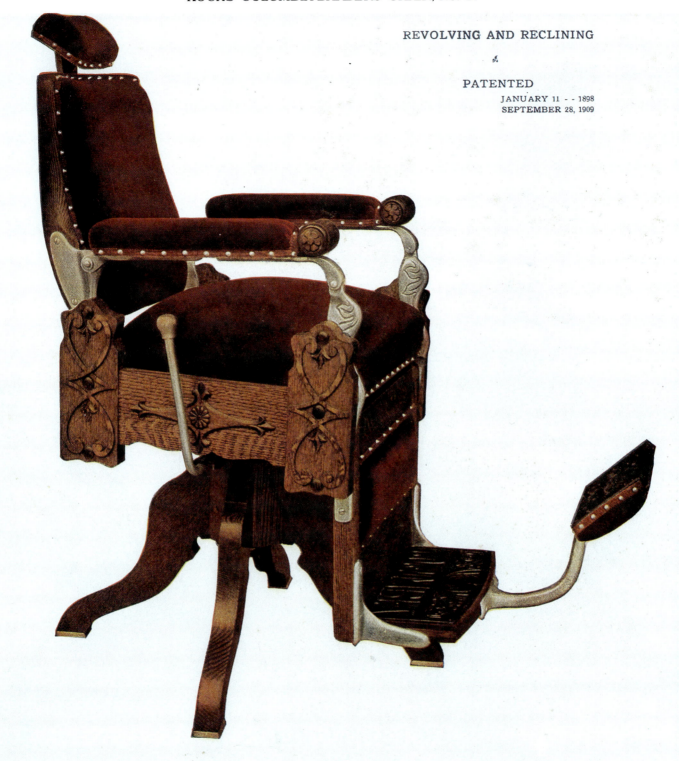

REVOLVING AND RECLINING

PATENTED
JANUARY 11 - - 1898
SEPTEMBER 28, 1909

Made of selected oak, golden finish and upholstered with green or maroon leather or with crimson or green mohair plush. Nickel-plated trimmings. Solid brass feet. Equipped with revolving and reclining mechanism controlled by one lever. The chair revolves on a ball-bearing pin, eliminating friction and wear.

Price - - - - - - - - - $32.00

John Rieder & Co., 1912 catalog page.

BARBER CHAIRS

KOCHS' COLUMBIA CHAIR, No. 19.
REVOLVING AND RECLINING.

PATENTED DEC. 8, 1891, AND JAN. 11, 1898.

Made of quarter-sawed Oak, golden finish. Upholstered with Mohair Plush, crimson or green, or with Maroon Leather; nickel-plated trimmings. Brass feet.

PRICE, ... $37.00.

Theo. A. Kochs & Son, 1899 catalog page.

BARBER CHAIRS

KOCHS' GOLD MEDAL
HYDRAULIC BARBERS' CHAIR, No. 21.

RAISING AND LOWERING. REVOLVING AND RECLINING.

PATENTED DEC. 8, 1891; JAN. 11, 1898; FEB. 8, 1898.

Made of quarter-sawed Oak, golden finish, and highly polished. Upholstered with best quality Mohair Plush of any color desired, or with Maroon or Green Leather; patent adjustable head-rest; oxidized copper trimmings. The base of this chair is fitted with solid brass rim, polished, and is covered with figured quarter-sawed Oak to match the chair. This chair stands firmly alone.

PRICE, . . . $75.00.
SAME CHAIR IN MAHOGANY, PRICE, . . . $85.00.

We have cane seats for summer use to fit our Barbers' Chairs, at from $3.00 to $5.00, according to style.

Theo. A. Kochs & Son, 1903 catalog page.

BARBER CHAIRS
KOCHS' GRAND PRIZE HYDRAULIC BARBERS' CHAIR, No. 21

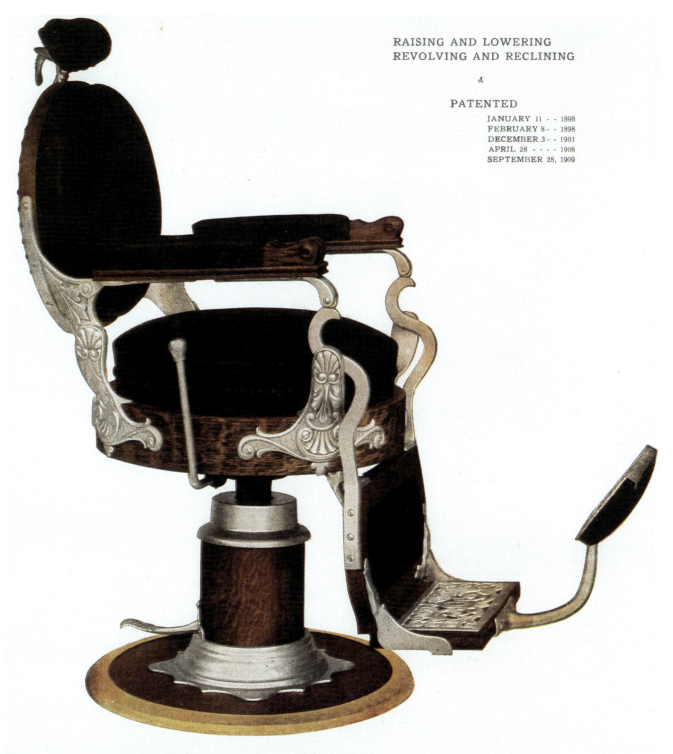

RAISING AND LOWERING
REVOLVING AND RECLINING

PATENTED
JANUARY 11 - - 1898
FEBRUARY 8 - - 1898
DECEMBER 3 - - 1901
APRIL 28 - - - - 1908
SEPTEMBER 28, 1909

Made of quarter-sawed oak of finest selection, golden finish. Upholstered with best quality leather, green or maroon. The improved adjustable head-rest is mounted on a nickel-plated steel stem which runs in a metal casing, insuring perfect rigidity. Nickel-plated trimmings. The base of this chair is fitted with a heavy cast-brass rim and is covered with quarter-sawed oak to match the chair. Equipped with foot-treadle hydraulic mechanism.

Price, as described - - - - - $75.00

John Rieder & Co., 1912 catalog page.

BARBER CHAIRS

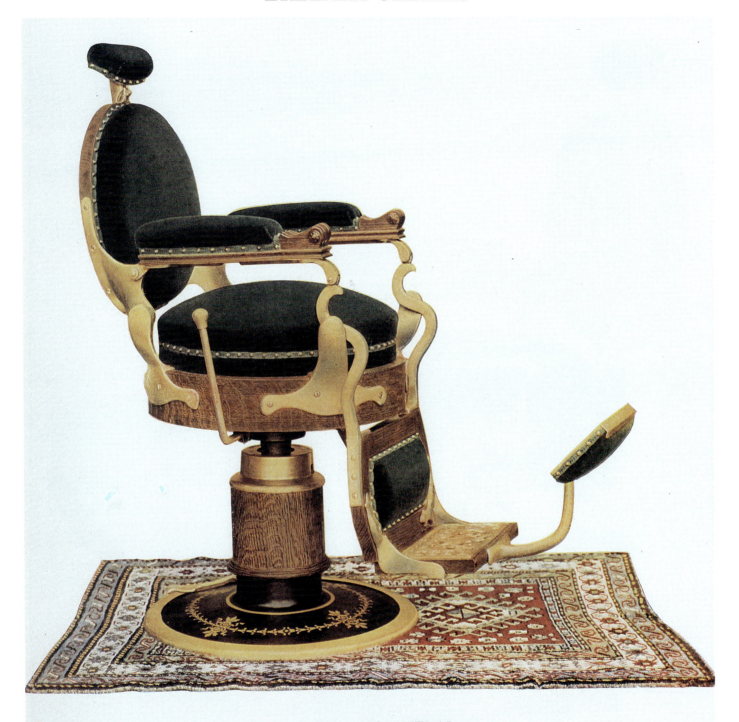

KOCHS' GOLD MEDAL
HYDRAULIC BARBERS' CHAIR, No. 23.

RAISING AND LOWERING.   REVOLVING AND RECLINING.

PATENTED DEC. 8, 1891; JAN. 11, 1898; FEB. 8, 1898.

Made of quarter-sawed Oak, golden finish. Upholstered with best quality Mohair Plush, crimsom or green, or with Maroon Leather. Patent adjustable head-rest; brass finished trimmings. The base of this chair is made of Iron, neatly japanned in Black and Gold and fitted with solid brass rim, polished. This chair stands firmly alone.

PRICE, ... $70.00.

Theo. A. Kochs & Son, 1903 catalog page.

BARBER CHAIRS

KOCHS' GOLD MEDAL
HYDRAULIC BARBERS' CHAIR, No. 24.

RAISING AND LOWERING.   REVOLVING AND RECLINING.

PATENTED DEC. 8, 1891; JAN. 11, 1898; FEB. 8, 1898.

Made of quarter-sawed Oak, golden finish. Upholstered with Mohair Plush, crimson, green or maroon, or with Maroon Leather; nickel-plated trimmings. Brass feet.

PRICE . . . $42.00.

Theo. A. Kochs & Son, 1899 catalog page.

BARBER CHAIRS

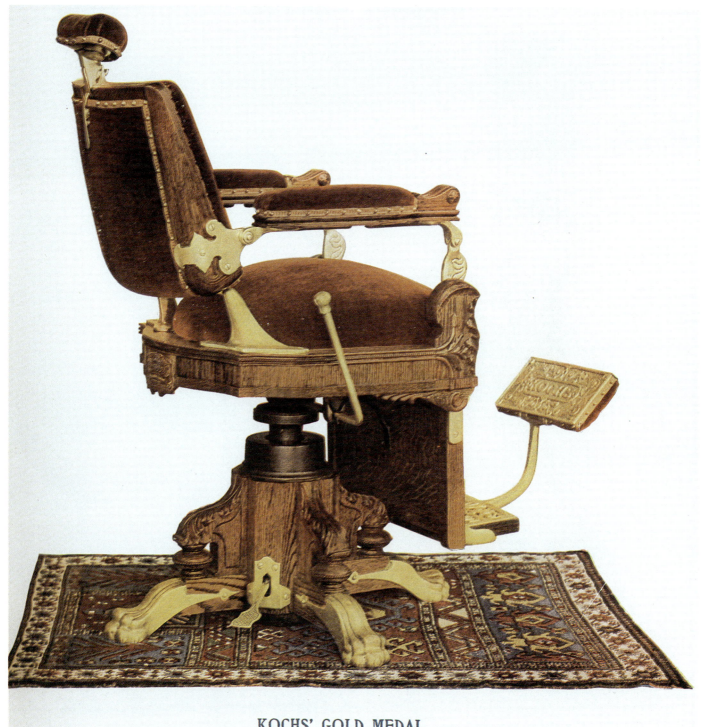

KOCHS' GOLD MEDAL
HYDRAULIC BARBERS' CHAIR, No. 25.

RAISING AND LOWERING.   REVOLVING AND RECLINING.

PATENTED DEC. 8, 1891; JAN. 11, 1898; FEB. 8, 1898.

Made of quarter-sawed Oak, golden finish. Upholstered with best quality Mohair Plush, crimson, green or old gold, or with Maroon Leather. Patent adjustable head-rest; brass finished trimmings. Solid brass feet.

PRICE, . . . $60.00.

When chairs are upholstered with leather, we cover the head-rest with plush, unless otherwise ordered. Plush head-rests prevent the towel from slipping.

Theo. A. Kochs & Son, 1899 catalog page.

BARBER CHAIRS

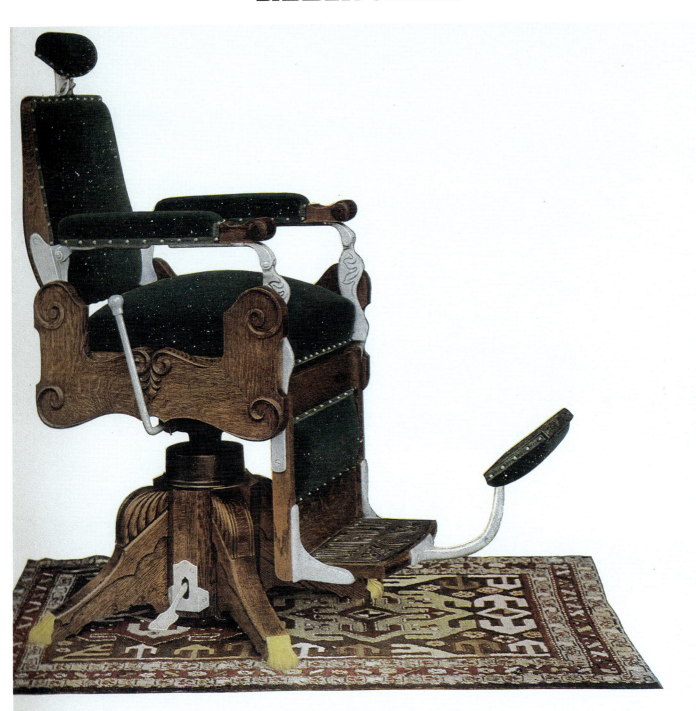

KOCHS' GOLD MEDAL
HYDRAULIC BARBERS' CHAIR, No. 26.

RAISING AND LOWERING.   REVOLVING AND RECLINING.

PATENTED DEC. 8, 1891; JAN. 11, 1898; FEB. 8, 1898.

Made of quarter-sawed Oak, golden finish. Covered with Mohair Plush, crimson or green, or with Maroon Leather; nickel-plated trimmings. Patent adjustable head-rest. Brass feet.

PRICE, ... $43.50.

We have cane seats for summer use to fit our Barbers' Chairs, at from $3.00 to $5.00, according to style.

Theo. A. Kochs & Son, 1899 catalog page.

BARBER CHAIRS

KOCHS' GOLD MEDAL
HYDRAULIC BARBERS' CHAIR, No. 27.

RAISING AND LOWERING.   REVOLVING AND RECLINING.

PATENTED DEC. 8, 1891; JAN. 11, 1898; FEB. 8, 1898.

Made of quarter-sawed Oak, golden finish. Patent adjustable head-rest; trimmings on this chair brass finished. Ornaments solid brass. Upholstered with best quality Mohair Plush, crimson or green, or with Maroon Leather. The base of this chair is fitted with solid brass rim, polished, and is covered with figured quarter-sawed Oak to match the chair. This chair stands firmly alone.

PRICE, ... $62.50.

Theo. A. Kochs & Son, 1903 catalog page.

BARBER CHAIRS

KOCHS' GOLD MEDAL
HYDRAULIC BARBERS' CHAIR, No. 28.

RAISING AND LOWERING.　　　　REVOLVING AND RECLINING

PATENTED DEC. 8, 1891; JAN. 11, 1898; FEB. 8, 1898.

This chair is of a plain and pleasing pattern and made of Oak, quarter-sawed and golden finish. Upholstered with best quality Mohair Plush, green or crimson, or with Maroon Leather. Oxidized copper trimmings. Patent adjustable head-rest. The base of this chair is made of iron, neatly japanned in black and gold and fitted with rubber rim. This chair stands firmly alone.

PRICE　.　.　.　.　$58.00.

Theo. A. Kochs & Son, 1903 catalog page.

BARBER CHAIRS

KOCHS' PEDESTAL COLUMBIA CHAIR, No. 34.
REVOLVING AND RECLINING.
PATENTED DEC. 8, 1891, AND JAN. 11, 1898.

Made of quarter-sawed Oak, golden finish, with iron base neatly japanned in black and gold. This chair stands firmly alone. Upholstered with Mohair Plush, crimson or green, or with Maroon Leather; nickel-plated trimmings. The rim on the base of this chair is made of rubber.

PRICE, ... $37.50.

We have cane seats for summer use to fit our Barbers' Chairs, at from $3.00 to $5.00, according to style.

Theo. A. Kochs & Son, 1903 catalog page.

BARBER CHAIRS

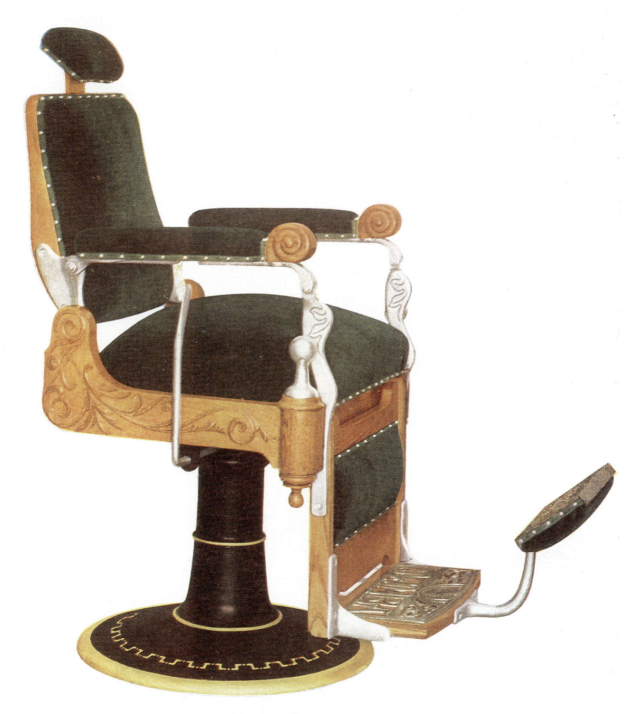

KOCHS' PEDESTAL COLUMBIA CHAIR, No. 35.
REVOLVING AND RECLINING.
PATENTED DEC. 8, 1891 AND JAN. 11, 1898.

Made of quarter-sawed Oak, finely finished, with iron base neatly japanned in black and gold. This chair stands firmly alone, and it is not necessary to fasten it to the floor. Upholstered with Mohair Plush, crimson, green or old gold, or with Maroon Leather.

PRICE, . . . $38.00.

THE RIM ON THE BASE OF THIS CHAIR IS BRONZE JAPANNED.

Loeffler & Sykes Co., 1902 catalog page.

BARBER CHAIRS

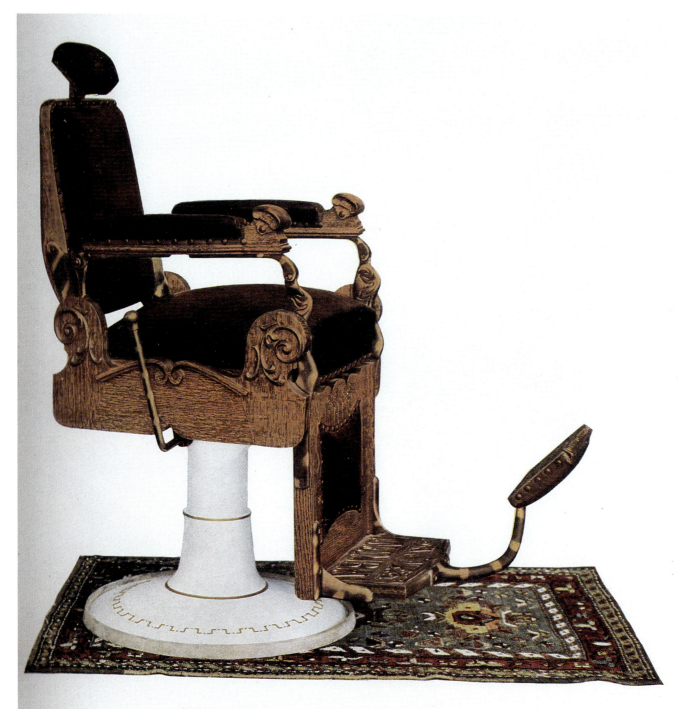

KOCHS' PEDESTAL COLUMBIA CHAIR, No. 36.
REVOLVING AND RECLINING.
PATENTED DEC. 8, 1891, AND JAN. 11, 1898.

Made of quarter-sawed Oak, golden finish, with iron base neatly japanned in white and gold. This chair stands firmly alone. Upholstered with Mohair Plush, crimson or green, or with Maroon Leather; oxidized copper trimmings. The rim on the base of this chair is made of rubber.

PRICE, ... $42.00.

NO. 39. Same chair, with black and gold japanned base. PRICE, $40.00.

Theo. A. Kochs & Son, 1903 catalog page.

BARBER CHAIRS

KOCHS' PEDESTAL COLUMBIA CHAIR, No. 37.
REVOLVING AND RECLINING.
PATENTED DEC. 8, 1891, AND JAN. 11, 1898.

Made of quarter-sawed Oak, golden finish; with iron base neatly japanned in black and gold. This chair stands firmly alone. Upholstered with Mohair Plush, crimson or green, or with Maroon Leather; oxidized copper trimmings. The rim on the base of this chair is made of metal, oxidized copper finish.

PRICE, ... $39.00

When chairs are upholstered with leather, we cover the head-rest with plush, unless otherwise ordered. Plush head-rests prevent the towel from slipping.

Theo. A. Kochs & Son, 1903 catalog page.

BARBER CHAIRS
KOCHS' PEDESTAL, COLUMBIA BARBERS' CHAIR, No. 47

REVOLVING AND RECLINING

PATENTED
JANUARY 11 - - 1898
SEPTEMBER 28, 1909

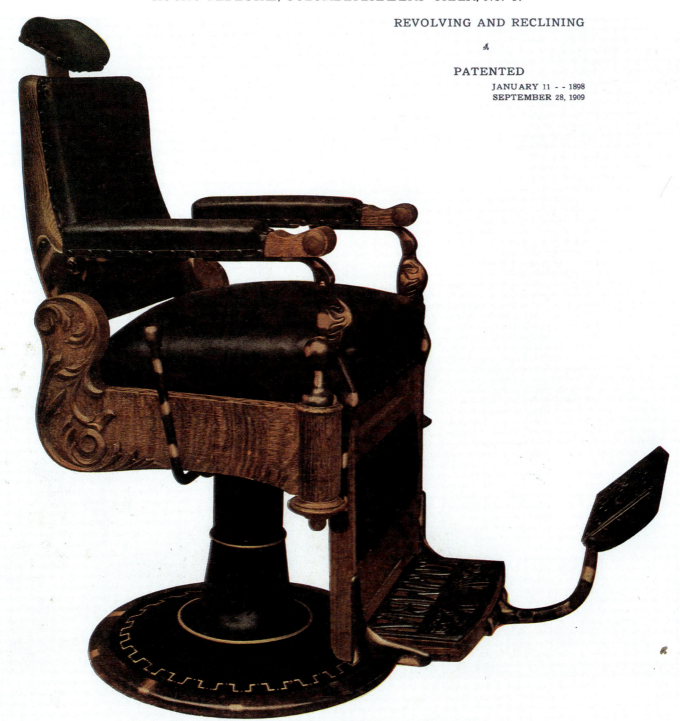

Made of selected quarter-sawed oak, golden finish, and equipped with revolving and reclining mechanism. The chair revolves on a ball-bearing pin, eliminating friction and wear. Upholstered with green or maroon leather or with crimson or green mohair plush. Oxidized copper finished trimmings. The base of this chair is made of iron, neatly japanned in black with gold decoration, and is fitted with a metal rim, oxidized copper finish.

Price - - - - - - - - $41.00

John Rieder & Co., 1912 catalog page.

BARBER CHAIRS
KOCHS' GRAND PRIZE HYDRAULIC BARBERS' CHAIR No. 50

RAISING AND LOWERING
REVOLVING AND RECLINING

PATENTED
DECEMBER 8, 1891
JANUARY 11 - 1898
FEBRUARY 8, 1898
DECEMBER 3, 1901
NOVEMBER 15, 1904
APRIL 28 - 1908

Made of mahogany of choice selection, highly finished. Upholstered with best grain leather, green or black. Nickel-plated trimmings. Polished brass heel-plate. The stem of the improved adjustable head-rest is made of malleable iron, nickel-plated, and runs in a groove to hold it rigid. The base is made of iron, white enameled, and fitted with a heavy cast-brass rim, polished. The design of this chair combines comfort to the customer and great convenience to the barber on account of its round seat-frame.

Price, in mahogany, as shown   -   - $75.00

John Rieder & Co., 1912 catalog page.

BARBER CHAIRS

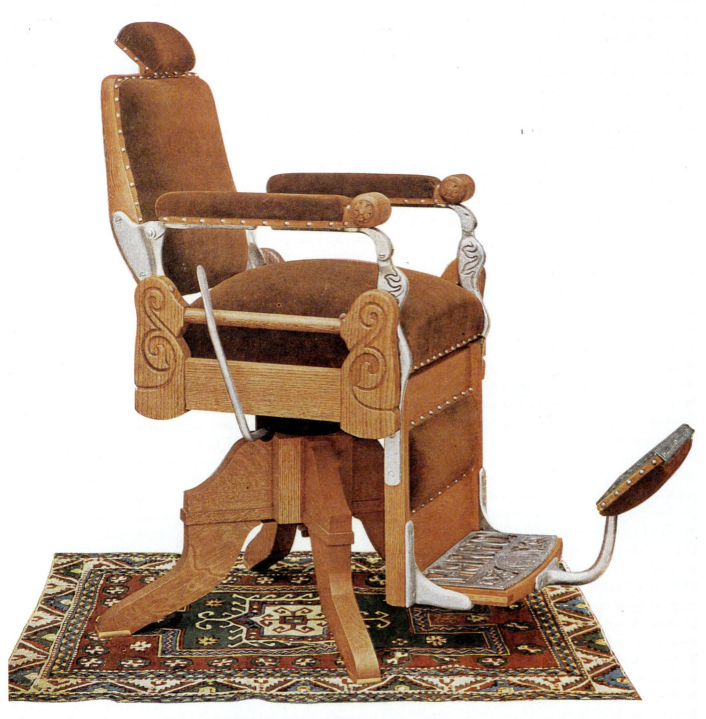

KOCHS' COLUMBIA, No. 53,
REVOLVING AND RECLINING.
BARBERS' CHAIR.
Patented—Dec. 8, 1891, and Jan. 11, 1898—Patented.

Made of Oak (golden finish) only. Covered with Mohair Plush, crimson, old gold or green.
The metal feet used upon this chair are made of solid brass.

PRICE, - - - $28.00

Theo A. Kochs Co., 1897 catalog page.

BARBER CHAIRS

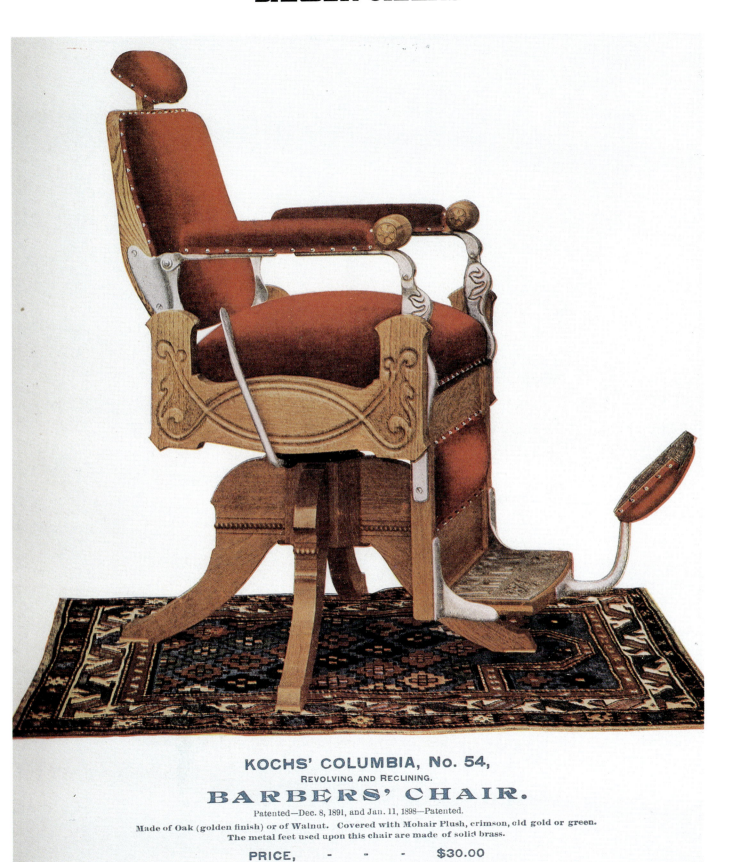

Theo. A. Kochs & Son, 1899 catalog page.

BARBER CHAIRS

KOCHS' COLUMBIA, No. 58,
REVOLVING AND RECLINING.
BARBERS' CHAIR.
Patented—Dec. 8, 1891, and Jan. 11, 1898—Patented.
Made of Oak (golden finish) only. Covered with Mohair Plush, crimson, old gold or green.
The metal feet used upon this chair are made of solid brass.

PRICE, - - - $33.00

Theo. A. Kochs & Son, 1899 catalog page.

BARBER CHAIRS

KOCHS' COLUMBIA, No. 59,
REVOLVING AND RECLINING.
BARBERS' CHAIR.
Patented—Dec. 8, 1891, and Jan. 11, 1898—Patented.

Made of Oak (golden finish) only. Covered with Mohair Plush, crimson, old gold or green, or with maroon leather. The metal feet used upon this chair are made of solid brass.

PRICE, - - - $36.00

Theo. A. Kochs & Son, 1899 catalog page.

BARBER CHAIRS
KOCHS' GRAND PRIZE HYDRAULIC BARBERS' CHAIR, No. 60

RAISING AND LOWERING
REVOLVING AND RECLINING
SLIDING SEAT
STATIONARY ARMS

PATENTED
DECEMBER 8, 1891
JANUARY 11 - 1898
FEBRUARY 8, 1898
DECEMBER 3, 1901
APRIL 28 - 1908

Our original design of 1908 in "Art Nouveau." Made of selected quarter-sawed oak, golden finish. The raised carving executed in a most artistic manner. On the smooth surfaces of the seat-frame, outside and inside, are displayed the rich figures of the carefully selected quarter-sawed veneer. Upholstered with finest quality grain leather, light green, dark green or black. Solid cast-brass foot-rest and foot-board plates. Brass heel-plate on leg-rest and polished solid brass rim on base, which is overlaid with quarter-sawed oak to match the chair. All other metal parts highly nickel-plated. The stem of the improved adjustable head-rest is made of malleable iron, nickel-plated, and runs in a groove to hold it rigid.

Price, as described - - - - $110.00

John Rieder & Co., 1912 catalog page.

BARBER CHAIRS

KOCHS' COLUMBIA, NO. 61,
REVOLVING ∴ AND ∴ RECLINING ∴ BARBERS' ∴ CHAIR.

Patented Dec. 8, 1891.

Made of Oak (antique finish) Only, Price, covered with Mohair Plush, Crimson, Maroon, Green or Old Gold - - $30.00

The metal feet used upon this chair are made of solid brass.

Theo. A. Kochs Co., 1897 catalog page.

BARBER CHAIRS

KOCHS' COLUMBIA, NO. 62,
REVOLVING ∴ AND ∴ RECLINING ∴ BARBERS' ∴ CHAIR.
Patented Dec. 8, 1891.

Made of Oak (antique finish) or of Walnut. Price, covered with Mohair Plush, Crimson, Maroon, Green or Old Gold, and with Nickel Plated trimmings, - - - - - - - - - $35.00
The metal feet used upon this chair are made of solid brass.

Theo. A. Kochs Co., 1897 catalog page.

BARBER CHAIRS

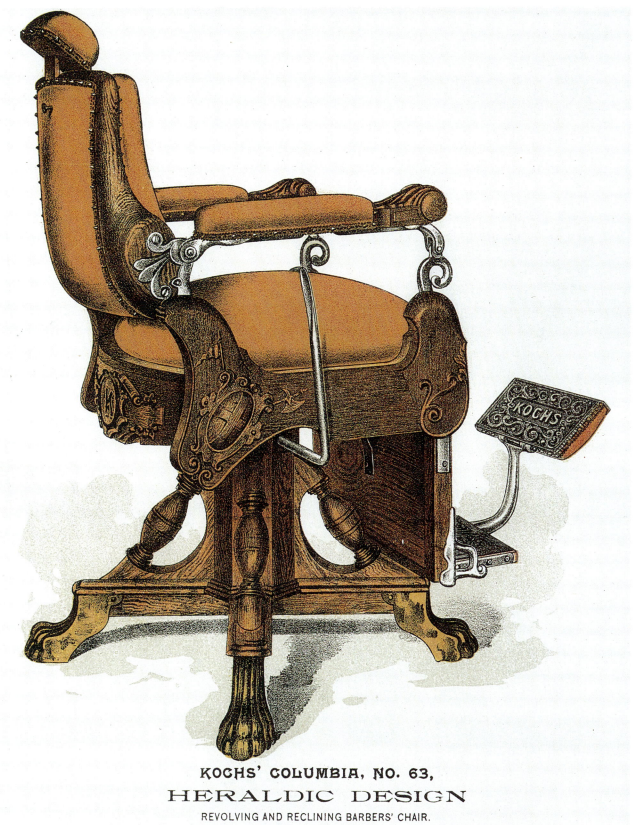

KOCHS' COLUMBIA, NO. 63,
HERALDIC DESIGN
REVOLVING AND RECLINING BARBERS' CHAIR.
Patented Dec. 8, 1891.

Made of Oak (antique finish) Only. Price, covered with best Mohair Plush, Crimson, Green or Old Gold, - - - $52.00

Theo. A. Kochs Co., 1897 catalog page.

BARBER CHAIRS

KOCHS' COLUMBIA, NO. 64,
REVOLVING ∴ AND ∴ RECLINING ∴ BARBERS' ∴ CHAIR
Patented Dec. 8, 1891.

Made of Oak (antique finish) or of Walnut. Price, covered with Mohair Plush, Crimson, Maroon, Green or Old Gold, - - $45.00
The metal feet used upon this chair are made of solid brass.

Theo. A. Kochs Co., 1897 catalog page.

BARBER CHAIRS

KOCHS' COLUMBIA, NO. 65,
REVOLVING ∴ AND ∴ RECLINING ∴ BARBERS' ∴ CHAIR.
Patented Dec. 8, 1891.

Made of Oak (antique finish) or of Walnut. Price, covered with Mohair Plush, Crimson, Maroon, Green or Old Gold, and with Nickel Plated trimmings, - - - - - - - - $30.00

Theo. A. Kochs Co., 1897 catalog page.

BARBER CHAIRS

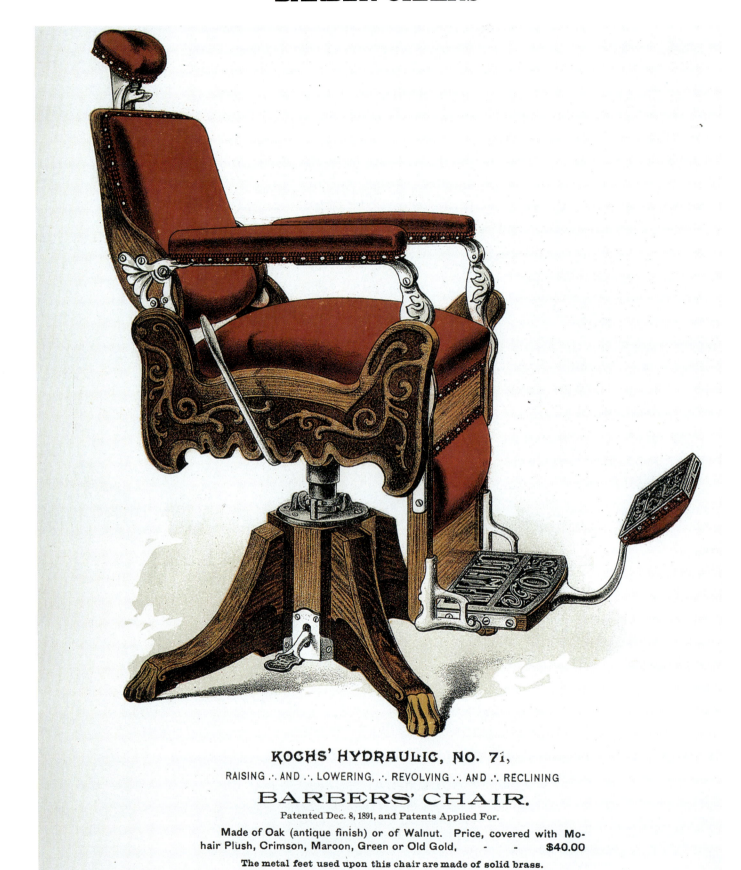

KOCHS' HYDRAULIC, NO. 71,
RAISING ∴ AND ∴ LOWERING, ∴ REVOLVING ∴ AND ∴ RECLINING
BARBERS' CHAIR.
Patented Dec. 8, 1891, and Patents Applied For.

Made of Oak (antique finish) or of Walnut. Price, covered with Mohair Plush, Crimson, Maroon, Green or Old Gold, - - $40.00

The metal feet used upon this chair are made of solid brass.

Theo. A. Kochs Co., 1897 catalog page.

BARBER CHAIRS

KOCHS' HYDRAULIC, NO. 72,

RAISING ∴ AND ∴ LOWERING, ∴ REVOLVING ∴ AND ∴ RECLINING

BARBERS' CHAIR.

Patented Dec. 8, 1891, and Patents Applied For.

Made of Oak (antique finish) or of Walnut. Price, covered with Mohair Plush, Crimson, Maroon, Green or Old Gold. - - $48.00

The metal feet used upon this chair are made of solid brass.

Theo. A. Kochs Co., 1897 catalog page.

BARBER CHAIRS

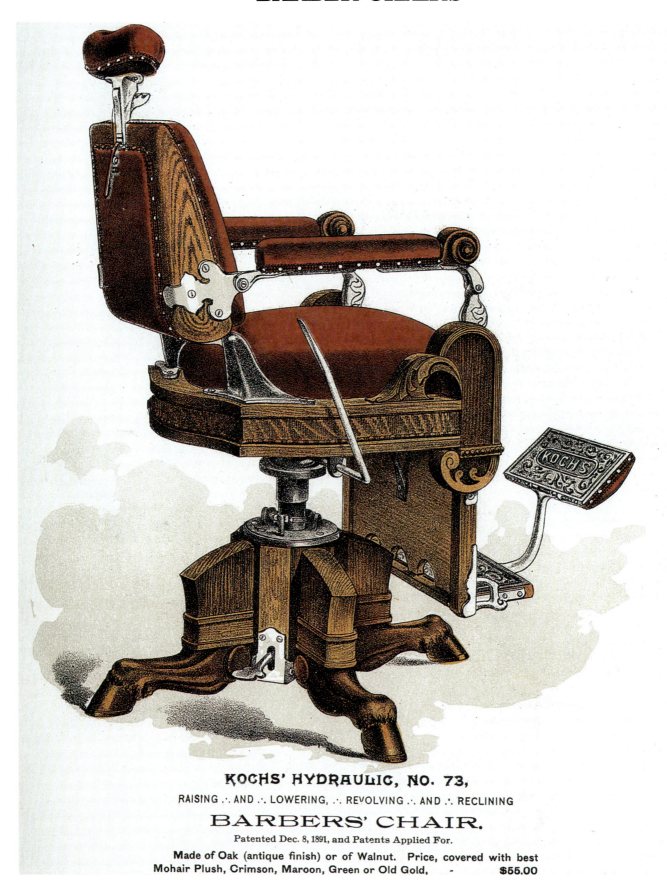

Theo. A. Kochs Co., 1897 catalog page.

BARBER CHAIRS

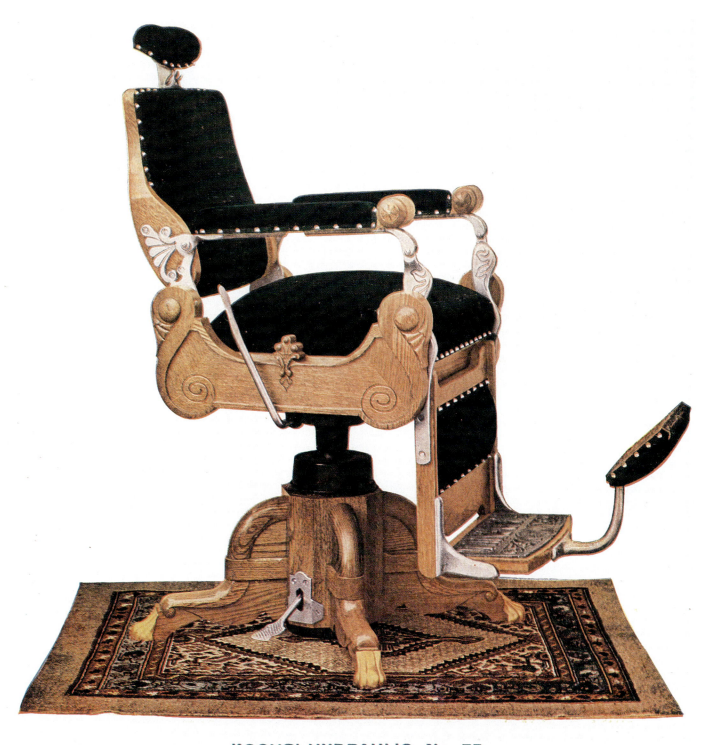

KOCHS' HYDRAULIC, No. 75,
RAISING AND LOWERING   REVOLVING AND RECLINING
BARBERS' CHAIR.
Patented—Dec. 8, 1891 -:- Jan. 11, 1898 -:- Feb. 8, 1898—Patented.

Made of quarter-sawed Oak (golden finish) or of Walnut. Covered with Mohair Plush, crimson, old gold or green, or with maroon leather. The metal feet used upon this chair are made of solid brass.

PRICE, - - - $45.00

Theo. A. Kochs & Son, 1899 catalog page.

BARBER CHAIRS

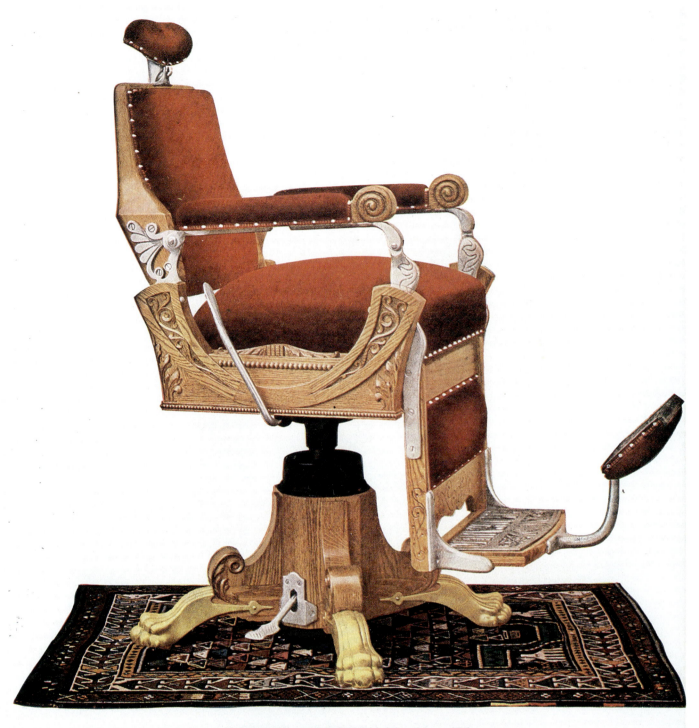

KOCHS' HYDRAULIC, No. 76,
RAISING AND LOWERING. REVOLVING AND RECLINING.
BARBERS' CHAIR.
Patented—Dec. 8, 1891 -:- Jan. 11, 1898 -:- Feb. 8, 1898—Patented.
Design Patented, Dec. 20, 1898.

Made of Oak (golden finish) only. Covered with Mohair Plush, crimson, old gold or green, or with maroon leather. The metal feet used upon this chair are made of solid brass.
This is absolutely the finest chair ever offered for the money.

PRICE, - - - $50.00

Theo. A. Kochs & Son, 1899 catalog page.

BARBER CHAIRS

KOCHS' GOLD MEDAL
HYDRAULIC BARBERS' CHAIR, No. 79.

RAISING AND LOWERING.   REVOLVING AND RECLINING.

PATENTED DEC. 8, 1891; JAN. 11, 1898; FEB. 8, 1898.

Made of quarter-sawed Oak, golden finish. Upholstered with Mohair Plush, crimson or green, or with Maroon Leather; nickel-plated trimmings. The base of this chair is fitted with metal rim, oxidized copper finish, and is covered with figured quarter-sawed Oak to match the chair. This chair stands firmly alone.

PRICE, ... $47.00.

Theo. A. Kochs & Son, 1903 catalog page.

BARBER CHAIRS
KOCHS' GRAND PRIZE HYDRAULIC BARBERS' CHAIR, No. 80

RAISING AND LOWERING
REVOLVING AND RECLINING
SLIDING SEAT
STATIONARY ARMS

PATENTED
DECEMBER 8, 1891
JANUARY 11 - 1898
FEBRUARY 8, 1898
DECEMBER 3, 1901
APRIL 28 - 1908

Our original design of 1908 in "Art Nouveau." Made of oak, covered with choicest quartered oak veneer, evenly matched to show the fine figures, both inside and outside of seat-frame. Superb hand carving, golden finish. Base of chair is overlaid with quarter-sawed oak and fitted with heavy cast-brass rim, polished. Solid cast-brass foot-rest and foot-board plates. All other metal parts highly nickel-plated. The stem of the improved adjustable head-rest is made of malleable iron, nickel-plated, and runs in a groove to hold it rigid.

Price, as described - - - - - $120.00

John Rieder & Co., 1912 catalog page.

BARBER CHAIRS

KOCHS' GOLD MEDAL
HYDRAULIC BARBERS' CHAIR, No. 83.

RAISING AND LOWERING.   REVOLVING AND RECLINING.

PATENTED DEC. 8, 1891; JAN. 11, 1898; FEB. 8, 1898.

Made of quarter-sawed Oak, golden finish. Upholstered with Mohair Plush, crimson or green, or with Maroon Leather; nickel-plated trimmings. The base of this chair is made of iron, neatly japanned in black and gold and fitted with metal rim, oxidized copper finish. This chair stands firmly alone.

PRICE, ... $47.00.

Theo. A. Kochs & Son, 1903 catalog page.

BARBER CHAIRS

KOCHS' GOLD MEDAL
HYDRAULIC BARBERS' CHAIR, No. 85.

RAISING AND LOWERING.   REVOLVING AND RECLINING.

PATENTED DEC. 8, 1891; JAN. 11, 1898; FEB. 8, 1898.

Made of quarter-sawed Oak, golden finish. Upholstered with best quality Mohair Plush, green or crimson, or with Maroon Leather; nickel-plated trimmings; patent adjustable headrest. The base of this chair is made of iron, neatly japanned in black and gold and fitted with solid brass rim, polished. This chair stands firmly alone.

PRICE, ... $60.00.

Theo. A. Kochs & Son, 1903 catalog page.

BARBER CHAIRS

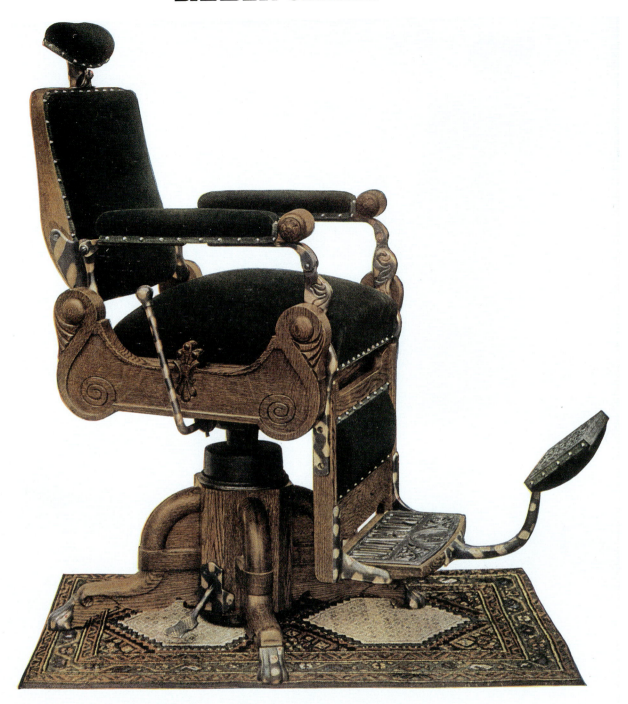

KOCHS' GOLD MEDAL
HYDRAULIC BARBERS' CHAIR, No. 86.

RAISING AND LOWERING.   REVOLVING AND RECLINING.

PATENTED DEC. 8, 1891; JAN. 11, 1898; FEB. 8, 1898.

Made of quarter-sawed Oak, golden finish. Upholstered with best quality Mohair Plush, crimson or green, or with Maroon Leather; oxidized copper trimmings. Patent adjustable head-rest. Brass feet oxidized.

PRICE, ... $45.00.

When chairs are upholstered with leather, we cover the head-rest with plush, unless otherwise ordered. Plush head-rests prevent the towel from slipping.

Theo. A. Kochs & Son, 1899 catalog page.

BARBER CHAIRS

KOCHS' GOLD MEDAL
HYDRAULIC BARBERS' CHAIR, No. 87.
RAISING AND LOWERING. REVOLVING AND RECLINING.
PATENTED DEC. 8, 1891; JAN. 11, 1898; FEB. 8, 1898.

Made of quarter-sawed Oak, golden finish. Upholstered with best quality Mohair Plush, crimson or green, or with Green or Maroon Leather; oxidized copper trimmings; patent adjustable head-rest. The base of this chair is fitted with solid brass rim, oxidized copper finish, and is covered with figured quarter-sawed Oak to match the chair. This chair stands firmly alone.

PRICE, ... $57.50.

Theo. A. Kochs & Son, 1903 catalog page.

BARBER CHAIRS
KOCHS' GRAND PRIZE HYDRAULIC BARBERS' CHAIR, No. 88

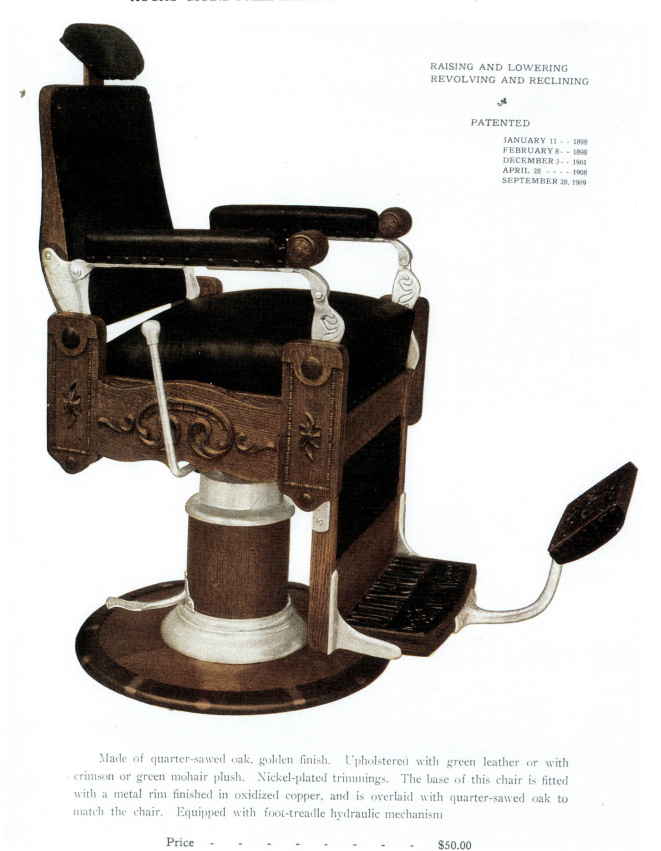

RAISING AND LOWERING
REVOLVING AND RECLINING

PATENTED

JANUARY 11 - - 1898
FEBRUARY 8 - - 1898
DECEMBER 3 - - 1901
APRIL 28 - - - - 1908
SEPTEMBER 28, 1909

Made of quarter-sawed oak, golden finish. Upholstered with green leather or with crimson or green mohair plush. Nickel-plated trimmings. The base of this chair is fitted with a metal rim finished in oxidized copper, and is overlaid with quarter-sawed oak to match the chair. Equipped with foot-treadle hydraulic mechanism

Price - - - - - - - - - $50.00

John Rieder & Co., 1912 catalog page.

BARBER CHAIRS

KOCHS' GOLD MEDAL
HYDRAULIC BARBERS' CHAIR, No. 89.

RAISING AND LOWERING.　　　　　REVOLVING AND RECLINING.

PATENTED DEC. 8, 1891; JAN. 11, 1898; FEB. 8, 1898.

Made of quarter-sawed Oak, golden finish. Upholstered with best quality Mohair Plush, crimson or green, or with Green Leather; nickel-plated trimmings; patent adjustable head-rest. The base of this chair is made of iron, neatly japanned in black and gold and fitted with rubber rim. This chair stands firmly alone.

PRICE,　.　.　.　.　$50.00.

Theo. A. Kochs & Son, 1903 catalog page.

BARBER CHAIRS
KOCHS' GRAND PRIZE HYDRAULIC BARBERS' CHAIR, No. 90

ORIGINAL DESIGN 1908

RAISING AND LOWERING
REVOLVING AND RECLINING

PATENTED
DECEMBER 8, 1891
JANUARY 11 - 1898
FEBRUARY 8, 1898
DECEMBER 3, 1901
APRIL 23 - 1908

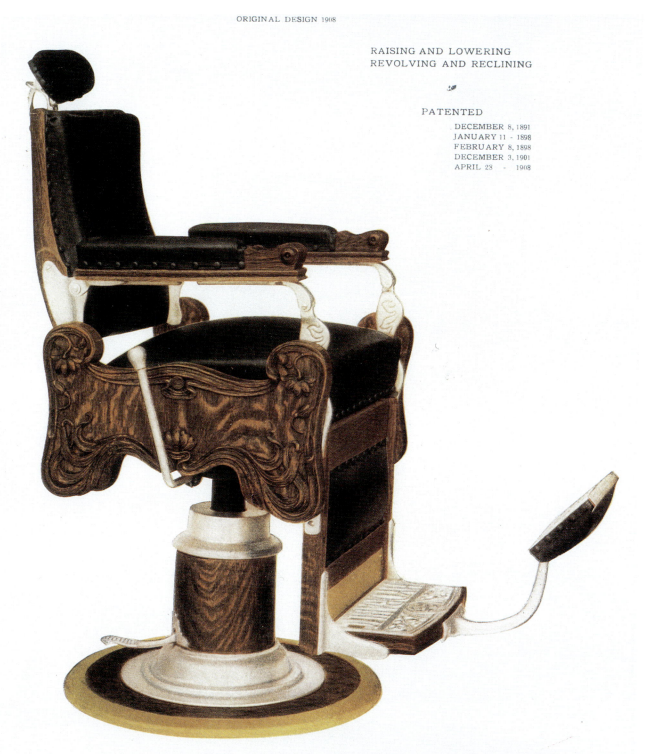

Made of choicest quarter-sawed oak, highly finished in golden oak and upholstered with best quality grain leather, green or black. Metal trimmings highly nickel-plated. The base is covered with figured quarter-sawed oak to match the chair and is fitted with a solid cast-brass rim. Polished brass heel plate. Patent adjustable head-rest with nickel-plated malleable-iron stem. This chair is tastefully designed in "Art Nouveau" style and presents quiet and pleasing outlines, giving the chair a dignified appearance.

Price, as described - - - - $75.00

John Rieder & Co., 1912 catalog page.

BARBER CHAIRS

KOCHS' HYDRAULIC, No. 92,

RAISING AND LOWERING.   REVOLVING AND RECLINING.

BARBERS' CHAIR.

Patented—Dec. 8, 1891 -:- Jan. 11, 1898 -:- Feb. 8, 1898—Patented.

Made of Oak (golden finish) only, with Lion's Head ornaments made of polished brass. Covered with Mohair Plush, crimson, old gold or green, or with maroon leather. The metal feet used upon this chair are made of solid brass.

PRICE, - - - $48.00

Theo. A. Kochs & Son, 1899 catalog page.

BARBER CHAIRS

KOCHS' HYDRAULIC, No. 93.

RAISING AND LOWERING   REVOLVING AND RECLINING

BARBERS' CHAIR.

Patented—Dec. 8, 1891 -:- Jan. 11, 1898 -:- Feb. 8, 1898—Patented.

Made of Oak (golden finish) only. Covered with Mohair Plush, crimson, old gold or green, or with maroon leather. The metal feet used upon this chair are made of solid brass.

PRICE, - - - $60.00

Theo. A. Kochs & Son, 1899 catalog page.

BARBER CHAIRS

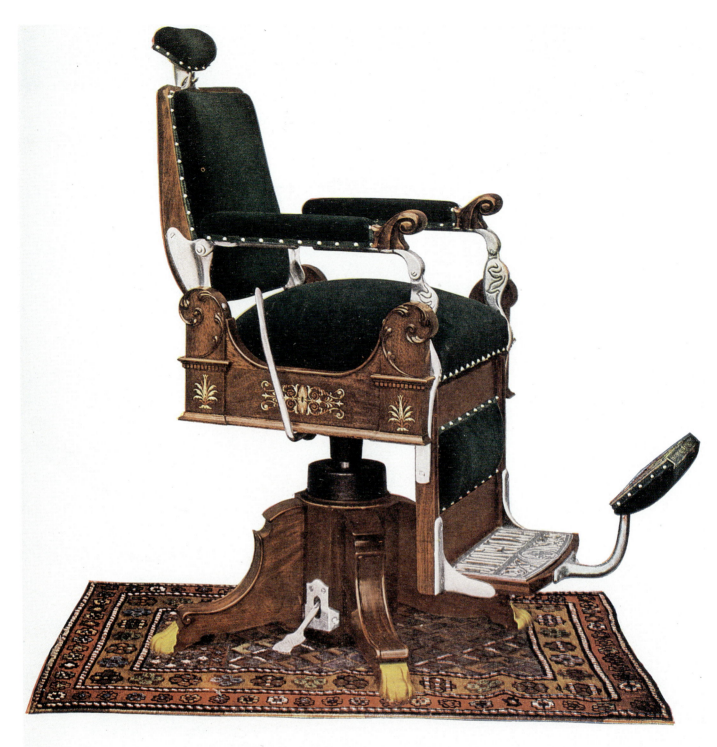

KOCHS' HYDRAULIC, No. 94,

RAISING AND LOWERING   REVOLVING AND RECLINING

BARBERS' CHAIR.

Patented—Dec. 8, 1891 -:- Jan. 11, 1898 -:- Feb. 8, 1898—Patented.

Made of Mahogany only. Beautiful Marquetry decoration having the appearance of inlaid woods.
Covered with best quality Mohair Plush, any desired color or with leather of any color.
The metal feet used upon this chair are made of solid brass.

PRICE,   - - - $70.00

Theo. A. Kochs & Son, 1899 catalog page.

BARBER CHAIRS

KOCHS' HYDRAULIC, No. 95,
RAISING AND LOWERING   REVOLVING AND RECLINING
BARBERS' CHAIR.
Patented—Dec. 8, 1891 -:- Jan. 11, 1898 -:- Feb. 8, 1898—Patented.

Made of Oak (golden finish) only. Covered with best quality Mohair Plush, crimson, old gold, green, or any desired color, or with leather of any color. The metal feet used upon this chair are made of solid brass.

PRICE,   -   -   - $75.00

Theo. A. Kochs & Son, 1899 catalog page.

BARBER CHAIRS

Theo. A. Kochs & Son, 1899 catalog page.

BARBER CHAIRS

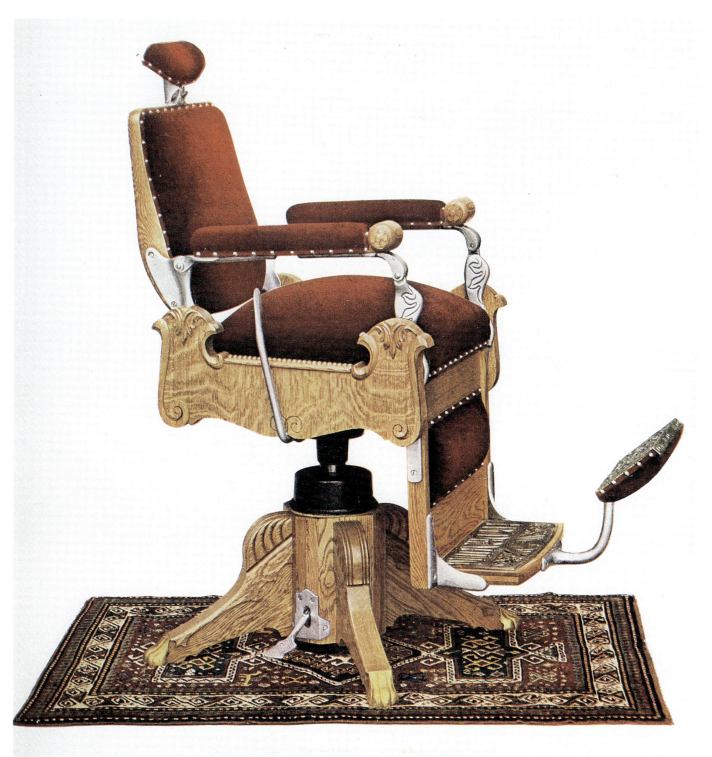

KOCHS' HYDRAULIC, No. 98,

RAISING AND LOWERING   REVOLVING AND RECLINING

BARBERS' CHAIR.

Patented—Dec. 8, 1891 -:- Jan. 11, 1898 -:- Feb. 8, 1898—Patented.

Made of quarter-sawed Oak (golden finish) only. Covered with Mohair Plush, crimson, old gold or green. The metal feet used upon this chair are made of solid brass.

PRICE, - - - $42.50

Theo. A. Kochs & Son, 1899 catalog page

BARBER CHAIRS

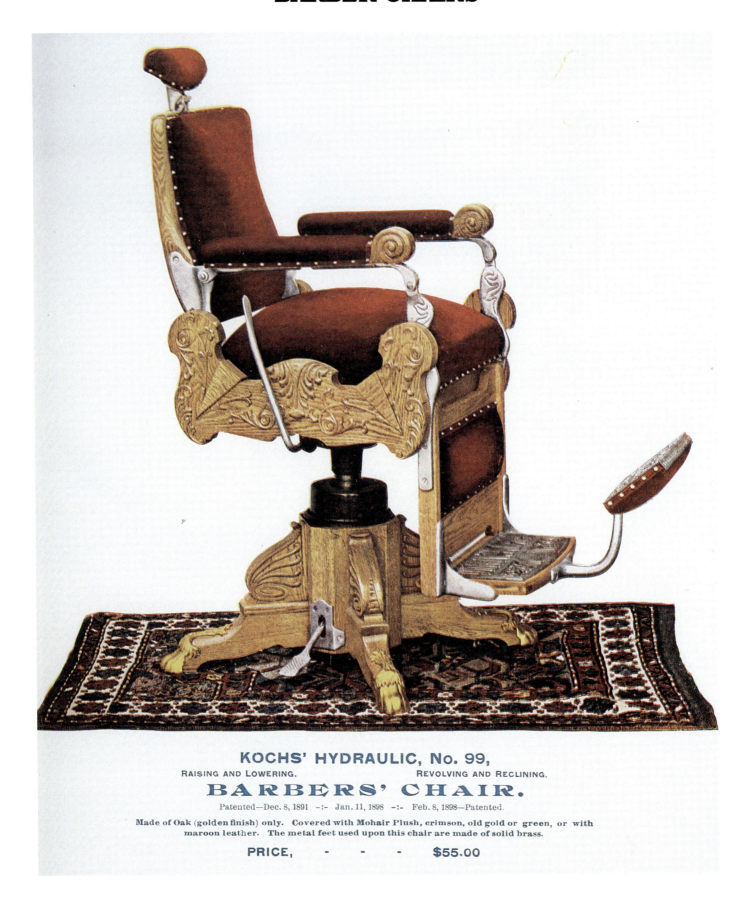

Theo. A. Kochs & Son, 1899 catalog page.

BARBER CHAIRS
KOCHS' PEDESTAL COLUMBIA BARBERS' CHAIR, No. 100

REVOLVING AND RECLINING

PATENTED
JANUARY 11 -- 1898
SEPTEMBER 28, 1909

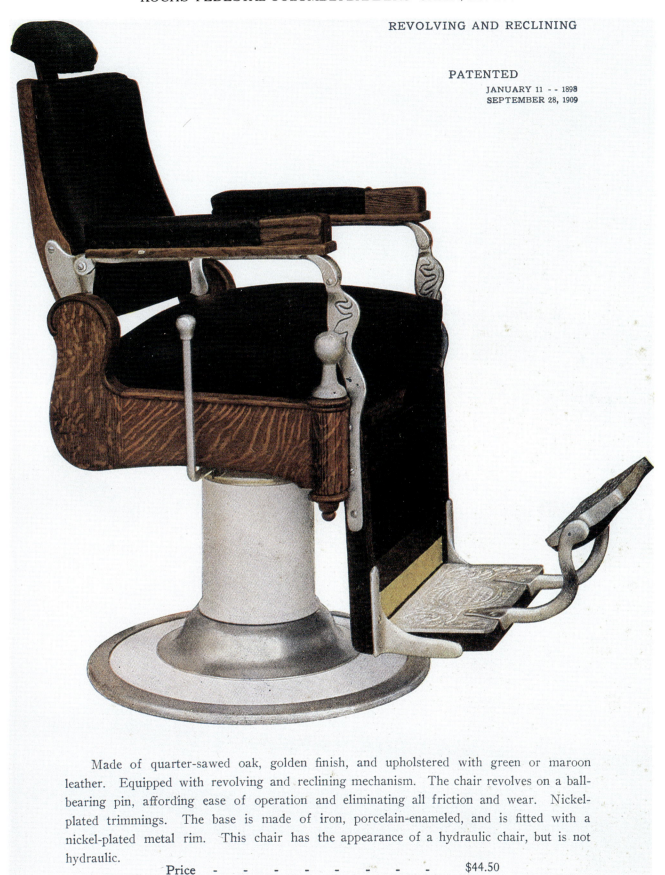

Made of quarter-sawed oak, golden finish, and upholstered with green or maroon leather. Equipped with revolving and reclining mechanism. The chair revolves on a ball-bearing pin, affording ease of operation and eliminating all friction and wear. Nickel-plated trimmings. The base is made of iron, porcelain-enameled, and is fitted with a nickel-plated metal rim. This chair has the appearance of a hydraulic chair, but is not hydraulic.

Price - - - - - - - - - $44.50

John Rieder & Co., 1912 catalog page.

BARBER CHAIRS

KOCHS' PEDESTAL HYDRAULIC CHAIR, No. 102.

RAISING AND LOWERING. REVOLVING AND RECLINING.

PATENTED DEC. 8, 891; JAN. 11, 1898; FEB. 8, 1898.

Made of Oak, finely finished. Iron Base neatly japanned to harmonize, and fitted with brass rim. This chair stands firmly alone, and it is not necessary to fasten it to the floor. Upholstered with best quality Mohair Plush, crimson, green or old gold, or with maroon leather.

PRICE, . . . $50.00.

THE BASE OF THIS CHAIR IS FITTED WITH SOLID BRASS RIM.

Loeffler & Sykes Co., 1902 catalog page.

BARBER CHAIRS

KOCHS' PEDESTAL HYDRAULIC CHAIR, No. 103.

RAISING AND LOWERING. REVOLVING AND RECLINING.

PATENTED DEC. 8, 1891; JAN. 11, 1898; FEB. 8, 1898.

Made of Oak, highly finished. Iron Base neatly japanned to harmonize, and fitted with brass rim. This chair stands firmly alone, and it is not necessary to fasten it to the floor. Upholstered with best quality Mohair Plush, crimson, green or old gold, or with maroon leather.

PRICE, . . . $65.00.

THE BASE OF THIS CHAIR IS FITTED WITH SOLID BRASS RIM.

Loeffler & Sykes Co., 1902 catalog page

BARBER CHAIRS
KOCHS' PEDESTAL COLUMBIA BARBERS' CHAIR, No. 105

PATENTED
DECEMBER 8, 1891
JANUARY 11 - 1898
OTHER PATENTS PENDING

This chair is equipped with our one lever mechanism for revolving and reclining, which is very simple, durable in construction and easily handled. Made both of mahogany and oak of the choicest selection, highly polished. Upholstered with green or black leather. Nickel-plated trimmings. Polished brass heel-plate. Patent adjustable head-rest with nickel-plated malleable iron stem. The base is of iron, white enameled and fitted with an ornamental metal rim, nickel-plated. This chair has been adopted by many steamship lines and is also in use in Pullman cars; it is admired by many who prefer a rather plain but well finished chair.

Price, mahogany, as illustrated, - - $53.00

John Reider & Co., 1912 catalog page.

BARBER CHAIRS

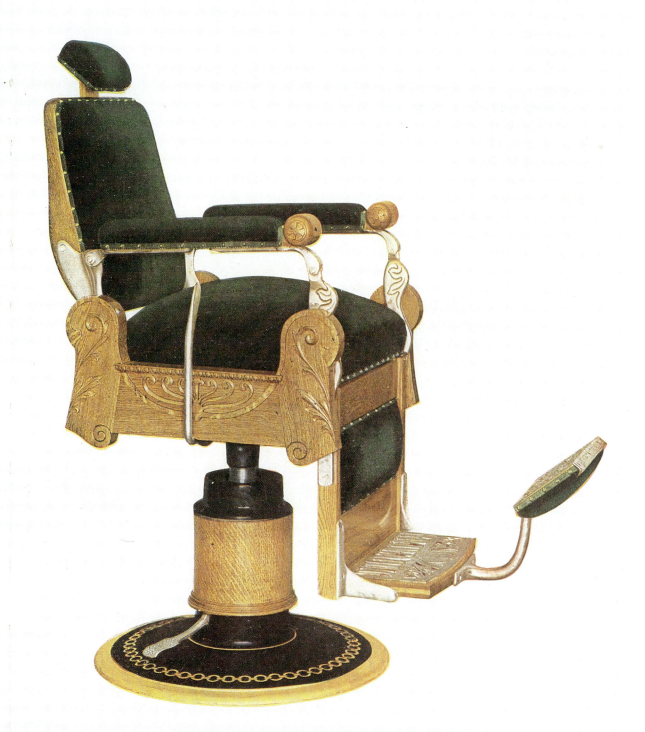

KOCHS' PEDESTAL HYDRAULIC CHAIR, No. 107.

RAISING AND LOWERING.   REVOLVING AND RECLINING.

PATENTED DEC. 8, 1891; JAN. 11, 1898; FEB. 8, 1898.

Made of Oak, finely finished, with iron base neatly japanned in black and gold. This chair stands firmly alone, and it is not necessary to fasten it to the floor. Upholstered with Mohair Plush, crimson, green or old gold.

PRICE, . . . $45.00.

THE RIM ON THE BASE OF THIS CHAIR IS BRONZE JAPANNED.

Loeffler & Sykes Co., 1902 catalog page.

BARBER CHAIRS

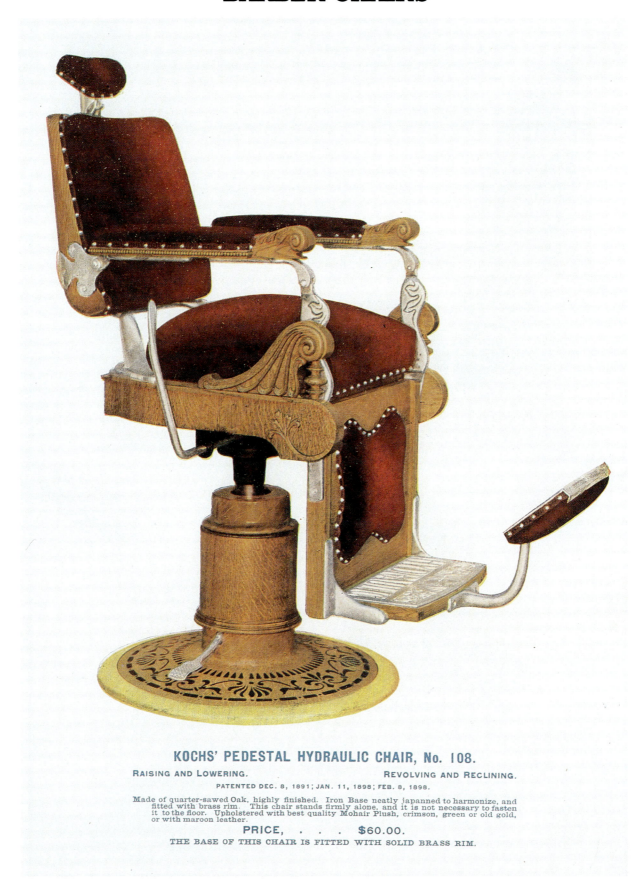

KOCHS' PEDESTAL HYDRAULIC CHAIR, No. 108.

RAISING AND LOWERING. REVOLVING AND RECLINING.

PATENTED DEC. 8, 1891; JAN. 11, 1898; FEB. 8, 1898.

Made of quarter-sawed Oak, highly finished. Iron Base neatly japanned to harmonize, and fitted with brass rim. This chair stands firmly alone, and it is not necessary to fasten it to the floor. Upholstered with best quality Mohair Plush, crimson, green or old gold, or with maroon leather.

PRICE, . . . $60.00

THE BASE OF THIS CHAIR IS FITTED WITH SOLID BRASS RIM.

Loeffler & Sykes Co., 1902 catalog page.

BARBER CHAIRS

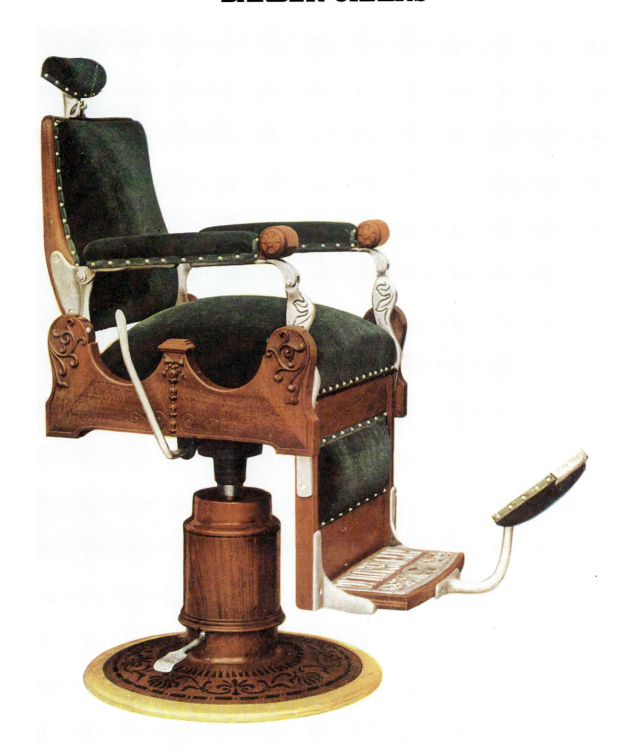

KOCHS' PEDESTAL HYDRAULIC CHAIR, No. 109.

RAISING AND LOWERING.   REVOLVING AND RECLINING.

PATENTED DEC. 8, 1891; JAN. 11, 1898; FEB. 8, 1898.

Made of Mahogany, highly finished. Iron Base neatly japanned to harmonize, and fitted with brass rim. This chair stands firmly alone, and it is not necessary to fasten it to the floor. Upholstered with best quality Mohair Plush, or with leather of any desired color.

PRICE, . . . $75.00.

THE BASE OF THIS CHAIR IS FITTED WITH SOLID BRASS RIM.

Loeffler & Sykes Co., 1902 catalog page.

BARBER CHAIRS
KOCHS' ONE LEVER HYDRAULIC BARBERS' CHAIR, No. 135

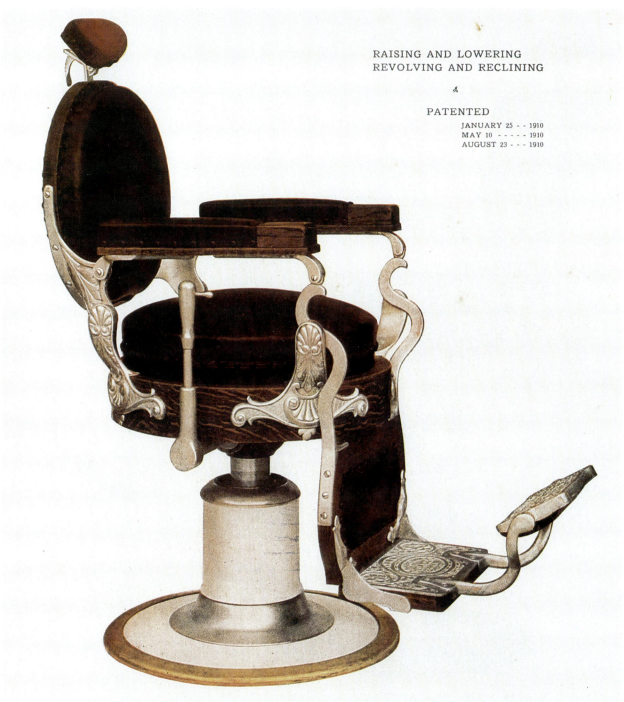

RAISING AND LOWERING
REVOLVING AND RECLINING

PATENTED
JANUARY 25 - - 1910
MAY 10 - - - - - 1910
AUGUST 23 - - - 1910

Made of selected quarter-sawed oak, golden finish. Upholstered with best quality leather, green, black or antique maroon. The above illustration shows the chair covered with antique maroon leather. Nickel-plated trimmings. The improved adjustable head-rest is mounted on a nickel-plated steel stem which runs in a metal casing, insuring perfect rigidity. The base of this chair is made of iron, porcelain-enameled, and is fitted with a heavy cast-brass rim. Equipped with one-lever hydraulic mechanism.

    Price, as described - - - - - $75.00
    Price, made of mahogany - - - - 85.00

John Rieder & Co., 1912 catalog page.

BARBER CHAIRS
KOCHS' ONE LEVER HYDRAULIC BARBERS' CHAIR, No. 152

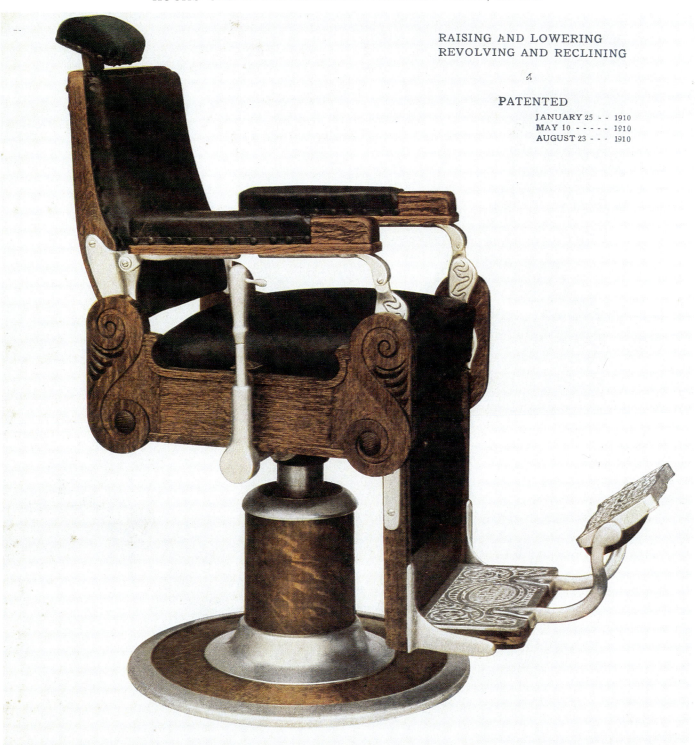

RAISING AND LOWERING
REVOLVING AND RECLINING

PATENTED
JANUARY 25 - - 1910
MAY 10 - - - - - 1910
AUGUST 23 - - - 1910

Made of quarter-sawed oak, golden finish. Upholstered with green or black or maroon leather. Nickel-plated trimmings. The base of this chair is fitted with a nickel-plated metal rim and is overlaid with quarter-sawed oak to match the chair. Equipped with one-lever hydraulic mechanism.

Price - - - - - - - - - $53.00

John Rieder & Co., 1912 catalog page.

BARBER CHAIRS
KOCHS' ONE LEVER HYDRAULIC BARBERS' CHAIR, No. 160

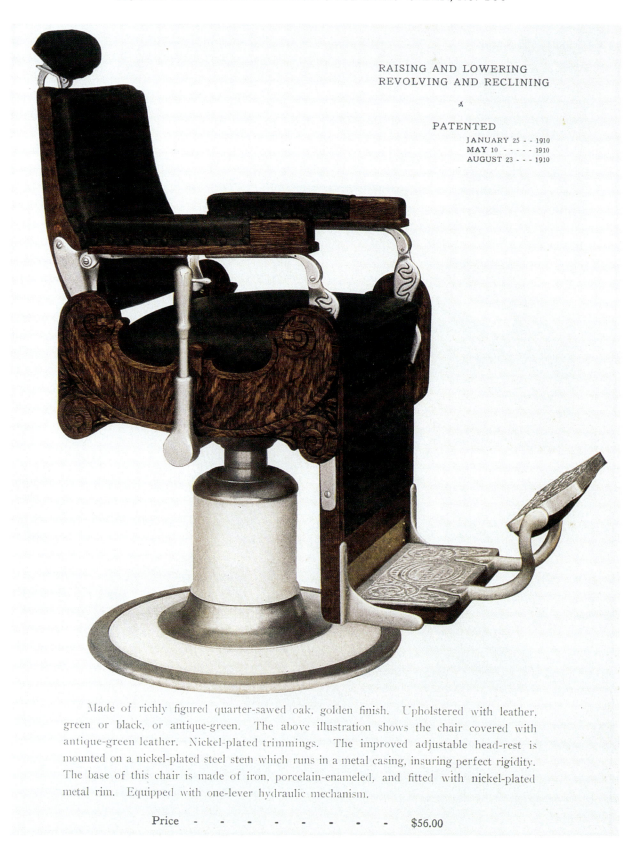

RAISING AND LOWERING
REVOLVING AND RECLINING

PATENTED
JANUARY 25 - - - 1910
MAY 10 - - - - - 1910
AUGUST 23 - - - 1910

Made of richly figured quarter-sawed oak, golden finish. Upholstered with leather, green or black, or antique-green. The above illustration shows the chair covered with antique-green leather. Nickel-plated trimmings. The improved adjustable head-rest is mounted on a nickel-plated steel stem which runs in a metal casing, insuring perfect rigidity. The base of this chair is made of iron, porcelain-enameled, and fitted with nickel-plated metal rim. Equipped with one-lever hydraulic mechanism.

Price - - - - - - - - - $56.00

John Rieder & Co., 1912 catalog page.

BARBER CHAIRS
KOCHS' VULCAN REVOLVING BARBERS' CHAIR, No. 165

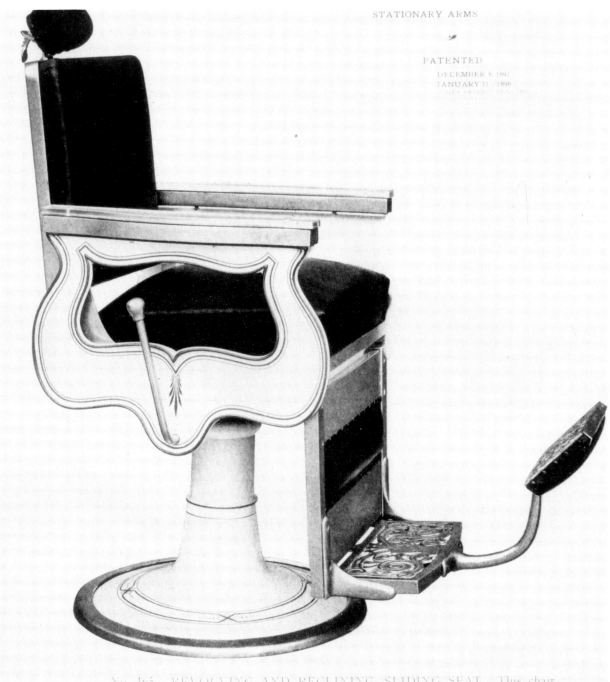

No. 165. REVOLVING AND RECLINING, SLIDING SEAT. This chair is equipped with our one lever mechanism for revolving and reclining, which is very simple, durable in construction and easily handled. It is made of iron, enameled in white and gold. Upholstered with best quality leather, green or black, or with woven cane. Metal trimmings are highly nickel-plated, including the metal rim upon the base. Adjustable head-rest. The seat slides forward as the chair is reclined, the arms remaining stationary. Glass arms, as shown, or leather arms, as illustrated on opposite page.   Price - - - - - - - - - $70.00

No. 186. RAISING AND LOWERING, REVOLVING AND RECLINING, SLIDING SEAT. This chair is identically the same as No. 165, excepting in the base, which is like the one on Chair No. 171, illustrated on the opposite page. It is also fitted with our well known hydraulic mechanism for raising and lowering, fully guaranteed. Solid cast brass rim, polished. Glass or leather arms.

John Rieder & Co., 1912 catalog page.

BARBER CHAIRS
KOCHS' ONE LEVER HYDRAULIC BARBERS' CHAIR, No. 168

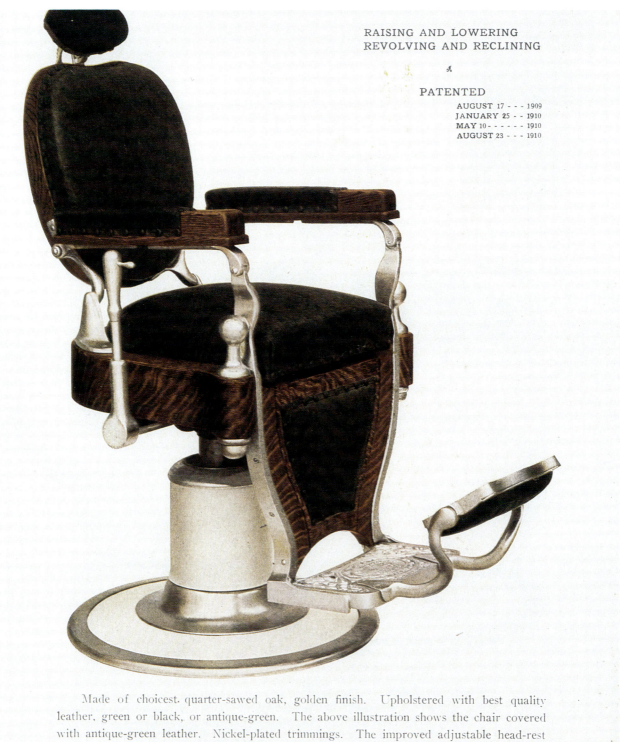

RAISING AND LOWERING
REVOLVING AND RECLINING

PATENTED
AUGUST 17 - - - 1909
JANUARY 25 - - 1910
MAY 10 - - - - - 1910
AUGUST 23 - - - 1910

Made of choicest, quarter-sawed oak, golden finish. Upholstered with best quality leather, green or black, or antique-green. The above illustration shows the chair covered with antique-green leather. Nickel-plated trimmings. The improved adjustable head-rest is mounted on a nickel-plated steel stem which runs in a metal casing, insuring perfect rigidity. The base of this chair is made of iron, porcelain-enameled, and is fitted with nickel-plated metal rim. The chair is so constructed as to afford great convenience to the barber and comfort to the customer. Equipped with one-lever hydraulic mechanism.

Price - - - - - - - - - $68.00

John Rieder & Co., 1912 catalog page.

BARBER CHAIRS
KOCHS' VULCAN HYDRAULIC BARBERS' CHAIR, No. 171

RAISING AND LOWERING
REVOLVING AND RECLINING
SLIDING SEAT
STATIONARY ARMS

PATENTED
DECEMBER 8, 1891
JANUARY 11 - 1898
FEBRUARY 8, 1898
APRIL 28 - 1908

This chair is fitted with our one lever mechanism for revolving and reclining and also with our improved hydraulic mechanism for raising and lowering, fully guaranteed. It is made of iron, enameled in white and gold. Upholstered with best grain leather, green or black, or with woven cane. All of the metal trimmings are highly nickel-plated and the base is fitted with a solid brass rim, polished. Adjustable headrest. The seat slides forward as the chair is reclined, the arms remaining stationary. This chair can be furnished with leather arms as shown above, or with glass arms as illustrated on opposite page.

Price - - - - - - - - $90.00

John Rieder & Co., 1912 catalog page.

BARBER CHAIRS

KOCHS' GOLD MEDAL
HYDRAULIC BARBERS' CHAIR, No. 302.

RAISING AND LOWERING.   REVOLVING AND RECLINING.

PATENTED DEC. 8, 1891; JAN. 11, 1898; FEB. 8, 1898.

Made of quarter-sawed Oak, golden finish. Upholstered with best quality Mohair Plush of any color desired, or with Leather; oxidized copper trimmings. Patent adjustable head-rest. The base of this chair is fitted with solid brass rim, oxidized copper finish, and is covered with figured quarter-sawed Oak to match the chair. This chair stands firmly alone.

PRICE, ... $70.00.

Theo. A. Kochs & Son, 1903 catalog page.

BARBER CHAIRS
KOCHS' GRAND PRIZE HYDRAULIC BARBERS' CHAIR, No. 331

REVOLVING AND RECLINING

PATENTED
DECEMBER 8, 1891
JANUARY 11 - 1898
FEBRUARY 8, 1898
DECEMBER 3, 1901
APRIL 28 - 1908

This chair is made of selected quarter-sawed oak and also of mahogany, highly finished. Upholstered with best grain leather, green or black. Nickel-plated trimmings. Patent adjustable head-rest with nickel-plated, malleable-iron stem. The base of the chair is covered with the wood to match the chair and is fitted with a heavy cast-brass rim, polished.

Price, quarter-sawed oak, golden finish, $85.00

John Rieder & Co., 1912 catalog page.

BARBER CHAIRS

KOCHS' GOLD MEDAL
HYDRAULIC BARBERS' CHAIR, No. 340.

RAISING AND LOWERING.   REVOLVING AND RECLINING.

PATENTED DEC. 8, 1891; JAN. 11, 1898; FEB. 8, 1898.

Made of quarter-sawed Oak, golden finish. Upholstered with best quality Mohair Plush, crimson or green, or with Green or Maroon Leather; oxidized copper trimmings; patent adjustable head-rest. The base of this chair is fitted with solid brass rim, oxidized copper finish, and is covered with figured quarter-sawed Oak to match the chair. This chair stands firmly alone.

PRICE, ... $65.00.

Theo. A. Kochs & Son, 1903 catalog page.

BARBER CHAIRS
KOCHS' GRAND PRIZE HYDRAULIC BARBERS' CHAIR, No. 345

RAISING AND LOWERING
REVOLVING AND RECLINING

PATENTED
JANUARY 11 - - 1898
FEBRUARY 8 - - 1898
DECEMBER 3 - - 1901
APRIL 28 - - - - 1908
SEPTEMBER 28, 1909

Made of selected quarter-sawed oak, golden finish. Upholstered with best quality leather, green, black or maroon. Fitted with improved adjustable head-rest, which is mounted on a steel stem running in a metal casing, insuring perfect rigidity. Oxidized copper finished trimmings. The base of this chair is fitted with a heavy cast-brass rim and is covered with quarter-sawed oak to match the chair. Equipped with foot-treadle hydraulic mechanism.

Price - - - - - - - - - $67.50

John Rieder & Co., 1912 catalog page.

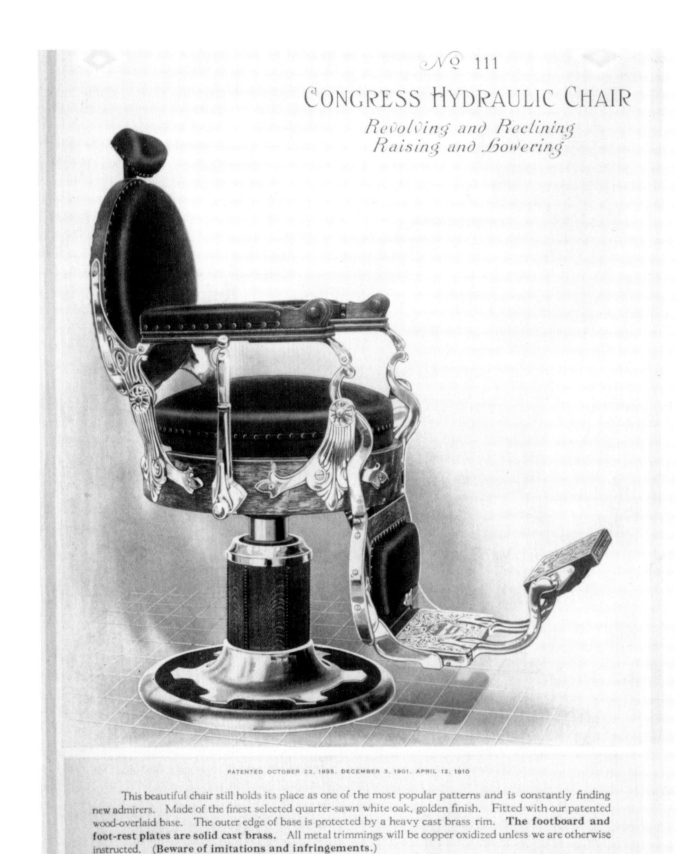

Koken Supply Co., 1911 catalog page.

BARBER CHAIRS
CONGRESS PEDESTAL HYDRAULIC CHAIR, No. 126 (patented 1901.)

Made of the finest selected quality quarter-sawn oak, golden finish. The base of the chair is not japanned or painted, but is overlaid with richly figured quarter-sawn oak to match the upper part. The outer edge is protected by a heavy polished cast brass rim. All other trimmings nickel plated. It stands alone.

Price	$60.00
" if required in Mahogany or other fancy woods, extra	10.00
" Cane Summer Seat, extra	3.00
" Cane Summer Seat in Mahogany, extra	5.00

Upholstered in plush or leather, any color.

Koken Supply Co., 1904 catalog page.

BARBER CHAIRS
CONGRESS ONE LEVER CHAIR, No. 130 (patented 1900)

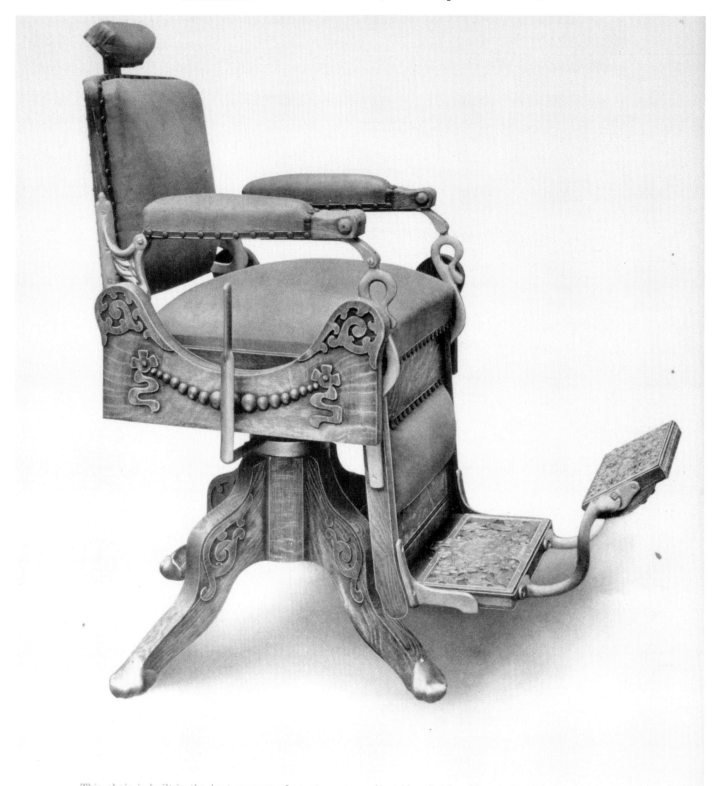

This chair is built in the best manner of quarter-sawn oak, golden finish. The mechanism is strong, simple and durable. The upholstering is good. Mohair plush or leather of any color is used for the cover. Nickel plated trimmings.

Price $35.00
" Summer Seat, extra 3.00

Koken Supply Co., 1904 catalog page.

BARBER CHAIRS
CONGRESS PEDESTAL HYDRAULIC CHAIR, No. 134 (patented 1901)

Made of the finest selected quarter-sawn oak, golden finish. Upholstered with best mohair plush or leather, any color. The base of this chair is not japanned or painted, but is overlaid with richly figured quarter-sawn oak to match the chair. The outer edge is protected by a heavy cast brass rim. The Chair stands alone.

Price	$80.00
" if required in Mahogany or other fancy woods, extra	10.00
" Cane Summer Seat, extra	5.00

Unless otherwise specified all trimmings will be furnished in our high grade copper-oxidized finish.

Koken Supply Co., 1904 catalog page.

BARBER CHAIRS
CONGRESS PEDESTAL HYDRAULIC CHAIR, No. 135

Pat. Dec. 8, 1891; Oct. 22, 1895; Dec. 3, 1901.

Made of the finest selected quarter-sawn oak, golden finish. Upholstered with best mohair plush or leather, any color. The base of this chair is not japanned or painted, but is overlaid with richly figured quarter-sawn oak to match the upper part. The outer edge is protected by a heavy cast brass rim copper oxidized. It stands alone.

Price	$70.00
" if required in Mahogany or other fancy woods, extra	10.00
" Cane Summer Seat, extra	5.00

Unless otherwise specified, all the trimmings of this chair will be copper oxidized.

Koken Supply Co., 1904 catalog page.

BARBER CHAIRS

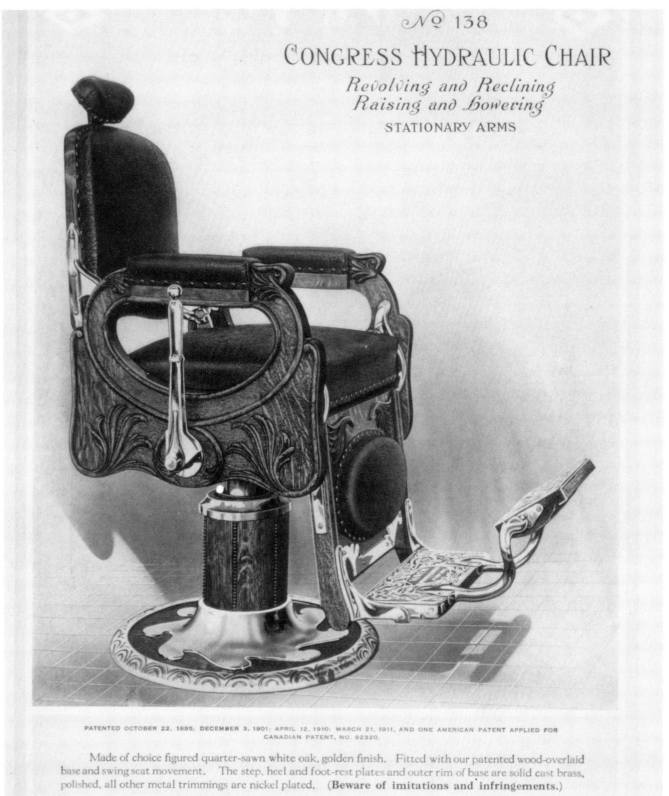

Koken Supply Co., 1911 catalog page.

BARBER CHAIRS
CONGRESS PEDESTAL HYDRAULIC CHAIR, No. 139

Pat. Dec. 8, 1891; Oct. 22, 1895; Dec. 3, 1901.

Made of the finest selected quality quarter-sawn oak, golden finish. Upholstered with best mohair plush or leather, any color. The base of the chair is not japanned or painted, but is overlaid with richly figured quarter-sawn oak to match the upper part. The outer edge is protected by a heavy cast brass rim copper oxidized. It stands alone.

Price...$75.00

Koken Supply Co., 1911 catalog page.

BARBER CHAIRS
CONGRESS PEDESTAL HYDRAULIC CHAIR, No. 140

Pat. Dec. 8, 1891; Oct. 22, 1895; Dec. 3, 1901.

Made of best quarter-sawn oak, golden finish. The base of this chair is not japanned or painted, but is overlaid with figured quarter-sawn oak to match the upper part. The outer edge is protected by a heavy cast brass rim. This chair stands alone.

Price $65.00
" if required in Mahogany or fancy cabinet woods, extra 10.00

Koken Supply Co., 1904 catalog page.

BARBER CHAIRS
CONGRESS PEDESTAL HYDRAULIC CHAIR, No. 141

Pat. Dec. 8, 1891; Oct. 22, 1895; Dec. 3, 1901.

Made of the finest selected quarter-sawn oak, golden finish. The base of this chair is not japanned or painted, but is overlaid with richly figured quarter-sawn oak to match the upper part. The outer edge is protected by a heavy polished cast brass rim. All other trimmings nickel plated. It stands alone.

Price...$62.50

Koken Supply Co., 1904 catalog page.

BARBER CHAIRS
CONGRESS PEDESTAL HYDRAULIC CHAIR, No. 142

Pat. Dec. 8, 1891; Oct. 22, 1895; Dec. 3, 1901.

Made of best quarter-sawn oak, golden finish. The base of this chair is not japanned or painted, but is covered with quarter-sawn oak to match the chair. The outer edge is protected with a heavy oxidized rim. This chair stands alone.

Price...$57.50

Koken Supply Co., 1904 catalog page.

BARBER CHAIRS

№ 143
Congress Hydraulic Chair
Revolving and Reclining
Raising and Lowering
STATIONARY ARMS

PATENTED OCTOBER 22, 1895; DECEMBER 3, 1901; APRIL 12, 1910; MARCH 21, 1911, AND ONE AMERICAN PATENT APPLIED FOR
CANADIAN PATENT, NO. 92320

Made of quarter-sawn white oak, golden finish. Fitted with our patented wood-overlaid base and swing seat movement. The metal step and foot-rest plates are finished in berlin lacquer. The outer rim of base and all other metal trimmings are copper oxidized in our superior style. **(Beware of imitations and infringements.)**

Price, in oak, upholstered with plush or leather, any color............$57.50
Price, in mahogany or other fancy cabinet woods, extra............10.00
Price, oak Summer seat, extra............3.00

Koken Supply Co., 1911 catalog page.

BARBER CHAIRS
CONGRESS PEDESTAL HYDRAULIC CHAIR No. 144

Pat. Dec. 8, 1891; Oct. 22, 1895; Dec. 3, 1901.

Made of the finest selected quality quarter-sawn oak, golden finish. The base of this chair is not japanned or painted, but is overlaid with richly figured quarter-sawn oak to match the upper part. The outer edge is protected by a heavy polished cast brass rim. Other parts nickel plated. It stands alone.

Price, upholstered in plush or leather, any color............................$55.00

Koken Supply Co., 1904 catalog page.

BARBER CHAIRS
CONGRESS PEDESTAL HYDRAULIC CHAIR, No. 145

Pat. Dec. 8, 1891; Oct. 22, 1895; Dec. 3, 1901.

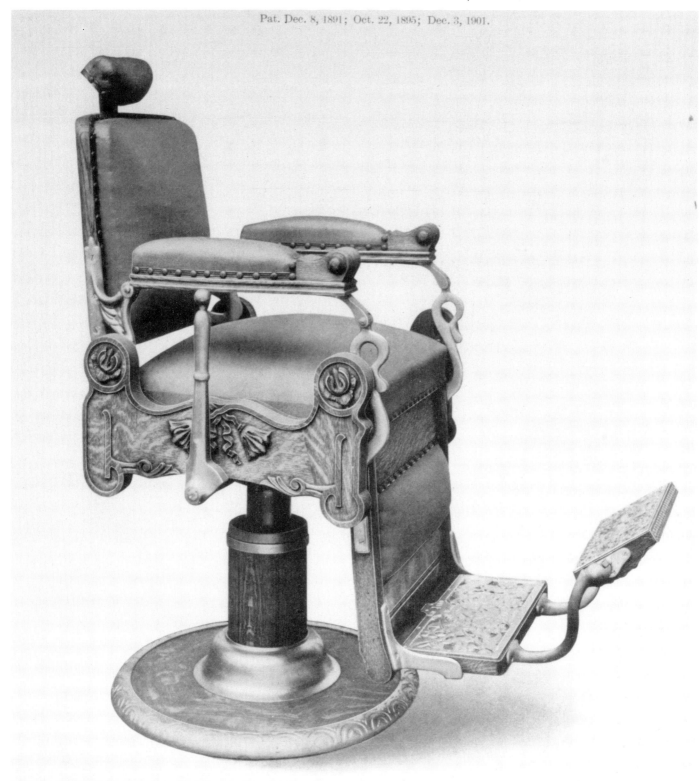

Made of the best quarter-sawn oak, golden finish. The base of this chair is not painted or japanned, but is overlaid with a paneling of quarter-sawn oak, and the outer edge is protected by an oxidized metal rim. Other parts nickel plated. This chair stands alone.

Price, upholstered in plush or leather, any color...$52.50

Koken Supply Co., 1904 catalog page.

BARBER CHAIRS

Koken Supply Co., 1911 catalog page.

BARBER CHAIRS

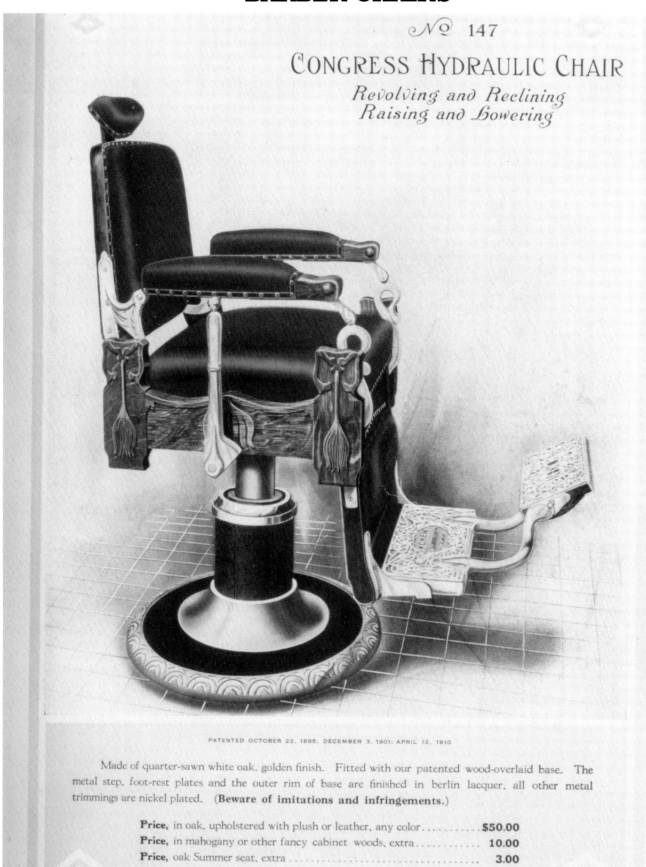

№ 147
Congress Hydraulic Chair
*Revolving and Reclining
Raising and Lowering*

PATENTED OCTOBER 22, 1895; DECEMBER 3, 1901; APRIL 12, 1910

Made of quarter-sawn white oak, golden finish. Fitted with our patented wood-overlaid base. The metal step, foot-rest plates and the outer rim of base are finished in berlin lacquer, all other metal trimmings are nickel plated. **(Beware of imitations and infringements.)**

Price, in oak, upholstered with plush or leather, any color............ $50.00
Price, in mahogany or other fancy cabinet woods, extra............ 10.00
Price, oak Summer seat, extra....................... 3.00

Koken Supply Co., 1911 catalog page.

BARBER CHAIRS

№ 149
Congress Hydraulic Chair
*Revolving and Reclining
Raising and Lowering*

PATENTED OCTOBER 22, 1895; APRIL 12, 1910

A very desirable chair for warm climates. Made of quarter-sawn white oak, golden finish. Fitted with our celebrated hydraulic mechanism. The ventilator castings for back and the shoes are solid cast brass, polished. The metal step and foot-rest plates are finished in berlin lacquer, all other metal trimmings are nickel plated.

Catalogue showing several other patterns of cane seat and back chairs will be sent on application.

Price, in oak, with cane seat, back and apron, as shown	$45.00
Price, in oak, completely upholstered with plush or leather, any color, instead of cane	45.00
Price, in mahogany or other fancy cabinet woods, extra	10.00
Price, oak Summer seat for upholstered chair, extra	3.00

Koken Supply Co., 1911 catalog page.

BARBER CHAIRS
CONGRESS PEDESTAL ONE LEVER CHAIR, NO. 150 (Patented 1901)

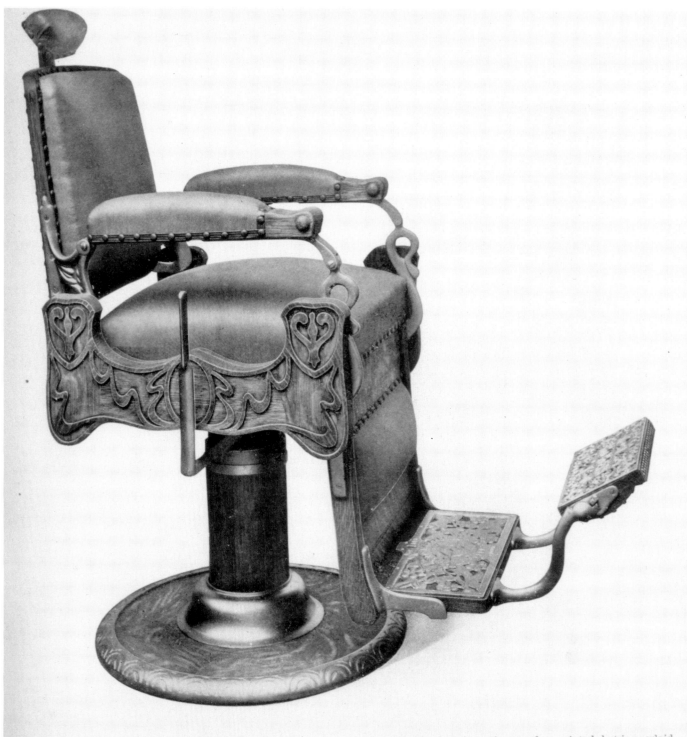

Made of the finest selected quarter-sawn oak, golden finish. The base of this chair is not japanned or painted, but is overlaid with figured quarter-sawn oak to match the chair. The outer edge is protected by an embossed metal rim finished in Berlin Lacquer. Other parts nickel plated. We apply our one lever mechanism for revolving and reclining, which is positive and powerful, easily handled and satisfactory in every way.

Price, upholstered in plush or leather, any color..................$40.00
" Cane Summer Seat to fit this chair, extra.....................3.00

Koken Supply Co., 1904 catalog page.

BARBER CHAIRS

№151
CONGRESS ONE LEVER CHAIR
Revolving and Reclining

PATENTED OCTOBER 30, 1900; APRIL 12, 1910

Made of quarter-sawn white oak, golden finish. Fitted with our improved one-lever mechanism, which is simple, strong and reliable. The shoes are solid cast brass, polished. The metal step and foot-rest plates are finished in berlin lacquer, all other metal trimmings are nickel plated.

Price, in oak, upholstered with plush or leather, any color..........$34.00
Price, oak Summer seat, extra................................... 3.00

Koken Supply Co., 1911 catalog page.

BARBER CHAIRS

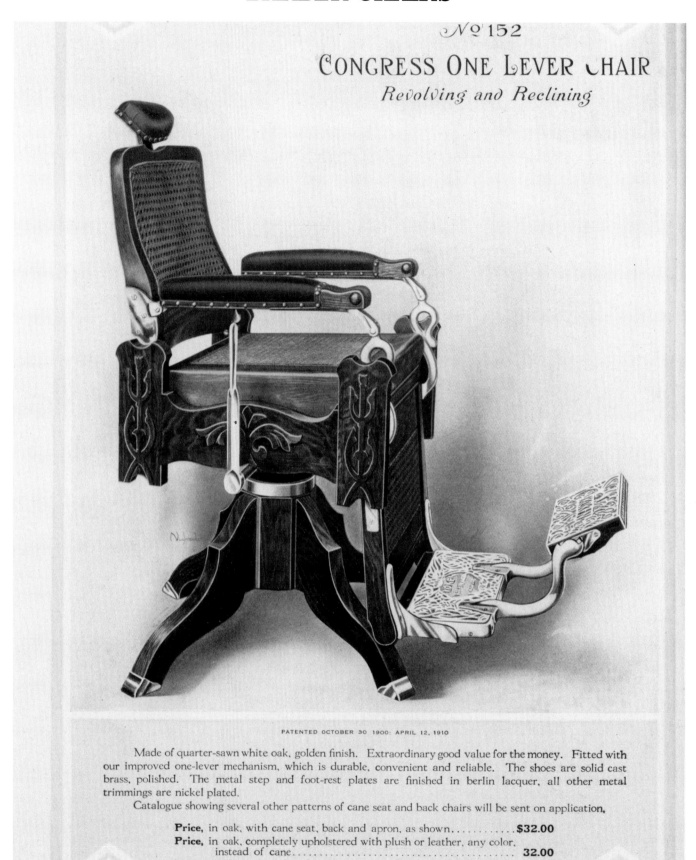

№ 152
CONGRESS ONE LEVER CHAIR
Revolving and Reclining

PATENTED OCTOBER 30 1900; APRIL 12, 1910

Made of quarter-sawn white oak, golden finish. Extraordinary good value for the money. Fitted with our improved one-lever mechanism, which is durable, convenient and reliable. The shoes are solid cast brass, polished. The metal step and foot-rest plates are finished in berlin lacquer, all other metal trimmings are nickel plated.

Catalogue showing several other patterns of cane seat and back chairs will be sent on application.

Price, in oak, with cane seat, back and apron, as shown............$32.00
Price, in oak, completely upholstered with plush or leather, any color, instead of cane... 32.00
Price, oak Summer seat, extra... 3.00

Koken Supply Co., 1911 catalog page.

BARBER CHAIRS

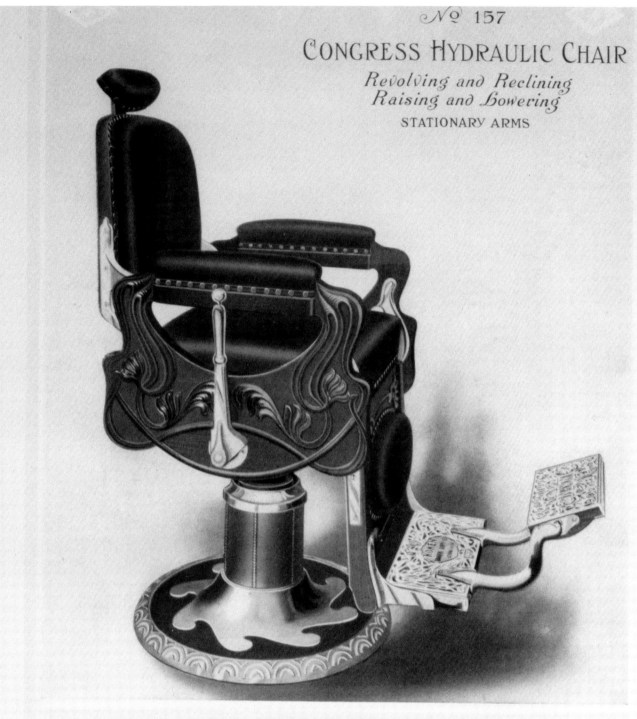

Koken Supply Co., 1911 catalog page.

BARBER CHAIRS

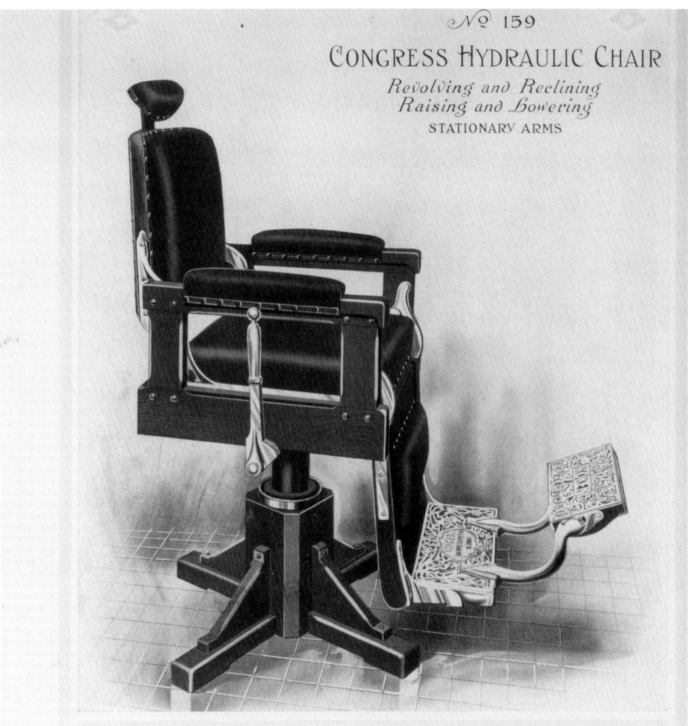

Koken Supply Co., 1911 catalog page.

BARBER CHAIRS

Koken Supply Co., 1911 catalog page.

BARBER CHAIRS

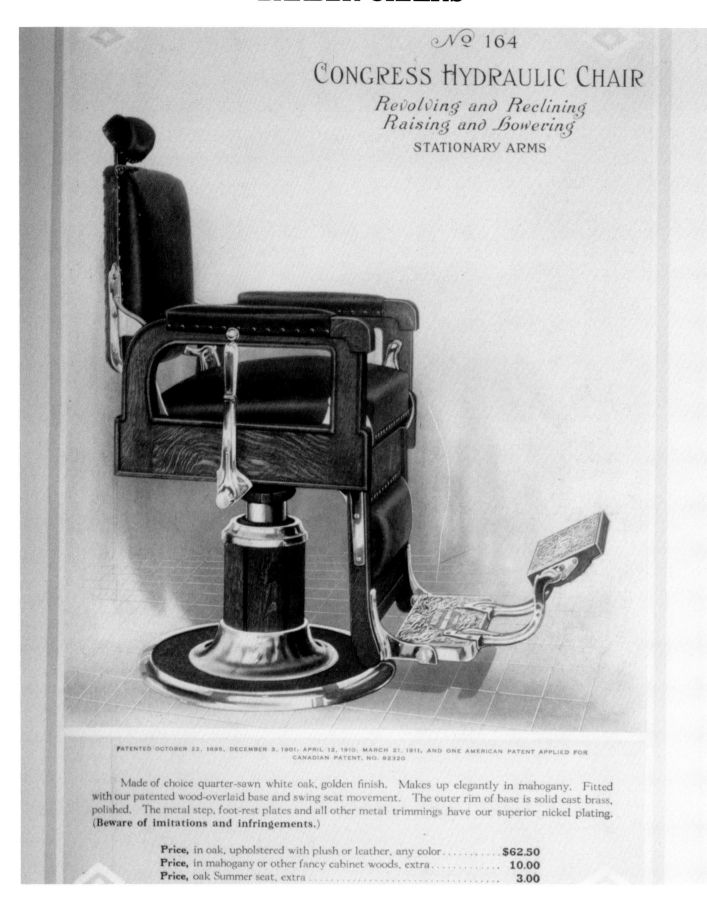

Koken Supply Co., 1911 catalog page.

BARBER CHAIRS

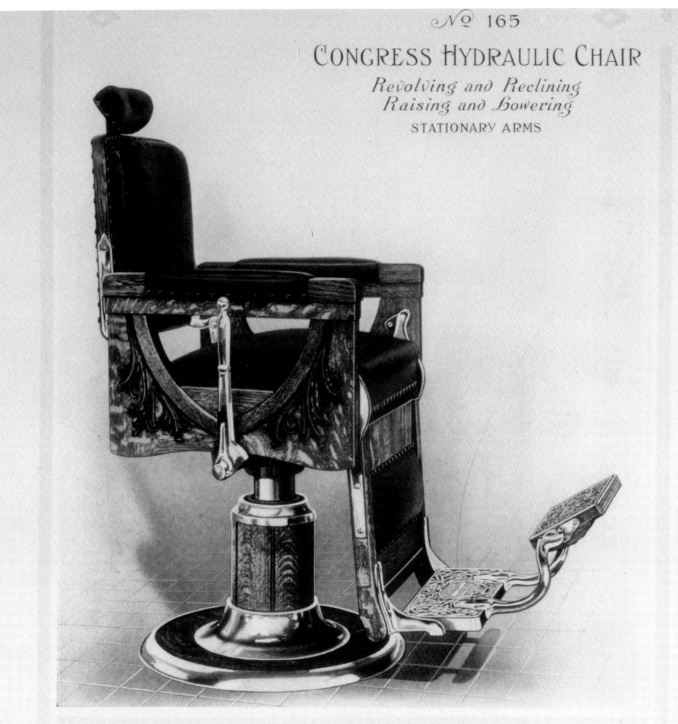

№ 165
CONGRESS HYDRAULIC CHAIR
Revolving and Reclining
Raising and Lowering
STATIONARY ARMS

PATENTED OCTOBER 22, 1895; DECEMBER 3, 1901; APRIL 12, 1910; MARCH 21, 1911; AND ONE AMERICAN PATENT APPLIED FOR
CANADIAN PATENT, NO. 92320

Made of choice quarter-sawn white oak, golden finish. Fitted with our patented wood-overlaid base and swing seat movement. The outer rim of base is solid cast brass, polished. The metal step and footrest plates are finished in berlin lacquer, all other metal trimmings are handsomely nickel plated. **(Beware of imitations and infringements.)**

Price, in oak, upholstered with plush or leather, any color $60.00
Price, in mahogany or other fancy cabinet woods, extra 10.00
Price, oak Summer seat, extra 3.00

Koken Supply Co., 1911 catalog page.

BARBER CHAIRS

№ 166
CONGRESS HYDRAULIC CHAIR
Revolving and Reclining
Raising and Lowering

PATENTED OCTOBER 22, 1895. DECEMBER 3, 1901. APRIL 12, 1910

Made of choice quarter-sawn white oak, golden finish. Fitted with our patented wood-overlaid base. The metal step, foot-rest plates, outer rim of base and all other metal trimmings have our superior nickel plating. **(Beware of imitations and infringements.)**

Price, in oak, upholstered with plush or leather, any color **$65.00**
Price, in mahogany or other fancy cabinet woods, extra 10.00
Price, oak Summer seat, extra 3.00

Koken Supply Co., 1911 catalog page

BARBER CHAIRS

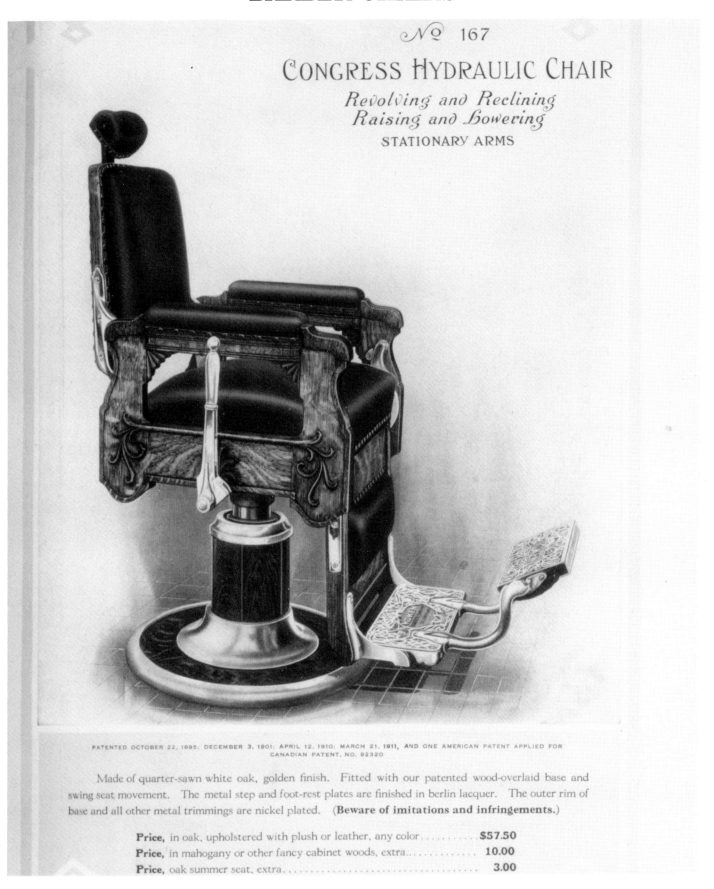

№ 167
Congress Hydraulic Chair
Revolving and Reclining
Raising and Lowering
STATIONARY ARMS

PATENTED OCTOBER 22, 1895; DECEMBER 3, 1901; APRIL 12, 1910; MARCH 21, 1911, AND ONE AMERICAN PATENT APPLIED FOR
CANADIAN PATENT, NO. 92320

Made of quarter-sawn white oak, golden finish. Fitted with our patented wood-overlaid base and swing seat movement. The metal step and foot-rest plates are finished in berlin lacquer. The outer rim of base and all other metal trimmings are nickel plated. **(Beware of imitations and infringements.)**

Price, in oak, upholstered with plush or leather, any color	$57.50
Price, in mahogany or other fancy cabinet woods, extra	10.00
Price, oak summer seat, extra	3.00

Koken Supply Co., catalog page

BARBER CHAIRS

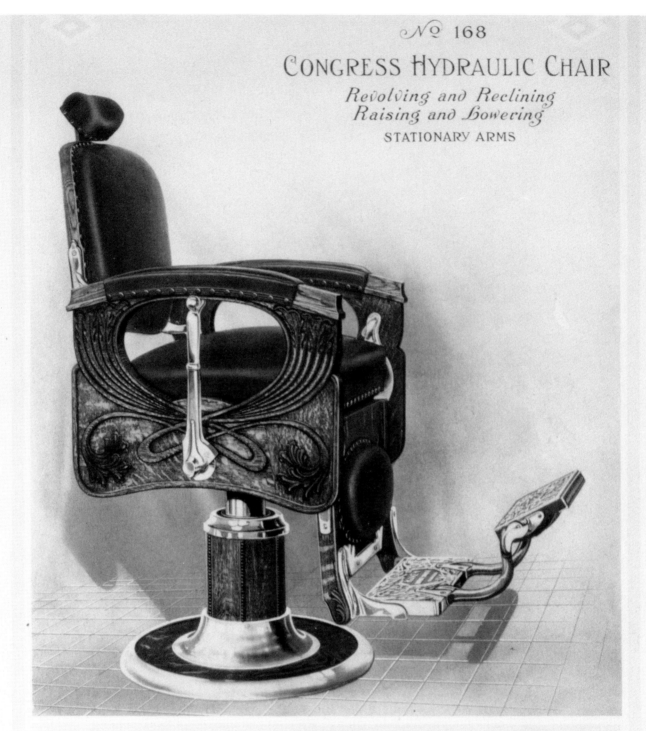

№ 168
CONGRESS HYDRAULIC CHAIR
Revolving and Reclining
Raising and Lowering
STATIONARY ARMS

PATENTED OCTOBER 22, 1895; DECEMBER 3, 1901; APRIL 12, 1910; MARCH 21, 1911, AND ONE AMERICAN PATENT APPLIED FOR
CANADIAN PATENT, NO. 92320

Made of quarter-sawn white oak, golden finish. Fitted with our patented wood-overlaid base and swing seat movement. The step, heel and foot-rest plates and the outer rim of base are solid cast brass, polished, all other metal trimmings are nickel plated. (**Beware of imitations and infringements.**)

Price, in oak, upholstered with best grain leather, any color.......$100.00
Price, in mahogany or other fancy cabinet woods, extra.......... 15.00
Price, oak Summer seat, extra 5.00
Price, mahogany Summer seat, extra 7.00

Koken Supply Co., 1911 catalog page.

BARBER CHAIRS

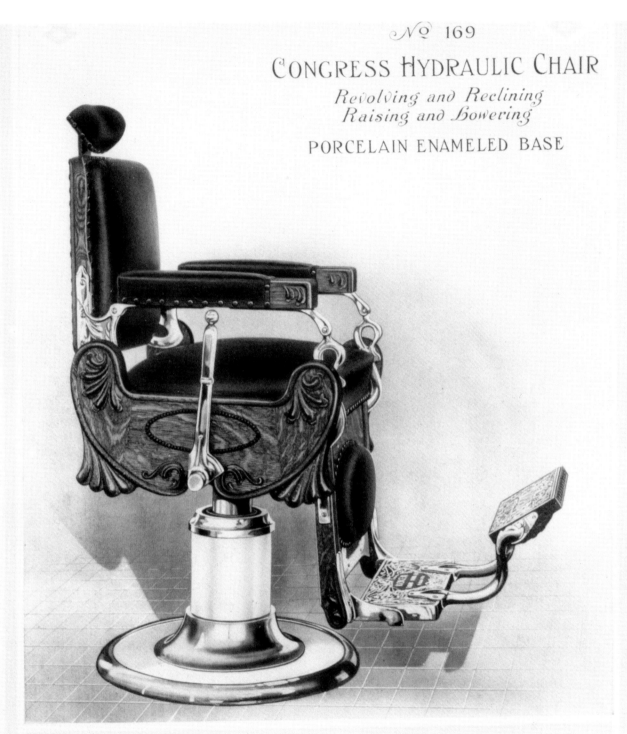

Koken Supply Co., 1911 catalog page.

BARBER CHAIRS

№ 170
Congress Pedestal One Lever Chair
Revolving and Reclining

PATENTED OCTOBER 30, 1900; DECEMBER 3, 1901; APRIL 12, 1910

Made of quarter-sawn white oak, golden finish. Fitted with our patented wood-overlaid base. The metal step and foot-rest plates and the outer rim of base are finished in berlin lacquer, all other metal trimmings are nickel plated. We apply our improved one-lever mechanism for revolving and reclining, which is positive and powerful, easily handled and satisfactory in every way.

Price, in oak, upholstered with plush or leather, any color............$42.50
Price, oak Summer seat, extra... 3.00

Koken Supply Co., 1911 catalog page.

BARBER CHAIRS

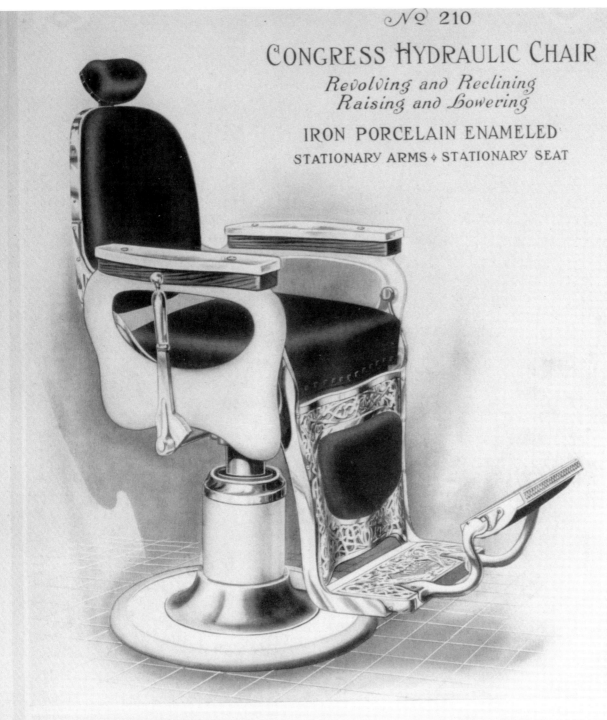

Koken Supply Co., 1911 catalog page.

BARBER CHAIRS

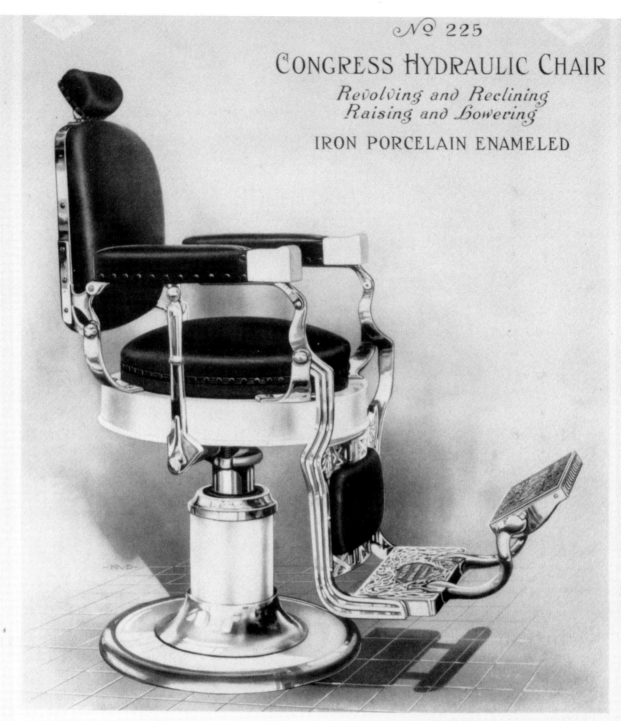

№ 225
Congress Hydraulic Chair
Revolving and Reclining
Raising and Lowering

IRON PORCELAIN ENAMELED

PATENTED OCTOBER 22, 1895; DECEMBER 3, 1901; APRIL 12, 1910; MAY 17, 1910. DESIGN PATENTED MAY 3, 1910.

The acme of barber chair construction. Strong and durable; artistic in appearance. The seat frame, pedestal drum and plate and hand-holds are made of iron, porcelain enameled. The spider, which supports the seat frame, and the side bars, which support the apron and footboard, are made of malleable iron. The step, the foot-rest plates and the outer rim of base are solid cast brass, polished. All other exposed metal parts are heavily nickel plated. It is fitted with all our patented improvements. (**Beware of imitations and infringements.**)

Price, as shown, upholstered with best grain leather, any color.......$85.00
Price, with mahogany ends on upholstered arms, instead of porcelain
    enameled, as shown... 85.00
Price, with marble or white glass arms, on mahogany blocks......... 90.00
Price, mahogany Summer seat, with cane weaving, extra........... 7.00

Koken Supply Co., 1911 catalog page.

BARBER CHAIRS

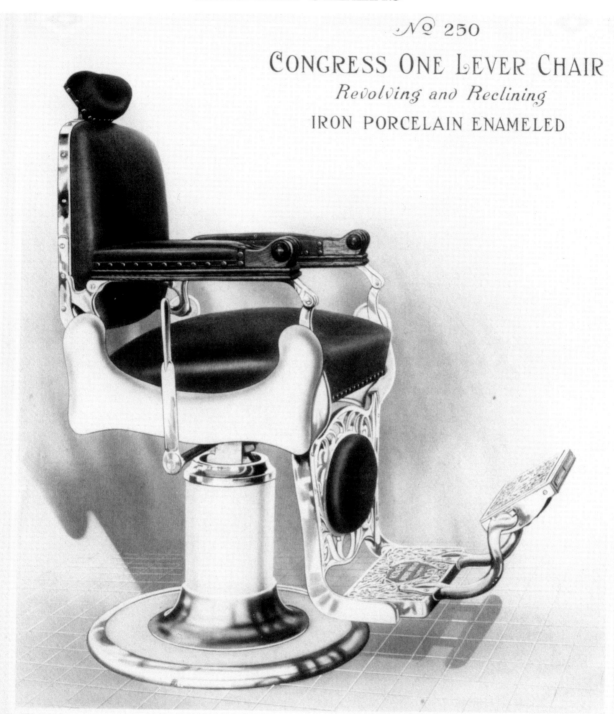

Koken Supply Co., 1911 catalog page.

BARBER CHAIRS

№ 500

CONGRESS HYDRAULIC CHAIR

*Revolving and Reclining
Raising and Lowering*

IRON PORCELAIN ENAMELED

PATENTED OCTOBER 22, 1895; DECEMBER 3, 1901; MARCH 1, 1910; APRIL 12, 1910; MAY 17, 1910; DECEMBER 6, 1910
DESIGN PATENT APPLIED FOR

The Barber Chair De Luxe. Octagon design. The richest and most attractive Porcelain Enameled Barber Chair ever offered to the trade. It is not only unique and attractive in its appearance, but is so constructed as to be exceptionally strong and durable. The seat frame, pedestal drum and plate and handholds, are made of iron, porcelain enameled. The step, the foot-rest plates and the outer rim of base are solid cast brass, polished. All other exposed metal parts are heavily nickel plated. It is fitted with all our patented improvements, including our patented sanitary paper-holding head-rest. (**Beware of imitations and infringements.**)

Price, as shown, upholstered with best grain leather, any color	$100.00
Price, with mahogany ends on upholstered arms, instead of porcelain enameled, as shown	100.00
Price, with marble or white glass arms, on mahogany blocks, extra	5.00
Price, mahogany Summer seat, with cane weaving, extra	7.50

Koken Supply Co., 1911 catalog page.

BARBER CHAIRS

Emil J. Paidar Co., 1925 catalog page.

BARBER CHAIRS

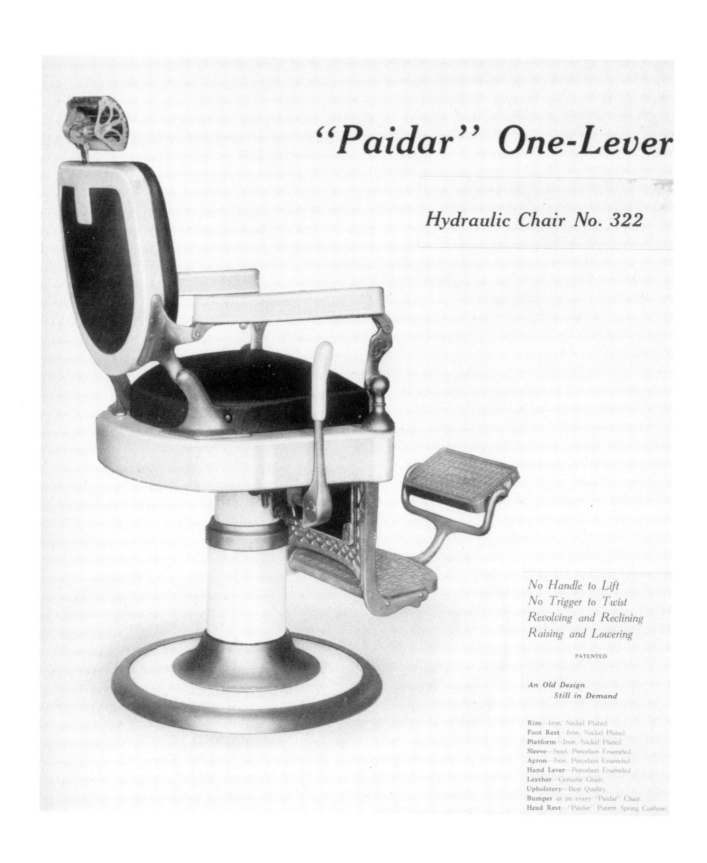

Emil J. Paidar Co., 1925 catalog page.

BARBER CHAIRS

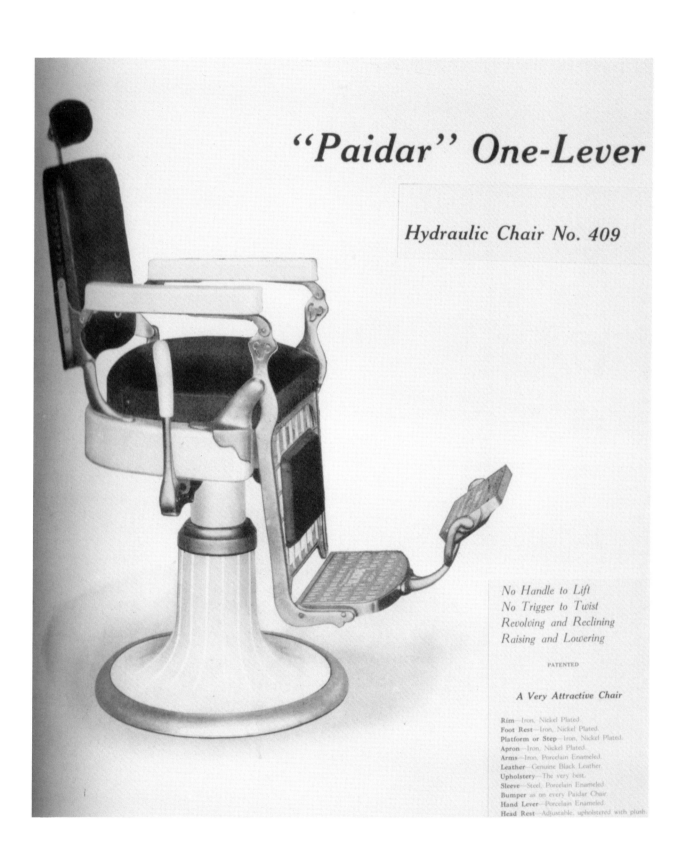

Emil J. Paidar Co., 1925 catalog page.

BARBER CHAIRS

Emil J. Paidar Co., 1932 catalog page.

Paidar BARBER SHOP EQUIPMENT

Paidar Hydraulic Chair No. 549

Paidar DUO-HYDRAULIC-CHAIR

GO-HIGH — GO-LOW

RAISES — LOWERS — REVOLVES — RECLINES

In this chair we offer one that is particularly attractive. The round seat makes it a little different than the average, but it is just as comfortable. This chair is made entirely of iron porcelain enamel. All exposed metal parts are highly nickel-plated, but may be had in chromium plate at a slight additional cost. It is fitted with the Paidar Duo-Hydraulic Mechanism which raises high enough for the tallest barber and goes low enough for the shortest.

Furnished complete with Radiap Spring Cushion Headrest, Porcelain Apron, Single Arm Footrest, Spring Bumper, Holder in Seat for Headrest, Towel Bar, Manicure Sockets, etc. Furnished in any of our regular colors of enamel or leather.

Always Furnished in Colors as Shown Unless Ordered Otherwise

"The Chair with the Longer Life"

BARBER CHAIRS

Paidar BARBER SHOP EQUIPMENT
Paidar Hydraulic Chair No. 821-C. E.

GO-HIGH — GO-LOW

Paidar DUO-HYDRAULIC-CHAIR

RAISES—LOWERS—REVOLVES—RECLINES

An unusual chair at a very moderate price made of iron porcelain enameled, including Seat Frame, Apron, Arms, Handle, Base and Sleeve. Back is surrounded by a German Silver Band. May be had in any of our regular colors of leather and enamel. Two-tone enamel may be had if desired in any combination of our regular colors. Exposed metal parts are nickel-plated, but may be had in chromium plate at a slight additional cost.

Complete in every respect including Paidar Duo-Hydraulic Mechanism, Radiap Spring Cushion Headrest, Porcelain Apron, Single Arm Footrest, Spring Bumper, Headrest Holder in seat, Towel Bar, Manicure Sockets and hole in Back to allow hair falling in Headrest slot to fall through.

Always Furnished in Colors as Shown Unless Ordered Otherwise

"The Chair with the Longer Life"

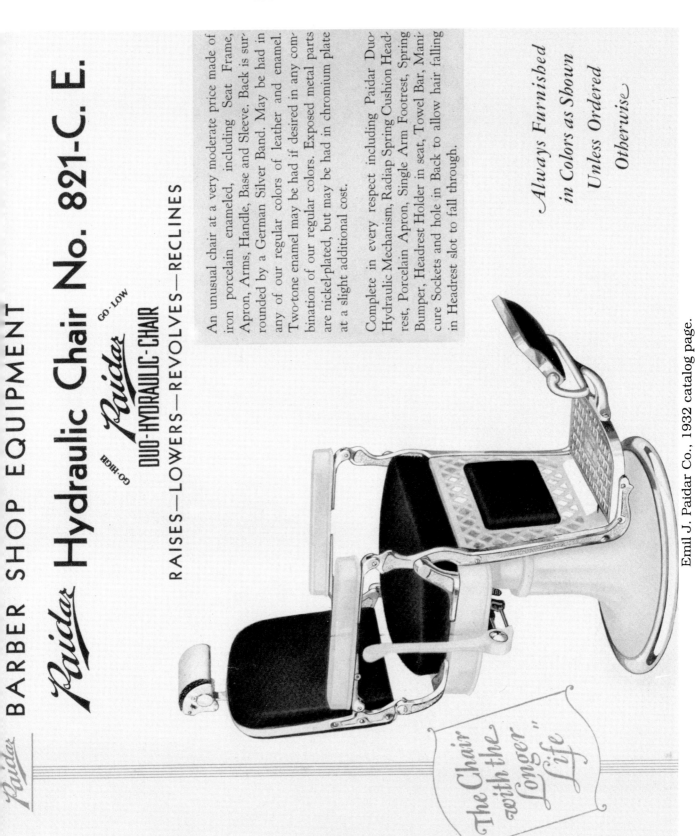

Emil J. Paidar Co., 1932 catalog page.

BARBER CHAIRS

Emil J. Paidar Co., 1932 catalog page.

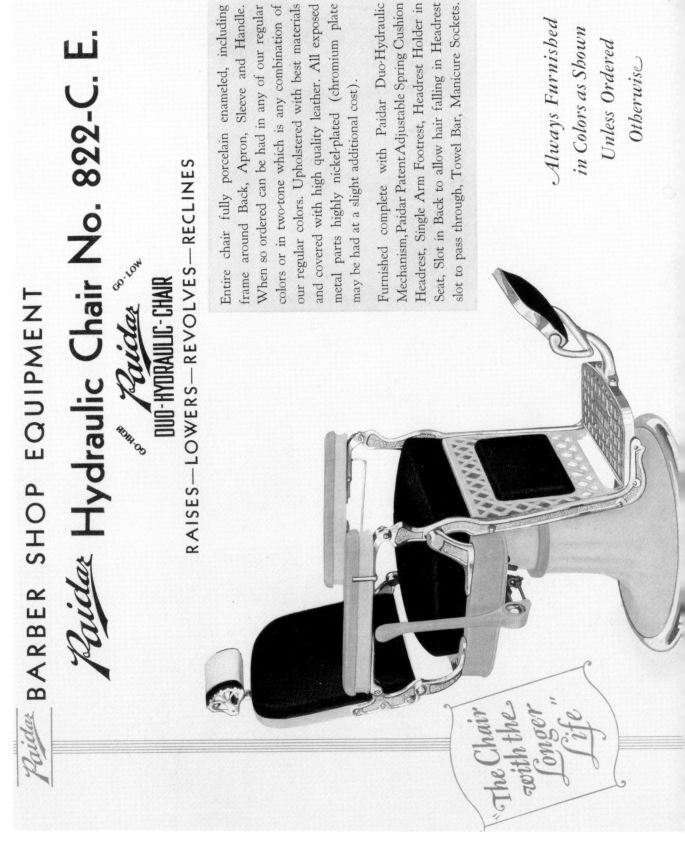

BARBER SHOP EQUIPMENT

Paidar Hydraulic Chair No. 822-C. E.

GO-HIGH — GO-LOW

Paidar DUO-HYDRAULIC-CHAIR

RAISES — LOWERS — REVOLVES — RECLINES

Entire chair fully porcelain enameled, including frame around Back, Apron, Sleeve and Handle. When so ordered can be had in any of our regular colors or in two-tone which is any combination of our regular colors. Upholstered with best materials and covered with high quality leather. All exposed metal parts highly nickel-plated (chromium plate may be had at a slight additional cost).

Furnished complete with Paidar Duo-Hydraulic Mechanism, Paidar Patent Adjustable Spring Cushion Headrest, Single Arm Footrest, Headrest Holder in Headrest, Slot in Back to allow hair falling in Headrest slot to pass through, Towel Bar, Manicure Sockets.

Always Furnished in Colors as Shown Unless Ordered Otherwise

"The Chair with the Longer Life"

BARBER CHAIRS

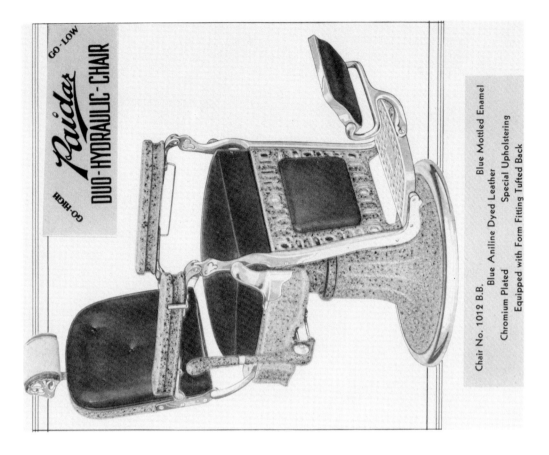

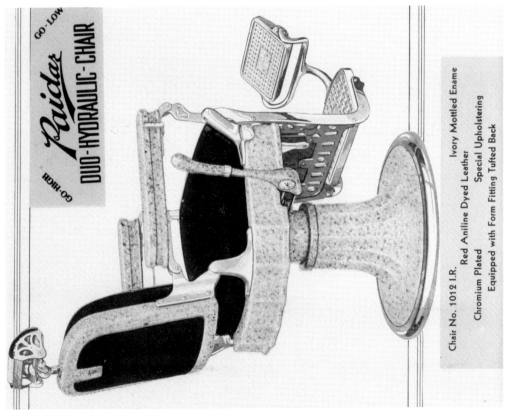

Both chairs from Emil J. Paidar Co., 1932 catalog page.

BARBER CHAIRS

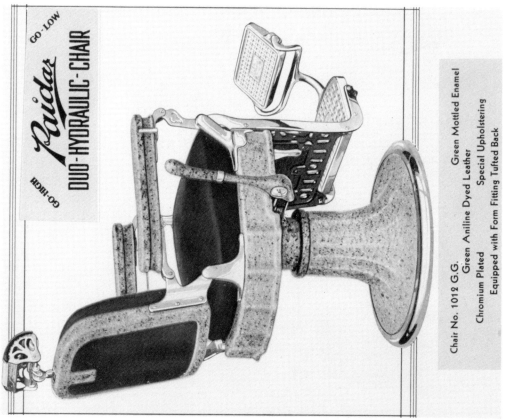

Both chairs from Emil J. Paidar Co., 1932 catalog page.

BARBER CHAIRS

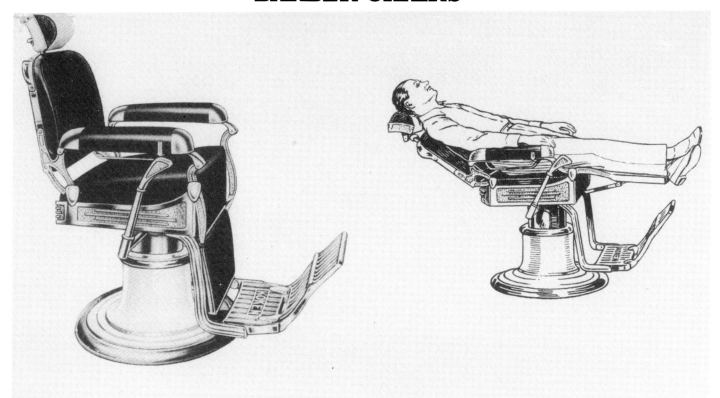

No. 754 SUPER LUXOR CHAIR

Upholstered with KOKEN'S exclusive DUNLOPILLO Cushions, covered in Top Grain Leather, this chair is the acme of comfort.

Heavy high-lighted Chrome Plated Seat Frame; Newly designed, perfect posture arms. KOKEN'S exclusive 10-inch range Hydraulic Lock. Large Porcelain Enameled Base. All castings Chrome Plated. Chair equipped with adjustable DUNLOPILLO Headrest and KOKEN'S patented, improved leg-rest which supports the legs when Chair is in reclined position.

THE SUPER LUXOR CHAIR . . THE BARBER CHAIR OF TOMORROW

No. 736 CHAIR

An exquisite All-Chrome Chair. Streamlined, form-fitting Back and Seat. Soft Spring Upholstery covered with Genuine Leather. Triple Chrome Plated Spun Copper Base. Perfect posture Chrome Plated Arms — cut out on sides, and upholstered to match seat. Seat Frame and all other castings, Triple Plated Chrome, except Foot Board and Foot Rest which are of Polished White Metal Alloy which will not turn brassy. KOKEN'S exclusive 10-inch range Hydraulic Lock and finger tip reclining.

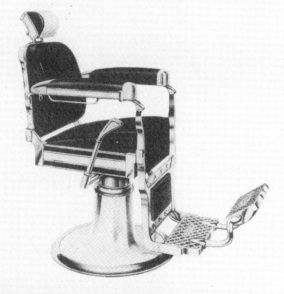

No. 735 CHAIR

Smartly designed, and colorful — a chair which will enhance the beauty of any shop. Polished Chrome Seat Frame carries colored Bakelite for beauty. Perfect posture Arms decorated with colored Bakelite to match Seat Frame. Porcelain Enameled Fluted Base. Soft Spring Upholstery. All Castings Triple Chrome Plated, except Footrest and Footstep which are made of White Metal Alloy. KOKEN'S exclusive DUNLOPILLO Headrest. 10-inch range Hydraulic Lock and finger tip reclining.

Buerger Bros. Supply Co., 1935 catalog page. (authorized Koken dealer)

BARBER CHAIRS

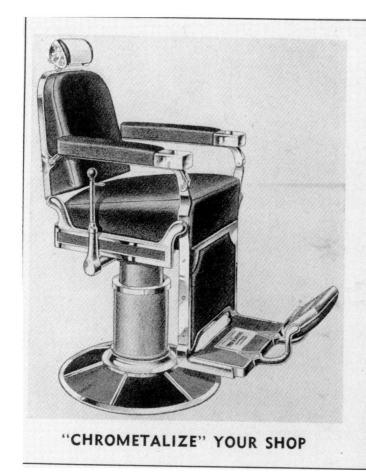

Classified Ad for Kochs Co., Model 1936 "CHROMETAL" barbers' chair
(Ad from 1936 "Barbers Journal" catalog page.)

BARBER CHAIRS

Summer Seats for Barber Chairs.

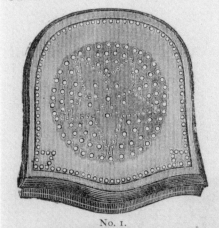

No. 1.

This Summer Seat is made to be used in the "Beauty" and "Pride of the West" Chairs. Price $2.00.

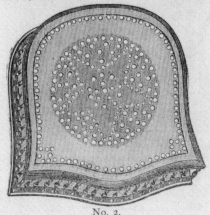

No. 2.

This is made for the "Novelty" and "Lady Gay." Price, $3.00.

Barbers having barber chairs of other make and wishing to procure Summer Seats for same can be accomodated by sending me the size of the bottom of upholstered seat, which can be easily done by laying a piece of strong paper on the bottom of upholstered seat, and trimming close with scissors.

Prices: No. 1, $2.50, No. 2, $3.50.

EUGENE BERNINGHAUS'
IMPROVED
Children's Hair Cutting Chair and Shampoo Stool

Shampoo Seat.

This Chair can be raised to any desired height by simply raising the seat. The spring (S) holds the same in position; the seat revolves wherever placed. By pulling the spring (S) the seat can be lowered. The back-rest (B) is loose and can be taken out if the child is too small. The back-rest (B) is veneered. The chair can also be used as a Shampoo Stool by taking off the upper part of chair and placing the other seat, which is also upholstered, on the stool; this makes it one of the most useful and convenient articles in a shop. No shop complete without it.

Covered in Plush, Carpet or Enameled Cloth, $6.00
Extra Seat for Shampoo Stool 1.00

Eugene Berninghaus Co., 1881 catalog page.

BARBER CHAIRS

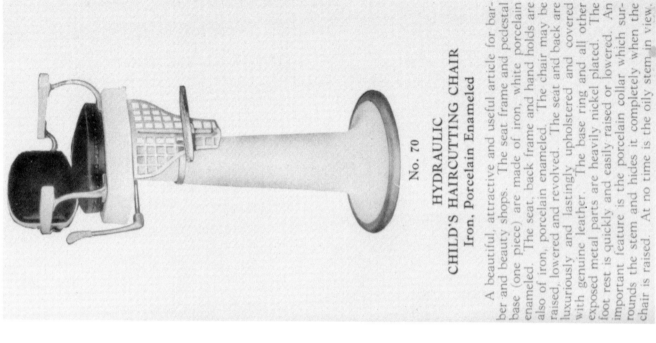

No. 70

**HYDRAULIC
CHILD'S HAIRCUTTING CHAIR
Iron, Porcelain Enameled**

A beautiful, attractive and useful article for barber and beauty shops. The seat frame and pedestal base (one piece) are made of iron, white porcelain enameled. The seat, back frame and hand holds are also of iron, porcelain enameled. The chair may be raised, lowered and revolved. The seat and back are luxuriously and lastingly upholstered and covered with genuine leather. The base ring and all other exposed metal parts are heavily nickel plated. The foot rest is quickly and easily raised or lowered. An important feature is the porcelain collar which surrounds the stem and hides it completely when the chair is raised. At no time is the oily stem in view.

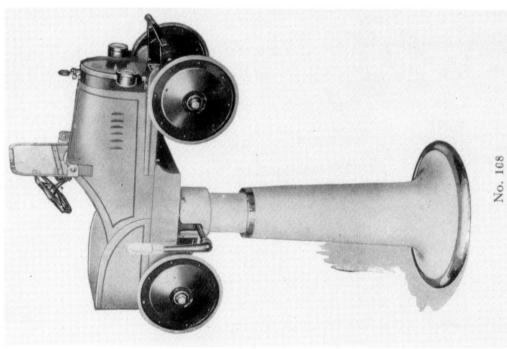

No. 108

**HYDRAULIC
CHILD'S AUTO HAIRCUTTING CHAIR
Iron, Porcelain Enameled**

Same as our No. 70, equipped with an auto made of metal painted blue in color, decorated with yellow striping. It is fitted with our hydraulic machine for raising, lowering and revolving. It is also fitted with a steel porcelain enameled sleeve which covers the oily stem.

Chairs made by Emil J. Paidar Co. (1925 catalog page.)

BARBER CHAIRS

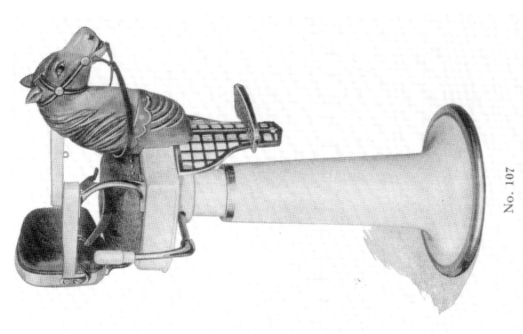

No. 107

HYDRAULIC
CHILD'S HAIRCUTTING CHAIR
Iron, Porcelain Enameled

Same as our No. 70. Fitted with a finely carved horse's head which can be removed when desired and as readily attached to the seat frame of the chair. This chair can be raised, lowered, and revolved. It is fitted with a steel porcelain enameled sleeve which covers the oily stem.

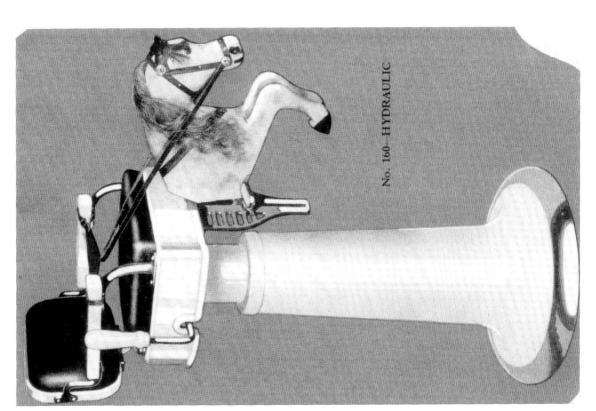

No. 160—HYDRAULIC

Hydraulic childs' chair No. 107 is by Emil J. Paidar Co. (1925). Chair No. 160 is a Hercules Hydraulic Chair. By Fred Dolle Inc. (1924).

141

BARBER CHAIRS

No. 17. CHILDREN'S SEAT

This seat is made of wood, entirely covered with imitation leather, and has an apron to cover the seat of the chair so as to protect it from the child's feet. This seat is made so that it has really three heights. When placed on the arm of the chair, as shown, it is at its highest. When reversed so the box is downward, it is about four inches lower. When placed on the cushion as outlined it is still lower.

No. 20. CHILDREN'S SEAT

Made to hang over the back of barber's chair. It is adjustable to three heights, and is very substantial. Nickel plated finish and seat of black leatherette.

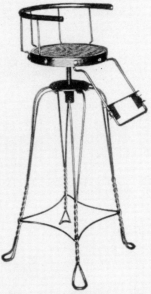

No. 500. HAIR CUTTING CHAIR

Made of steel wire, oxidized copper finish and adjustable for height. The seat is of oak.

Emil J. Paidar Co., 1925 catalog page

BARBER CHAIRS

No. 2 Child's Chair.
With cane seat, screw machinery.
Price,...................... $3.50
No. 7—Same as No. 2, but with upholstered seat 4.50

No. 466 Child's Chair.
Can be raised and lowered; adjustable foot-rest. Steel, oxidized finish. Polished oak seat.
Price,....................each, $5.50

No. 9 Child's Chair.
Made of Oak, Golden finish. Adjustable screw machine. Metal foot rest.
Price, ...$7.00

No. 8 Child's Hair Cutting Seat.
Is adjustable; to be hung over the back of a barber's chair. This raises the child to a convenient height. The feet rest on cushion seat of chair, protected by towel or otherwise. The hooks are nickel plated and rubber protected.
Each $3.50

No. 1 Folding Barber Chair.
Made of Oak, Golden finish, covered with velour, trimmed with fringe to match.
Price, ... $13.50

Koken Supply Co. 1910 catalog page.

BARBER CHAIRS

WAITING CHAIR, NO. 167.

Made of ELM (antique oak finish).

Price, per dozen $20.00

SHAMPOOING STOOL.

ANTIQUE OAK finish. Cane seat.

24 inches high.

Price $2.50

CHILDREN'S HAIR-CUTTING CHAIR, NO. 18.

Made of OAK (antique finish) only.

Cane Seat and Back, without Foot-rest $5.00
Plush Seat and Cane Back, without Foot-rest 6.00
Adjustable Foot-rest, extra 1.00

CHILDREN'S HAIR-CUTTING CHAIR, NO. 17.

Made of Hard Wood, ANTIQUE OAK finish only.

Cane Seat $3.25
Plush Seat 4.25

Theo. A. Kochs Co., 1897 catalog page.

BARBER CHAIRS

No. 80 Seating Chair.
Made of Oak, Chestnut Seat, Golden finish.
Price, ... each, $2.75

No. 85 Seating Chair.
Made of Rock Elm, Golden finish.
Price, ... per dozen, $16.00

No. 75 Seating Chair.
Made of Oak, Chestnut Seat, Golden finish.
Price, ... each, $3.25

No. 90 Seating Chair.
Made of Quarter-sawn Oak, Golden finish.
Price, ... each, $6.00

No. 465 Metal Chair.
Steel, copper oxidized finish; polished oak seat.
Price, ... each, $2.50

No. 71 Mission Style Chair.
Made of Quarter-sawn Oak, Golden finish.
Price, ... each, $6.50

No. 121 Shampoo Stool.
Made of Oak, Golden finish.
Height, 22 inches.
Price, ... each, $1.50

No. 464 Shampoo Stool.
Made of Steel, copper oxidized. Polished oak seat. Height, 22 inches.
Price, ... each, $2.25

No. 16 Shampoo Stool.
Vienna Bent Wood.
Height, 22 inches.
Price, ... each, $2.25

John Rieder & Co., 1910 catalog page.

BARBER CHAIRS

Koken Supply Co., 1904 catalog page.

WALL FIXTURES WITH MIRRORS

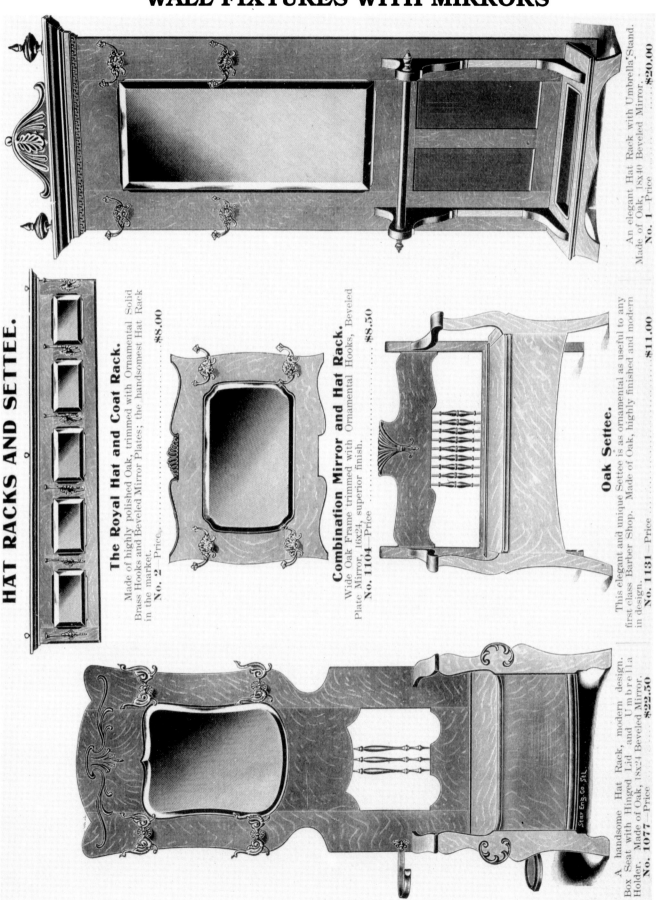

An elegant Hat Rack with Umbrella Stand. Made of Oak, 18x40 Beveled Mirror.
No. 1—Price $20.00

HAT RACKS AND SETTEE.

The Royal Hat and Coat Rack.
Made of highly polished Oak, trimmed with Ornamental Solid Brass Hooks and Beveled Mirror Plates; the handsomest Hat Rack in the market.
No. 2—Price $8.00

Combination Mirror and Hat Rack.
Wide Oak Frame trimmed with Ornamental Hooks, Beveled Plate Mirror, 16x24, superior finish.
No. 1104—Price $8.50

Oak Settee.
This elegant and unique Settee is as ornamental as useful to any first class Barber Shop. Made of Oak, highly finished and modern in design.
No. 1131—Price $11.00

A handsome Hat Rack, modern design. Box Seat with Hinged Lid and Umbrella Holder. Made of Oak, 18x24 Beveled Mirror.
No. 1077—Price $22.50

Koken Supply Co., 1904 catalog page.

WALL FIXTURES WITH MIRRORS

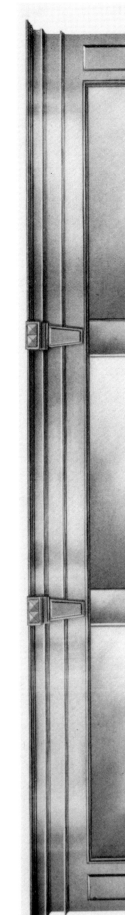

John Rieder & Co., 1911 catalog page.

MIRROR CASE, No. 375

Woodwork white-enameled in the best possible manner. French mirror plates, plain, 36 x 48, divided by 8-inch mirrors with rounded, polished edges, presenting a continuous mirror surface. Italian marble shelf and base. Cabinets fitted with Yale locks and glass knobs and supported by white-enameled steel brackets. The plain design and sanitary arrangement of this case combine to make it a very practical fixture at a moderate price. Height, 7 feet 9 inches.

PRICES

2-chair case, length 10 ft. 9 in.	$140.00
3-chair case, length 15 ft. 4 in.	203.00
4-chair case, length 19 ft. 11 in.	$266.00
5-chair case, length 24 ft. 7 in.	329.00

WALL FIXTURES WITH MIRRORS

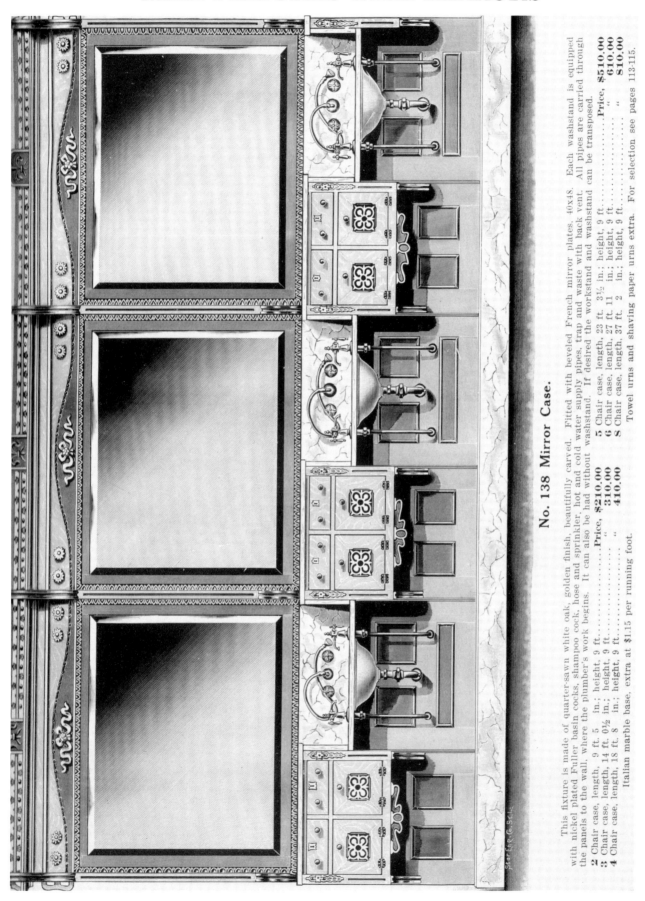

No. 138 Mirror Case.

This fixture is made of quarter-sawn white oak, golden finish, beautifully carved. Fitted with beveled French mirror plates, 40x48. Each washstand is equipped with nickel plated Fuller basin cocks, shampoo cock, hose and sprinkler, hot and cold water supply pipes, trap and waste with back vent. All pipes are carried through the panels to the wall, where the plumber's work begins. It can also be had without washstand. If desired the workstand and washstand can be transposed.

2 Chair case, length, 9 ft. 5   in.; height, 9 ft. ....Price, $210.00 5 Chair case, length, 23 ft. 3½ in.; height, 9 ft................Price, $510.00
3 Chair case, length, 14 ft. 0½ in.; height, 9 ft. .... "   310.00 6 Chair case, length, 27 ft. 11 in.; height, 9 ft................ "   610.00
4 Chair case, length, 18 ft. 8   in.; height, 9 ft. .... "   410.00 8 Chair case, length, 37 ft. 2   in.; height, 9 ft................ "   810.00

Italian marble base, extra at $1.15 per running foot. Towel urns and shaving paper urns extra. For selection see pages 113-115.

Koken Supply Co., 1910 catalog page.

WALL FIXTURES WITH MIRRORS

John Rieder & Co., 1912 catalog page.

MIRROR CASE, No. 225.

Made of quarter-sawed oak, golden finish. French mirror plates, beveled, size 36 x 40 and 15 x 36 and 8 x 18. Italian marble shelf. Sanitary workstands with open compartments for clean towels, shallow drawers for razors, shears and other small tools and large drawers fitted with Yale locks. Brass drawer knobs and handles and oxidized copper finished metal legs. Earthenware towel urns and Bohemian glass shaving-paper vases furnished with each case. Height, 8 feet 8 inches.

PRICES

2-chair case, length 10 ft. 2 in.	$146.00	4-chair case, length 19 ft. 3 in.	$270.00
3-chair case, length 14 ft. 9 in.	208.00	5-chair case, length 23 ft. 10 in.	332.00

150

WALL FIXTURES WITH MIRRORS

MIRROR CASE, No. 267

Made of quarter-sawed oak, golden finish. French mirror plates, beveled, size 36 x 48, connected by 6 x 36 beveled mirror strips. Beveled French plate mirror pillars at each end of the case, fitted with opaque glass electric light globes mounted on polished brass globe holders. Italian marble shelf. Sanitary open base with handsome work cabinets, each containing a compartment for clean towels, large drawer with Yale lock and smaller drawer for tools, etc. The cabinets are provided with doors opening on the side in place of the usual drop doors and all three sides of each cabinet are fitted with beveled, clear French plate panels. Polished solid brass hardware throughout. Bohemian shaving-paper vases and glazed earthen towel urns are furnished with the case. Height of Mirror Case, 8 feet 8 inches.

PRICES

2-chair case, length 11 ft. 4 in.	$201.00	4-chair case, length 20 ft. 2 in.	$349.00
3-chair case, length 15 ft. 9 in.	275.00	5-chair case, length 24 ft. 7 in.	423.00

John Rieder & Co., 1912 catalog page.

WALL FIXTURES WITH MIRRORS

SECTIONAL WALL FIXTURES

John Rieder & Co. 1912 catalog page.

MUG CASE No. 429

Made of quarter-sawed oak, golden finish. Holds forty-nine mugs. Furnished with glass doors. Drawers and shelf compartment in base. Height, 8 feet 4 inches; width, 4 feet.
Price $32.00

WALL FIXTURE No. 436

This fixture consists of a substantially constructed settee, made of selected quarter-sawed oak, 5 feet long, and a wall mirror equipped with a metal hat rack in oxidized copper finish. The mirror is French plate, beveled, size, 30 x 48. Golden oak finish.
Price, complete $58.50

HAT AND COAT RACK, No. 427

Made of quarter-sawed oak, golden finish. French mirror plate, beveled, 30 inches diameter. Furnished complete with double coat and hat hooks and glazed earthenware umbrella jar. Height, 8 feet 4 inches; width, 3 feet 10 inches.
Price, complete ... $36.00

WALL FIXTURE No. 436

This fixture consists of a substantially constructed settee, made of selected quarter-sawed oak, 5 feet long, and a wall mirror equipped with a metal hat rack in oxidized copper finish. The mirror is French plate, beveled, size, 30 x 48. Golden oak finish.
Price, complete $58.50

PERFUMERY CASE No. 430

Made of quarter-sawed oak, golden finish. Fitted with adjustable shelves and glass doors. Two drawers in base. Height, 8 feet 4 inches; width, 4 feet.
Price $35.00

Combinations of fixtures on the style of the above illustration add greatly to the appearance of the modern barber shop. It will be noticed that such a combination is composed of different pieces of furniture which are units in themselves, and it will be seen, therefore, that quite a variety of combinations for the purpose may be had by merely varying the arrangement of the different fixtures required.

By adding up the prices of the different pieces of furniture as quoted above, the total list price of the combination illustrated is $220.00; entire length, 21 feet.

A cheaper combination may be had, for instance, by using the hat and coat rack No. 427 in the center and No. 436 fixture on each side of the hat and coat rack. The list price of such a combination would be $153.00; length, 13 feet 6 inches.

Again it would be possible to place two or three No. 436 fixtures in a row, in which case the connections between the large mirrors will be made by smaller mirrors, thus furnishing a continuous mirror effect.

WALL FIXTURES WITH MIRRORS

MIRROR CASE, No. 380

This fixture presents every conceivable practical feature in Mirror Case construction and will add greatly to the appearance of the modern tonsorial shop. Italian marble wainscoting and shelves throughout. White enameled woodwork around the mirrors with Italian marble rail adjoining the shelves on the cabinets. White enameled work cabinets with drawers, fitted with mirror plates, glass knobs and Yale locks. Cabinets and towel shelve supported by nickel-plated brackets made of one-inch brass tubing. Vitreous china pedestal lavatories complete with nickel-plated brass supply and waste pipes. Fuller basin cocks and combination shampoo cocks with hose, sprinkler and sprinkler holders. Plain French mirror plates, 44 x 60, divided by beveled mirror strips. Beautiful ivory finish earthenware towel urns and vases are furnished with this Mirror Case. Height of the Mirror Case, 8 ft. 7 in.

PRICES

2-chair case, length 12 ft. 7 in.	$425.00	5-chair case, length 28 ft. 5 in.	$1,016.00
3-chair case, length 17 ft. 10 in.	622.00	6-chair case, length 33 ft. 9 in.	1,213.00
4-chair case, length 23 ft. 2 in.	819.00	7-chair case, length 39 ft.	1,410.00

John Rieder & Co., 1912 catalog page.

WALL FIXTURES WITH MIRRORS

Theo. A. Kochs Co., 1897 catalog page.

MIRROR CASE NO. 439.

END VIEW.

DESIGN PATENT APPLIED FOR.

Made of Oak (antique finish) only. French plates 30x48 and Ornamental French plates at top. 8 x 12, all beveled. Italian marble shelf. The lower compartment of each workstand is made with latticed front and perforated metal bottom, permitting a free circulation of air so that injury from damp towels is prevented. Height of mirror case, 8 ft. 8 in.

PRICES:

Arranged for 3 Chairs............................$235.00. Arranged for 4 Chairs..................$310.00. Arranged for 5 Chairs..................$385.00.
Length of 3-Chair Case, as shown above, 15 ft. 2 in.

WALL FIXTURES WITH MIRRORS

MIRROR CASE NO. 136.

Made of Oak (antique finish) only, Italian marble top. In this mirror case we use full size German plates, beveled, 18x40 and 24x30. Comparison should not be made with mirror cases quoted in other catalogues in which no size of plates is given. The lower compartments of this mirror case are made with perforated metal bottom and latticed front, permitting a free circulation of air, so that injury from damp towels is prevented. Heighth of case, 7 feet 11 inches.

PRICES:

Arranged for 2 Chairs.................$107.25. Arranged for 3 Chairs.................$150.00. Arranged for 4 Chairs.................$192.75.
Length of 3-Chair Case, as shown above, 15 ft. 5 in.

Theo. A. Kochs Co., 1897 catalog page.

WALL FIXTURES WITH MIRRORS

John Rieder & Co., 1912 catalog page.

MIRROR CASE, No. 348

Made of selected quarter-sawed oak, golden finish. French mirror plates, 40 x 54, plain, and 24 x 40, beveled. Italian marble wainscoting and shelves. Polished plate-glass shelves under the small mirror plates supported by solid brass brackets, highly nickel-plated. Heavy nickel-plated brackets made of 1-inch brass tubing under marble shelves. Vitreous china lavatories with backs and equipped complete with nickel-plated brass supply and waste pipes to wall and china handle hot and cold water faucets. Combination shampoo cocks with best quality rubber hose, shampoo sprinklers and sprinkler holders. Ivory-finish towel urns and blue Bohemian glass shaving paper vases are furnished: 10-inch pillars with ornamental caps and 12-inch glass globes complete with electric light socket and heavy rubber-covered electric feed wire. Height of case, 8 feet 6 inches.

PRICES

3-chair case, length 21 ft. 7 in.		$725.00
4-chair case, length 26 ft. 10 in.		910.00
5-chair case, length 32 ft. 2 in.		$1,085.00
6-chair case, length 37 ft. 5 in.		1,280.00

WALL FIXTURES WITH MIRRORS

John Rieder & Co., 1912 catalog page.

WALL FIXTURES WITH MIRRORS

Koken Supply Co., 1910 catalog page.

No. 173 Mirror Case.

A very handsome case that will add beauty to any barber shop. Made of quarter-sawn white oak in golden finish. French beveled mirrors, 30x48, 24x36 and 18x36 in. Italian marble shelves. One No. 27 patented cut-out towel urn and one No. 156 shaving paper urn to match, as shown, furnished with each section.

WALL FIXTURES WITH MIRRORS

No. 168 Sanitary Mirror Case.

This case is made of quarter-sawn white oak in golden finish. Beveled French mirrors, 36x48 and 12x26 in. Porcelain enameled lavatories, with 19x24-in. slab, 12x15 oval bowl and 10-in. back in one piece, hung on concealed brackets. This construction avoids the ugly, black, greasy cracks often found on marble wash stands and places this fixture in the forefront from a sanitary point of view. The cocks, supplies, wastes, etc., are heavily nickel plated and are furnished as shown. The work cabinets have Italian marble tops.

2 Chair case, length, 11 ft. 5 in.; height, 8 ft............Price,	$205.00
3 Chair case, length, 16 ft. 4 in.; height, 8 ft............ "	300.00
4 Chair case, length, 21 ft. 3 in.; height, 8 ft............ "	395.00
5 Chair case, length, 26 ft. 2 in.; height, 8 ft............Price,	$490.00
6 Chair case, length, 31 ft. 1 in.; height, 8 ft............ "	585.00
7 Chair case, length, 36 ft. 0 in.; height, 8 ft............ "	680.00

Italian marble base, extra at $1.15 per running foot. Towel urns and shaving paper urns extra, see pages 113-115 for selection.

Koken Supply Co., 1910 catalog page.

WALL FIXTURES WITH MIRRORS

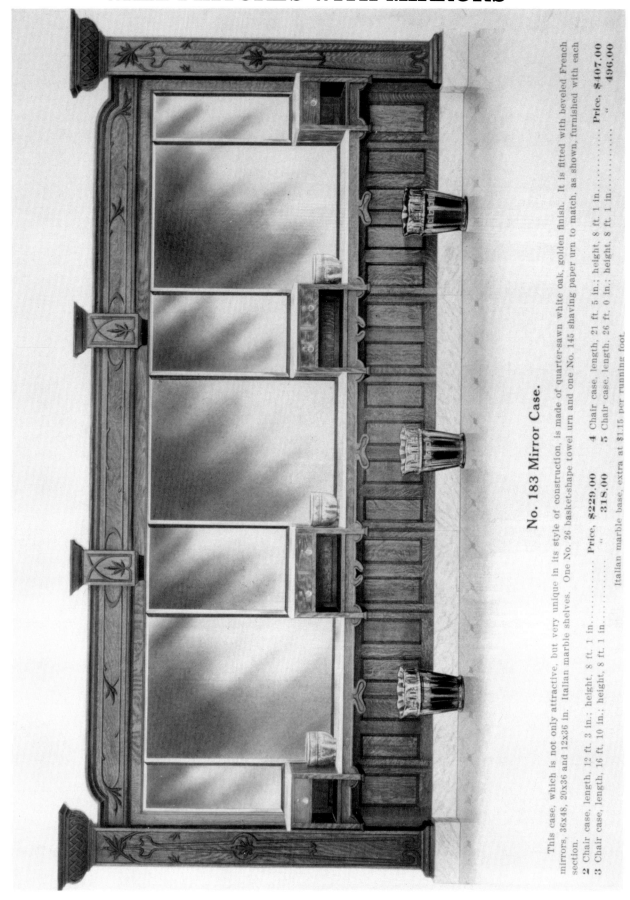

Koken Supply Co., 1910 catalog page.

No. 183 Mirror Case.

This case, which is not only attractive, but very unique in its style of construction, is made of quarter-sawn white oak, golden finish. It is fitted with beveled French mirrors, 36x48, 20x36 and 12x36 in. Italian marble shelves. One No. 26 basket-shape towel urn and one No. 145 shaving paper urn to match, furnished with each section.

2 Chair case, length, 12 ft. 3 in.; height, 8 ft. 1 in.	Price,	$229.00
3 Chair case, length, 16 ft. 10 in.; height, 8 ft. 1 in.	"	318.00
4 Chair case, length, 21 ft. 5 in.; height, 8 ft. 1 in.	"	407.00
5 Chair case, length, 26 ft. 0 in.; height, 8 ft. 1 in.	"	496.00

Italian marble base, extra at $1.15 per running foot.

WALL FIXTURES WITH MIRRORS

No. 171 Mirror Case.

This elegant case, with canopy top, is made of quarter-sawn white oak in beautiful golden finish. Beveled French mirrors, 36x48 and 8x36 in. Tennessee marble shelf. One No. 29 patented cut-out towel urn and one No. 157 shaving paper urn to match, as shown, are furnished with each section.

2 Chair case, length, 11 ft. 0 in.; height, 7 ft. 10 in............ Price, $169.00
3 Chair case, length, 15 ft. 7 in.; height, 7 ft. 10 in............ " 243.00
4 Chair case, length, 20 ft. 2 in.; height, 7 ft. 10 in............ " 317.00
5 Chair case, length, 24 ft. 9 in.; height, 7 ft. 10 in............ Price, $391.00
6 Chair case, length, 29 ft. 4 in.; height, 7 ft. 10 in............ " 465.00
7 Chair case, length, 33 ft. 11 in.; height, 7 ft. 10 in............ " 539.00

Marble base, extra at $1.15 per running foot.

Koken Supply Co., 1910 catalog page.

WALL FIXTURES WITH MIRRORS

MIRROR CASE, No. 249

Made of selected quarter-sawed oak. This mirror case is kept in stock in the golden oak finish; it can also be furnished in the English oak finish, which is much darker than the golden finish. When ordering please mention which finish is wanted. The massive pillars at each end of the case are 10 inches in diameter, and are made with richly carved caps. Plain French plates, 48 x 72, connected by beveled plates 12 x 48. Tennessee marble base and Italian marble shelves for cabinets. Towel urns and Bohemian glass shaving-paper vases are included in the price of the mirror case. Height of same, 9 feet 8 inches.

3-chair case, length 18 ft. 10 in.	$546.00	5-chair case, length 28 ft. 9 in.	$794.00
4-chair case, length 23 ft. 10 in.	670.00	6-chair case, length 33 ft. 9 in.	918.00

WALL FIXTURES WITH MIRRORS

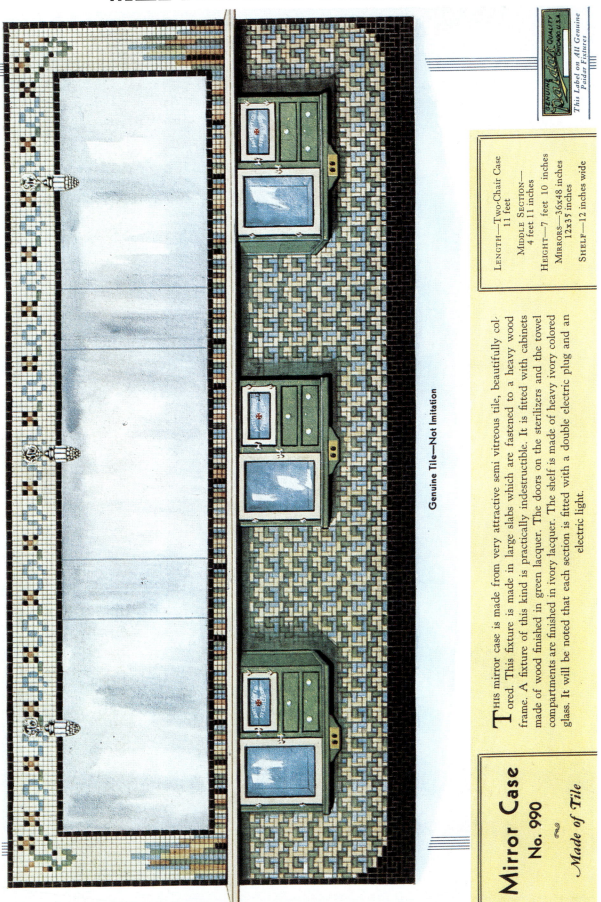

Genuine Tile—Not Imitation

Mirror Case No. 990

Made of Tile

This mirror case is made from very attractive semi vitreous tile, beautifully colored. This fixture is made in large slabs which are fastened to a heavy wood frame. A fixture of this kind is practically indestructible. It is fitted with cabinets made of wood finished in green lacquer. The doors on the sterilizers and the towel compartments are finished in ivory lacquer. The shelf is made of heavy ivory colored glass. It will be noted that each section is fitted with a double electric plug and an electric light.

Length—Two-Chair Case 11 feet
Middle Section— 4 feet 11 inches
Height—7 feet 10 inches
Mirrors—36x48 inches 12x35 inches
Shelf—12 inches wide

Emil J. Paidar Co., 1932 catalog page.

WALL FIXTURES WITH MIRRORS

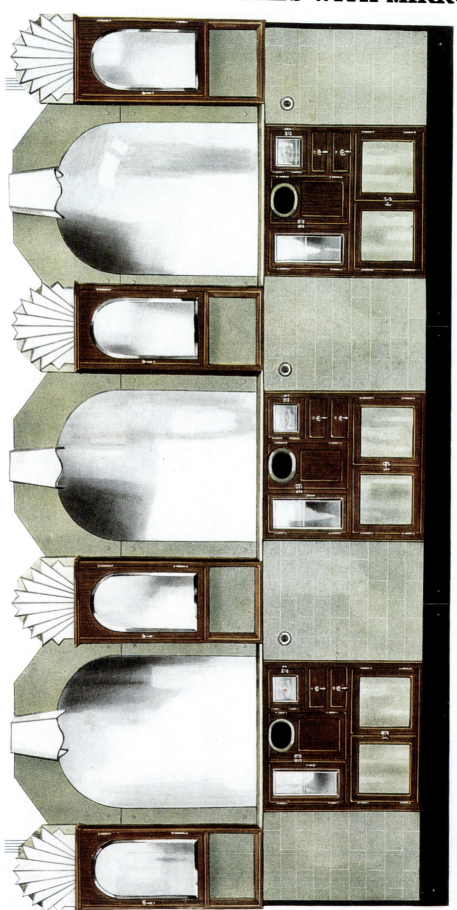

Emil J. Paidar Co., 1932 catalog page.

PARAMOUNT Mirror Case No. 2222
Made of Glass

A MODERNE fixture, built for utility, embodying the most modern lines. This fixture is built of turquoise green glass. The base along the floor is of black glass. The cabinets are of solid walnut, and are fitted with old silver trimmings. On top of each cabinet and over the center of each large mirror, is furnished a beautiful light fixture made of leaded white cathedral glass. Each fixture is furnished complete with Double Electric Outlet Plugs for each chair. The cabinets are fitted with a steel porcelain enamel towel hamper, a sterilizer, two drawers for tools, a compartment for clean towels, and in the bottom is a storage compartment. The upper cabinets are intended for the storage of clean towels and other supplies. Beneath each of the large mirrors is provided a 6-inch shelf. Lavatories can be put on this case.

LENGTH—Two-Chair Case 11 feet 6½ inches
MIDDLE SECTION— 5 feet 0¼ inch
DEPTH—Front to Rear 11½ inches
HEIGHT—8 feet 3¼ inches
LARGE MIRRORS—36x48 in.
SMALL MIRRORS—14x24 in.

WALL FIXTURES WITH MIRRORS

Emil J. Paidar Co., 1932 catalog page.

WALL FIXTURES WITH MIRRORS

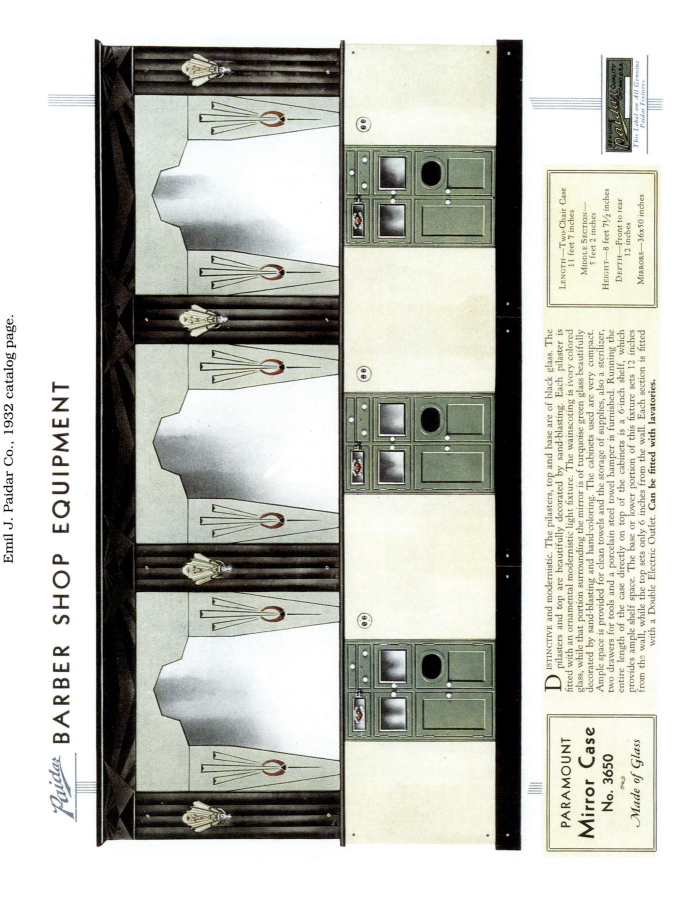

WALL FIXTURES WITH MIRRORS

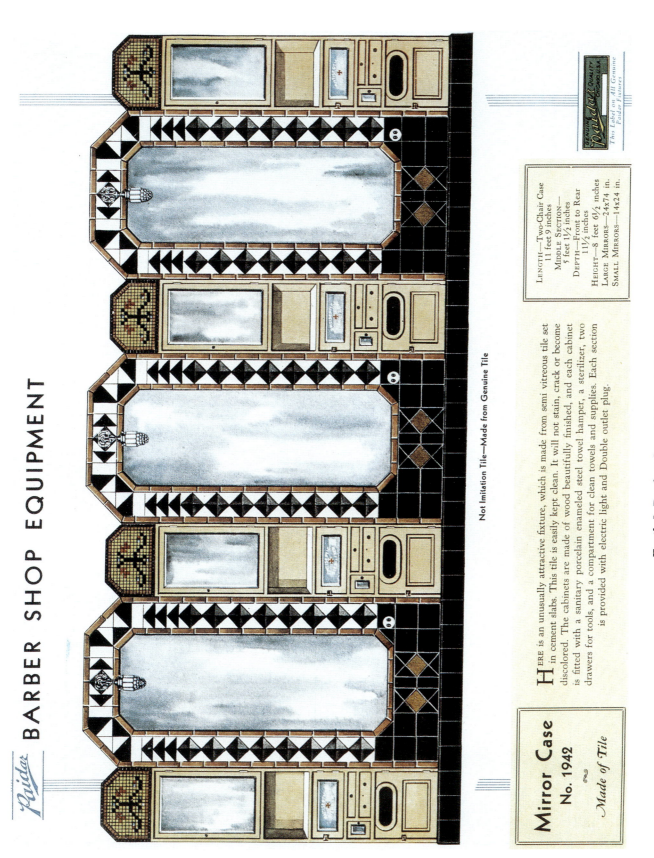

Emil J. Paidar Co., 1932 catalog page.

WALL FIXTURES WITH MIRRORS

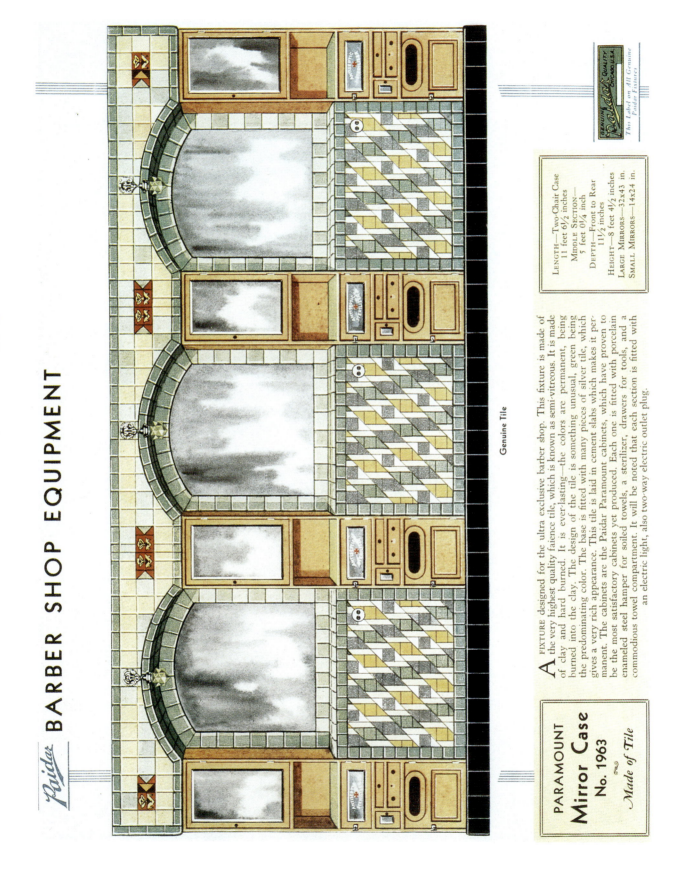

Emil J. Paidar Co., 1932 catalog page.

Paidar BARBER SHOP EQUIPMENT

Genuine Tile

PARAMOUNT Mirror Case No. 1963 *Made of Tile*

A FIXTURE designed for the ultra exclusive barber shop. This fixture is made of the very highest quality faience tile, which is known as semi-vitreous. It is made of clay and hard burned. It is ever-lasting—the colors are permanent, being burned into the clay. The design of the tile is something unusual, green being the predominating color. The base is fitted with many pieces of silver tile, which gives a very rich appearance. This tile is laid in cement slabs which makes it permanent. The cabinets are the Paidar Paramount cabinets, which have proven to be the most satisfactory cabinets yet produced. Each one is fitted with porcelain enameled steel hamper for soiled towels, a sterilizer, drawers for tools, and a commodious towel compartment. It will be noted that each section is fitted with an electric light, also two-way electric outlet plug.

LENGTH—Two-Chair Case 11 feet 6½ inches
MIDDLE SECTION—5 feet 0¼ inch
DEPTH—Front to Rear 11½ inches
HEIGHT—8 feet 4½ inches
LARGE MIRRORS—32x43 in.
SMALL MIRRORS—14x24 in.

WALL FIXTURES WITH MIRRORS

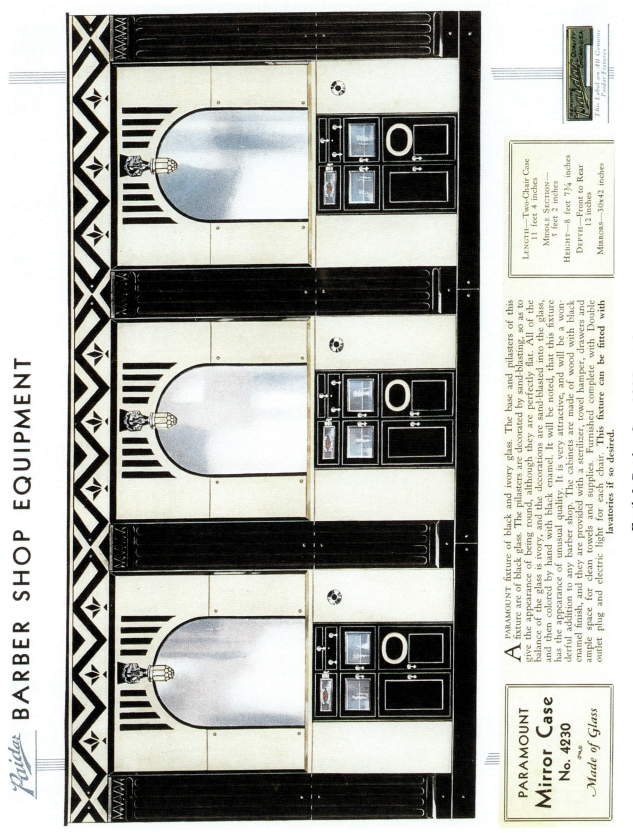

Paidar BARBER SHOP EQUIPMENT

PARAMOUNT Mirror Case No. 4230
Made of Glass

A PARAMOUNT fixture of black and ivory glass. The base and pilasters of this fixture are of black glass. The pilasters are decorated by sand-blasting, so as to give the appearance of being round, although they are perfectly flat. All of the balance of the glass is ivory, and the decorations are sand-blasted into the glass, and then colored by hand with black enamel. It will be noted, that this fixture has the appearance of unusual quality. It is very attractive, and will be a wonderful addition to any barber shop. The cabinets are made of wood with black enamel finish, and they are provided with a sterilizer, towel hamper, drawers and ample space for clean towels and supplies. Furnished complete with Double outlet plug and electric light for each chair. **This fixture can be fitted with lavatories if so desired.**

LENGTH—Two-Chair Case 11 feet 4 inches
MIDDLE SECTION— 5 feet 2 inches
HEIGHT—8 feet 7¾ inches
DEPTH—Front to Rear 12 inches
MIRRORS—30x42 inches

Emil J. Paidar Co., 1932 catalog page.

WALL FIXTURES WITH MIRRORS

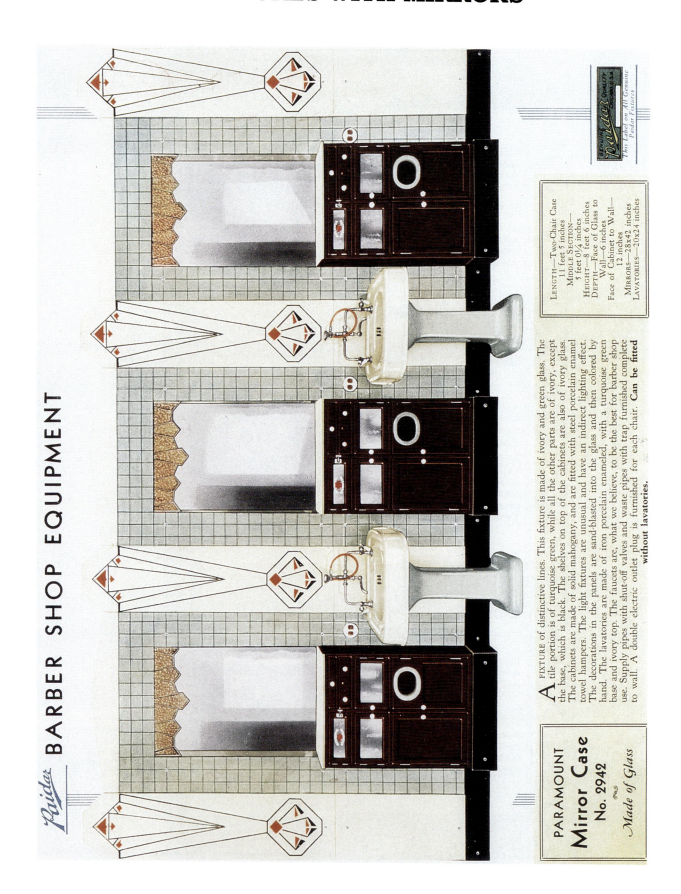

Emil J. Paidar Co., 1932 catalog page.

WALL FIXTURES WITH MIRRORS

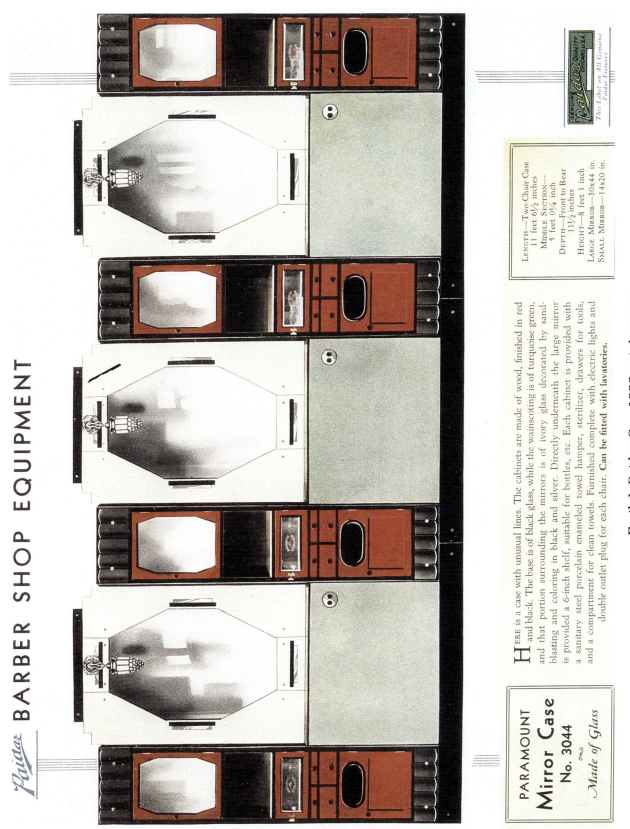

Emil J. Paidar Co., 1932 catalog page.

WALL FIXTURES WITH MIRRORS

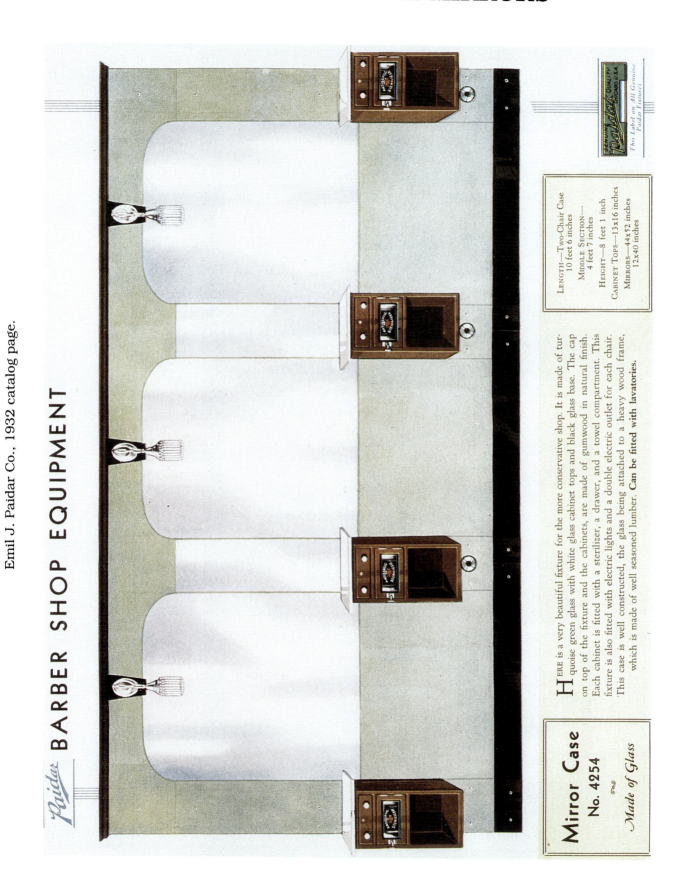

Emil J. Paidar Co., 1932 catalog page.

Mirror Case No. 4254
Made of Glass

Here is a very beautiful fixture for the more conservative shop. It is made of turquoise green glass with white glass cabinet tops and black glass base. The cap on top of the fixture and the cabinets, are made of gumwood in natural finish. Each cabinet is fitted with a sterilizer, a drawer, and a towel compartment. This fixture is also fitted with electric lights and a double electric outlet for each chair. This case is well constructed, the glass being attached to a heavy wood frame, which is made of well seasoned lumber. **Can be fitted with lavatories.**

Length—Two-Chair Case 10 feet 6 inches
Middle Section—4 feet 7 inches
Height—8 feet 1 inch
Cabinet Tops—13x16 inches
Mirrors—44x52 inches 12x40 inches

WALL FIXTURES WITH MIRRORS

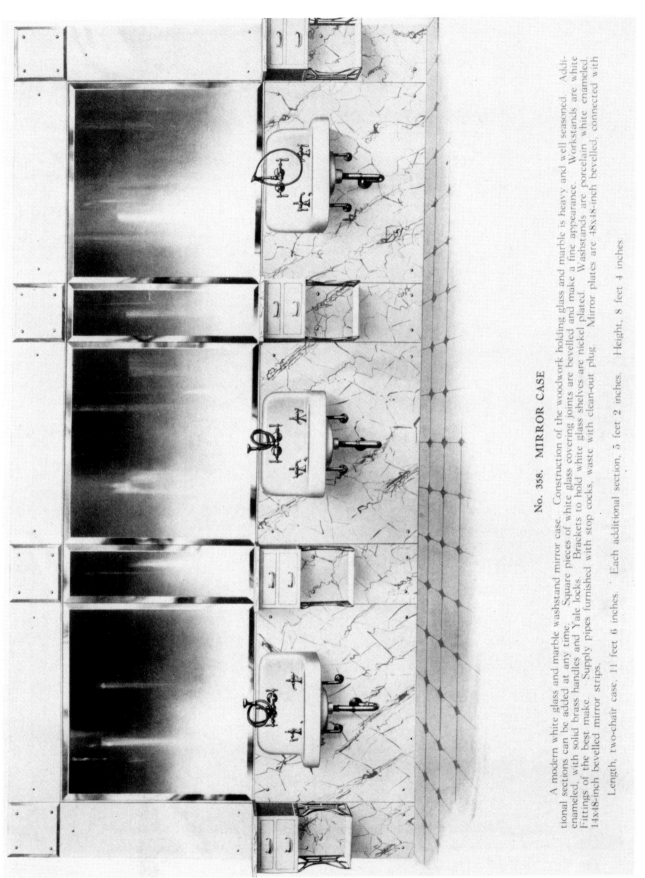

No. 358. MIRROR CASE

A modern white glass and marble washstand mirror case. Construction of the woodwork holding glass and marble is heavy and well seasoned. Additional sections can be added at any time. Square pieces of white glass covering joints are bevelled and make a fine appearance. Workstands are white enameled, with solid brass handles and Yale locks. Brackets to hold white glass shelves are nickel plated. Washstands are porcelain white enameled 14x18-inch bevelled mirror strips. Supply pipes furnished with stop cocks, waste with clean-out plug. Mirror plates are 48x18-inch bevelled, connected with 14x18-inch bevelled mirror strips.

Length, two-chair case, 11 feet 6 inches. Each additional section, 5 feet 2 inches. Height, 8 feet 4 inches.

Emil J. Paidar Co., 1932 catalog page.

WALL FIXTURES WITH MIRRORS

Emil J. Paidar Co., 1932 catalog page.

LAVATORIES & WASH STANDS

BARBERS' FURNITURE

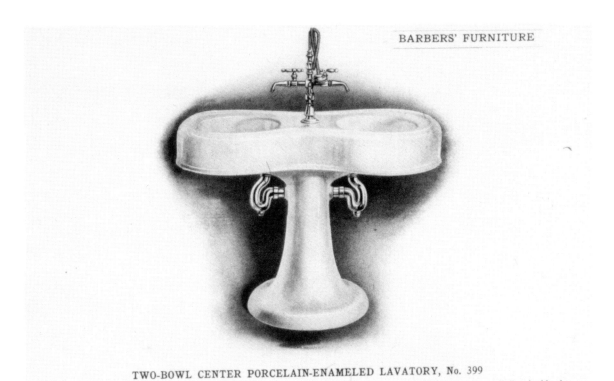

TWO-BOWL CENTER PORCELAIN-ENAMELED LAVATORY, No. 399

This lavatory is of modern design and especially suitable for the barber shop. It is fitted with nickel-plated Fuller double shampoo and basin cock and nickel-plated traps as shown. Shampoo sprinkler with rubber rim and hose furnished. Size of lavatory, 27 x 42. Size of bowls, 14 x 18.
Price $75.00

TWO-BOWL CENTER PORCELAIN-ENAMELED LAVATORY, No. 494

This lavatory is one of the latest patterns and especially made for barber shops. It is fitted with Ideal secret waste with china index. Fuller basin cocks. Improved Fuller shampoo cock with sprinkler holder attached. Shampoo sprinkler with rubber rim, including hose. Supply pipes with stock cocks. Waste pipe with bottle trap as shown to floor. All trimmings are brass, nickel-plated. Size of lavatory, 26 x 46. Size of bowls, 13 x 17.
Price $90.00

LAVATORIES & WASH STANDS

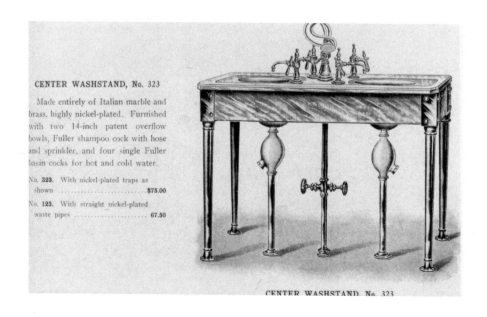

John Rieder & Co., 1912 catalog page.

LAVATORIES & WASH STANDS

No. 4765 C. E.—Size, 20 x 24. Bowl, 12 x 15
No. 4764 C. E.—Size, 22 x 28. Bowl, 13 x 16

Porcelain enameled pedestal washstand. Is an exceptionally good article for the price. The best of fittings are used including nickel plated waste and supply pipes to the floor. Made in two sizes.

Furnished in color as shown unless otherwise ordered.

We Recommend Pedestal Lavatories for Mirror Cases

No. 4772 C. E. Lavatory

Iron porcelain enameled furnished complete with waste and supply pipes to wall, also improved Rainbow Faucet.
Size, 19x27. Bowl, 11x15.

Furnished in color as shown unless otherwise ordered.

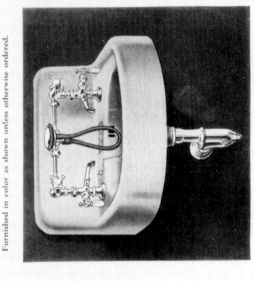

No. 1991 C. E. Porcelain Enameled Wall Lavatory

Fitted with Empaco shampoo fixture, nickel plated brass supply and waste pipes, P'trap with clean-out plug, rubber hose and sprinkler.
Size of lavatory 19x21 inches. Bowl 11x16 inches. Back

No. 4780 C. E.—20 x 24. Bowl, 12 x 15
No. 4781 C. E.—22 x 27. Bowl, 13 x 16

Porcelain enameled of best quality and fitted with low Empaco shampoo fixture. Pipes to floor, including S-trap with clean-out plug and waste. Also supply pipes with shut-off valves. Trimmings, heavy brass, nickel plated.

Furnished in color as shown unless otherwise ordered.

See Catalogue No. 32 for Other Lavatories.

Emil J. Paidar Co., 1932 catalog page.

LAVATORIES & WASH STANDS

ONE-BOWL CENTER PORCELAIN-ENAMELED LAVATORY, No. 441

One of the latest patterns, especially suitable for barber shops. Fitted with nickel-plated Fuller basin cocks and double Fuller shampoo cock with china handles, sprinkler-holder and best quality rubber hose and shampoo sprinkler with rubber rim. Nickel-plated supply pipes and waste pipe with P trap to floor.

Size of lavatory, 19 x 27. Size of bowl, 11 x 15.

Price, complete $46.25

ONE-BOWL CENTER PORCELAIN-ENAMELED LAVATORY, No. 442

One of the latest patterns, especially suitable for barber shops. Fitted with nickel-plated Fuller basin cocks and double Fuller shampoo cock with china handles, sprinkler-holder and best quality rubber hose and shampoo sprinkler with rubber rim. Nickel-plated supply pipes and waste pipe with P trap to floor.

Size of lavatory, 24 x 33. Size of bowl, 13 x 17.

Price, complete $51.50

BARBERS' FURNITURE

ONE-BOWL CENTER PORCELAIN-ENAMELED LAVATORY, No. 476

This lavatory is of liberal size, measuring 24 x 33. Fitted with Ideal secret waste with china index. Improved No. 11 combination shampoo and basin cock with sprinkler-holder attached, hose and shampoo sprinkler with rubber rim. Supply pipes with stop cocks, waste pipe with bottle trap to floor. All trimmings are brass, nickel-plated. Size of bowl, 13 x 17.

Price $60.00

ONE-BOWL CENTER PORCELAIN-ENAMELED LAVATORY, No. 438

This lavatory is gotten up in colonial style and offered at a very low price, considering the quality. It is fitted with secret waste, china index and No. 6 Fuller double basin cock. Shampoo sprinkler with rubber rim; also rubber hose is furnished. Supply pipes with stop cocks, waste pipe with bottle trap to floor. All trimmings are brass, nickel-plated. Size of lavatory, 20 x 24. Size of bowl, 12 x 15.

Price, complete as shown $48.00

John Rieder & Co., 1912 catalog page.

COMBINATION & MUG CASES
LOEFFLER & SYKES, ROCHESTER, N. Y.

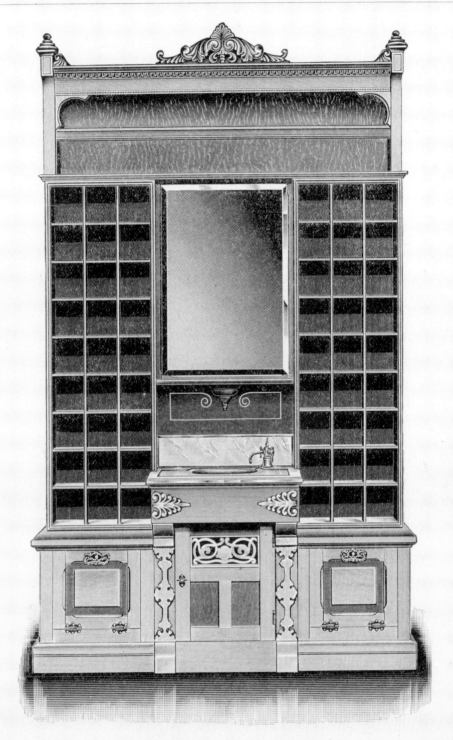

COMBINATION FIXTURE, No. 208.

Made of OAK, finely finished. A washstand, dressing glass and mug case combined, making a very useful piece of furniture. The washstand is furnished with Italian marble, 14 inch patent overflow bowl, and double Fuller basin cock for hot and cold water. German plate, 22 x 30, beveled. Height of fixture, 8 ft. 3 in.; width, 5 ft.

Price $55.00

Loeffler & Sykes, 1902 catalog page.

COMBINATION & MUG CASES

Eugene Berninghaus, 1882 catalog page.

COMBINATION & MUG CASES

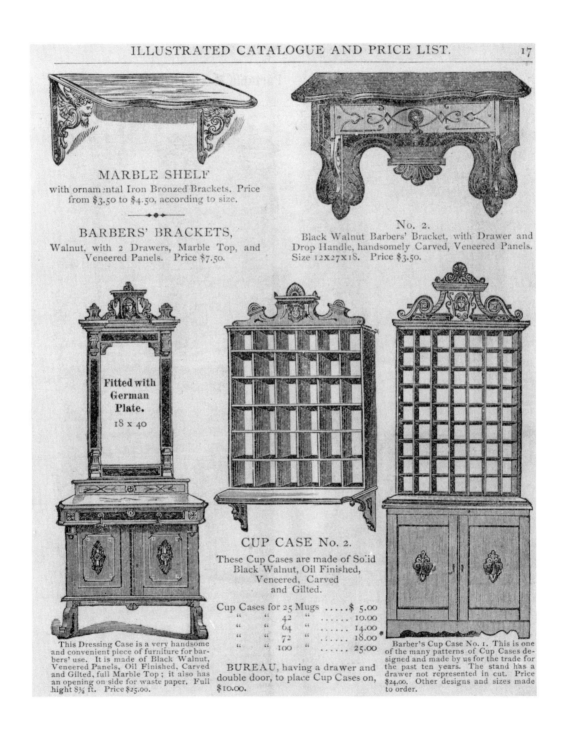

Eugene Berninghaus, 1882 catalog page.

COMBINATION & MUG CASES

LOEFFLER & SYKES, ROCHESTER, N. Y.

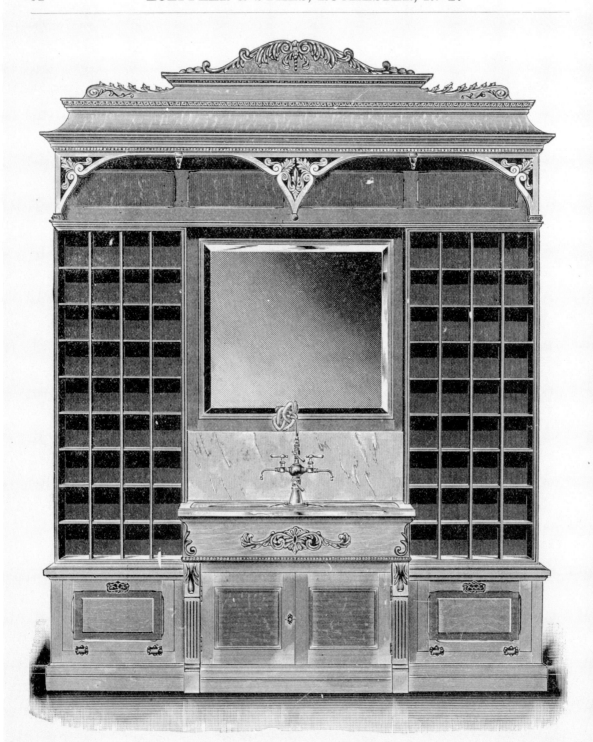

COMBINATION FIXTURE, No. 209.

Made of Oak, highly finished. This is a most useful combination of a washstand, mug cases and dressing mirror. The washstand is furnished with Italian marble, two 14-inch patent overflow bowls, and the Improved Combination Fuller Shampoo and Basin Cock. French Plate, 30 x 34, beveled. Height of fixture, 9 ft. 1 in.; width, 7 ft. 5 in.

Price $93.00

Loeffler & Sykes, 1902 catalog page.

COMBINATION & MUG CASES

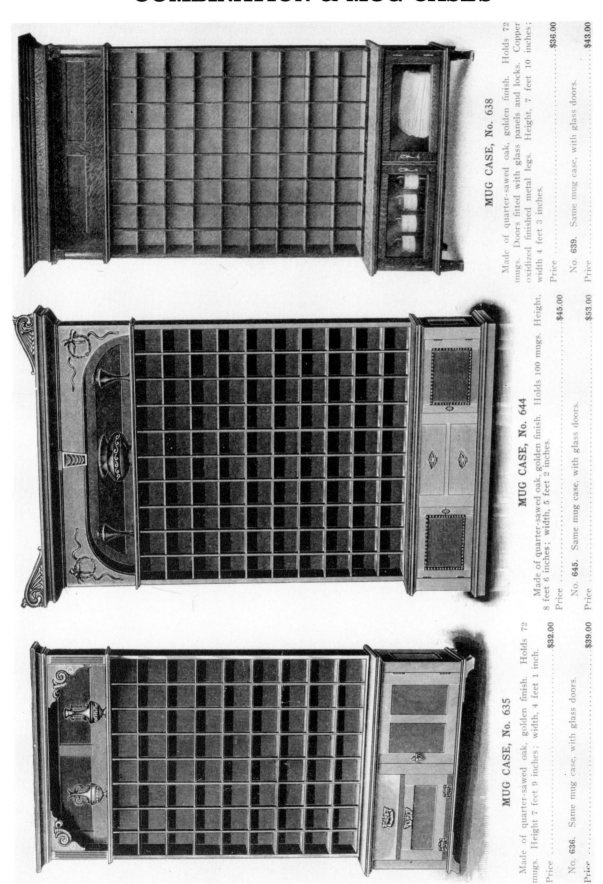

MUG CASE, No. 638

Made of quarter-sawed oak, golden finish. Holds 72 mugs. Doors fitted with glass panels and locks. Copper oxidized finished metal legs. Height, 7 feet 10 inches; width 4 feet 3 inches.
Price $36.00
No. 639. Same mug case, with glass doors.
Price $43.00

MUG CASE, No. 644

Made of quarter-sawed oak, golden finish. Holds 100 mugs. Height, 8 feet 6 inches; width, 5 feet 2 inches.
Price $45.00
No. 645. Same mug case, with glass doors.
Price $53.00

MUG CASE, No. 635

Made of quarter-sawed oak, golden finish. Holds 72 mugs. Height 7 feet 9 inches; width, 4 feet 1 inch.
Price $32.00
No. 636. Same mug case, with glass doors.
Price $39.00

COSTUMERS & COAT RACKS

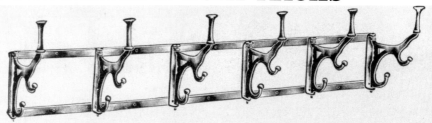

No. 517 Hat and Coat Rack.

Metal, oxidized copper finish, with 6 triple adjustable hooks that can be laid flat against the wall if desired.

Price, ...

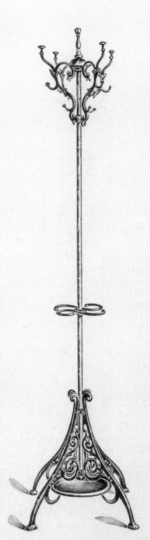

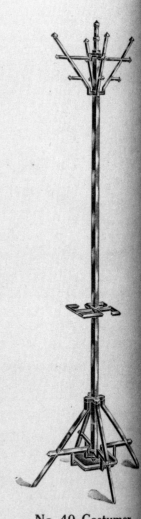

No. 34 Costumer.

Metal, oxidized copper finish, with umbrella holder, 4 side and 1 center hook.
Price, ...$5.50

No. 35—Same, with 6 side and 1 center hook.
Price. $6.50

No. 38 Costumer.

Metal, oxidized copper finish; extra heavy, with umbrella holder, 6 side and 1 center hook.

Price, ...$8.50

No. 40 Costumer.

Metal, oxidized copper finish; bars, with umbrella holder, 4 side 1 center hook.

Price, ...

Koken Supply Co., 1910 catalog page.

COSTUMERS & COAT RACKS

No. 518 Hat and Coat Rack.

Made of Quarter-sawn Oak, golden finish; fitted with two beveled Mirrors, 18x40, and three large, fancy double hooks; copper finish.

Price, 2 sections, as shown $29.50
Price, each additional section 12.50

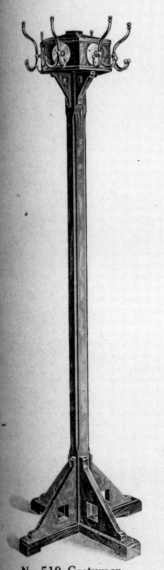

No. 519 Costumer.

Made of Quarter-sawn Oak, mission finish; equipped with 6 triple nickel-plated hooks.

Price, ... $15.00

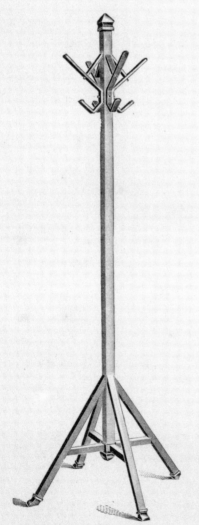

No. 520 Costumer.

Made of Brass, satin finish, with heavy base; has 4 double hooks.

Price, ... $16.00

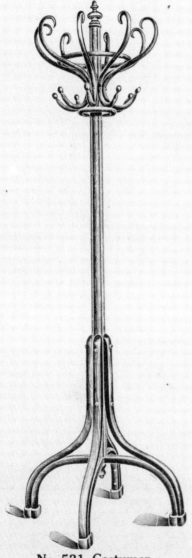

No. 521 Costumer.

Imported; made of Vienna bent oak wood; has 8 large double hooks.

Price, ... $13.50

Koken Supply Co., 1910 catalog page.

COSTUMERS & COAT RACKS

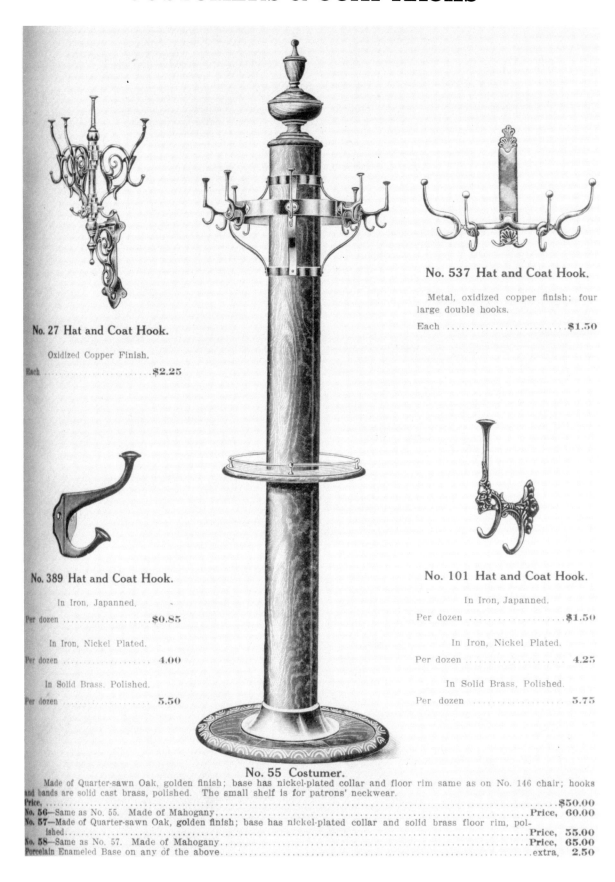

No. 27 Hat and Coat Hook.

Oxidized Copper Finish.

Each $2.25

No. 537 Hat and Coat Hook.

Metal, oxidized copper finish; four large double hooks.

Each $1.50

No. 389 Hat and Coat Hook.

In Iron, Japanned.

Per dozen $0.85

In Iron, Nickel Plated.

Per dozen 4.00

In Solid Brass. Polished.

Per dozen 5.50

No. 101 Hat and Coat Hook.

In Iron, Japanned.

Per dozen $1.50

In Iron, Nickel Plated.

Per dozen 4.25

In Solid Brass, Polished.

Per dozen 5.75

No. 55 Costumer.

Made of Quarter-sawn Oak, golden finish; base has nickel-plated collar and floor rim same as on No. 146 chair; hooks and bands are solid cast brass, polished. The small shelf is for patrons' neckwear.

Price, ... $50.00

No. 56—Same as No. 55. Made of Mahogany .... Price, 60.00

No. 57—Made of Quarter-sawn Oak, golden finish; base has nickel-plated collar and solid brass floor rim, polished .... Price, 55.00

No. 58—Same as No. 57. Made of Mahogany .... Price, 65.00

Porcelain Enameled Base on any of the above .... extra, 2.50

Koken Supply Co., 1910 catalog page.

SHOESHINE CHAIRS & RESTS

BARBERS' FURNITURE

No. 561

Width, 2 ft. 5 in.; depth, 3 ft. 9 in.

Price $51.00

No. 563

Width, 6 ft. 6 in.; depth, 3 ft. 9 in.

Price $116.00

These settees are made of selected quarter-sawed oak with paneled surfaces. Golden finish. Pink Tennessee marble slabs upon platforms. Seats and backs upholstered in green leather. The foot-rests are finished in oxidized copper. The drawers are provided with polished brass handles and Yale locks for the safe keeping of brushes and supplies during the porter's absence. These settees are massive in appearance, and not alone handsome pieces of furniture but also very comfortable, the upholstered seat and back and the wide arms affording a very restful position to the customer.

No. 562

Width, 4 ft. 5 in.; depth, 3 ft. 9 in. Made of selected quarter-sawed oak, golden finish, constructed and upholstered with leather the same as Nos. 561 and 563, described above.

Price $78.00

No. 546

Made of quarter-sawed oak, golden finish. Seat upholstered with leather. Tennessee marble slabs upon platforms. Foot-rests and legs copper oxidized finish. Yale locks on drawers. Length, 4 feet 1 in.

Price $62.00

John Rieder & Co., 1912 catalog page.

SHOESHINE CHAIRS & RESTS

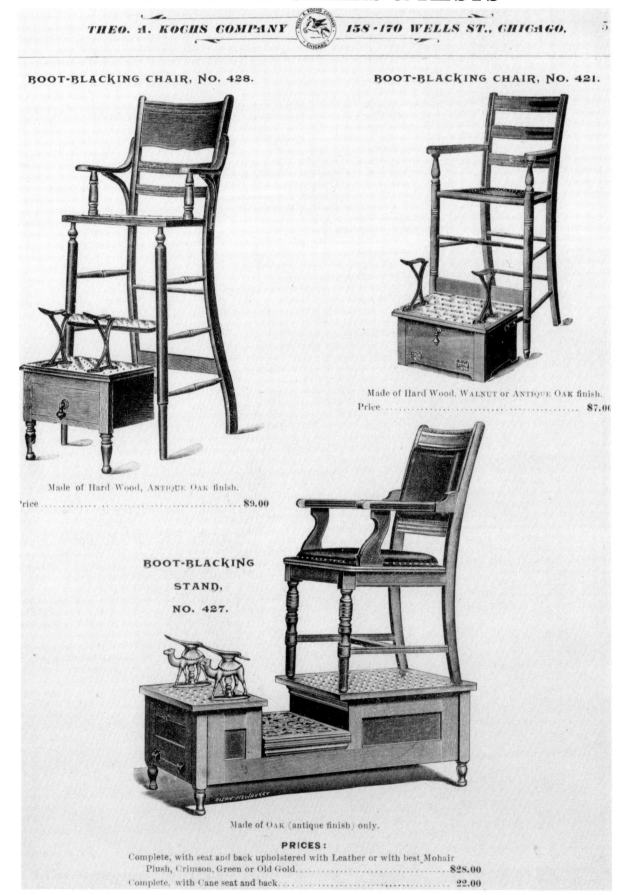

Theo. A. Kochs Co., 1897 catalog page.

SHOESHINE CHAIRS & RESTS

BARBERS' FURNITURE

No. 534. SHOESHINING STAND

Made of oak, golden finish. Top covered with sheet brass. Japanned foot-rests. This stand is proportioned so that the bootblack is seated while at work and the foot-rests project so that free action may be had when polishing the shoes. Length of stand, 2 feet 10 inches; width, 2 feet 2 inches.

PRICES
No. 534. Including chair $12.25
No. 535. Same stand without chair. 11.00

No. 538. SHOESHINING STAND

Made of hardwood, golden oak finish. Japanned foot-rests.
Price $8.75

No. 549. SHOESHINING STAND

Made of quarter-sawed oak, golden finish. This stand is so proportioned that the bootblack can stand while at work and still the chair is easily reached by the customer. Top covered with sheet brass. Nickel-plated foot-rests. Length, 3 feet 5 inches; width, 2 feet.

Price, complete with chair $21.00

No. 523. SHOESHINING STAND

Made entirely of steel, copper oxidized finish, oak seat and arms. Very practical and substantial.
Price $9.50

John Rieder & Co., 1912 catalog page.

SHOESHINE CHAIRS & RESTS

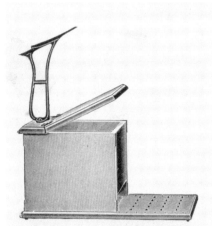

No. 493. SHINING STAND

For use upon revolving chairs. The box is made of oak, golden finish, and the footrest is nickel-plated.

Price $3.75

No. 501. SHINING STAND

Made of steel, copper oxidized finish. Polished oak seat. Footrest adjustable to any angle. Shelf under seat for brushes and polish. Very light and portable.

Price, complete $3.25

No. 550. SHINING STAND

For use at barber chair, golden oak, light weight, nickel-plated footrest.

Each $3.25

For Bootblacking Settees, Chairs and Stands, see pages 78 and 79.

BOOTBLACK FOOTRESTS

No. 234. Footrest, iron, nickel-plated, 15 inches high.

Each $1.25

No. 235. Footrest, iron, oxidized finish, 15 inches high.

Each $1.25

HANDY SHINING STANDS

Made of iron, japanned.

Each $2.00

THE ANCHOR SHOE HOLDER

Adjustable to all sizes of shoes. Effectual in stretching shoes. A convenient and practical article.

Each $1.00

Both pages from John Rieder & Co., 1912 catalog.

SHOESHINE CHAIRS & RESTS

No. 51 Foot-Rest.
Height, 8 inches.
Nickel plated .... each, $0.60
No. 51A—Japanned .... each, .30

No. 50 Foot-Rest.
Height, 8 inches.
Nickel plated .... each, $0.85
No. 50A—Bronzed ..... each, .50

No. 53 Foot-Rest.
Height, 15 inches.
Nickel plated .... each, $1.35
No. 53A—Japanned or bronzed .... each, .60

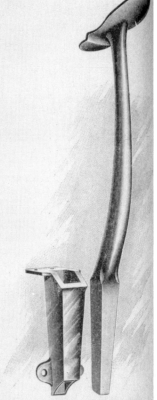

No. 55 Foot-Rest.
The pedestal can be removed the socket, as shown, making it cially convenient on a stand use ladies.
Height, 16 inches.
Nickel plated .... each, $
No. 55A—Japanned or bronzed .... each,

No. 52 Foot-Rest.
Height, 18 inches.
Nickel plated .... each, $2.50
No. 52A—Japanned or bronzed .... each, 1.00

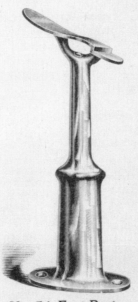

No. 54 Foot-Rest.
This rest is very massive.
Height, 18 inches.
Nickel plated .... each, $1.75
No. 54A—Japanned or bronzed .... each, .90

This cut shows No. 55 rem B. B. Foot-Rest, fitted to a B. B.

STERILIZERS

No. 1506—PORTABLE CABINET AND STERILIZER

A handsome and convenient sterilizing cabinet. Made of best grade seasoned lumber white enameled and mounted on easy-rolling casters. All sides are glass panels, except the front, which is beveled plate glass.

Height, 44 inches; width, 16 inches; depth, 12 inches.

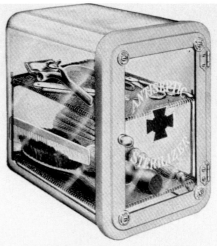

No. 769—ALL GLASS ANTISEPTIC TOOL STERILIZER

This will make an immediate appeal to the up-to-the-minute operator, as a practical as well as useful article. and an absolute necessity in every sanitary shop. A small piece of blotting paper in a glass tray is supplied with sterilizer, and is to be moistened with a fifteen percent solution of Formaldehyde. This case bears the endorsement of Health Departments and the Medical Profession. The insertion of rubber strips in the metal frame gives you an absolutely air-tight sterilizer. All metal parts are nickel-plated. Dimensions: 9¾ inches high, 7¼ inches wide, 10½ inches deep.

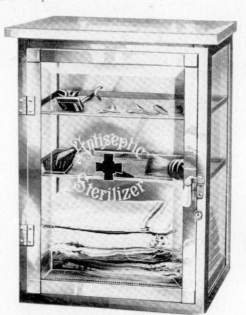

No. 1503—GLASS STERILIZER WITH METAL FRAME

This essential article is built to hold and sterilize combs, brushes and all necessary tools and towels. Comes with white glass top 12 x 16 inches, with beveled plate glass front panel, and double strength glass side panels. Height, 20 inches; width, 14¼ inches; depth 11½ inches. Easily fitted to old cases.

No. 428—MANICURE ATTACHMENT

No. 429—Manicure Bowl.
No. 430—Manicure Tray.
No. 431—Manicure Bracket.

Fred Dolle Inc., 1924 catalog page.

STERILIZERS

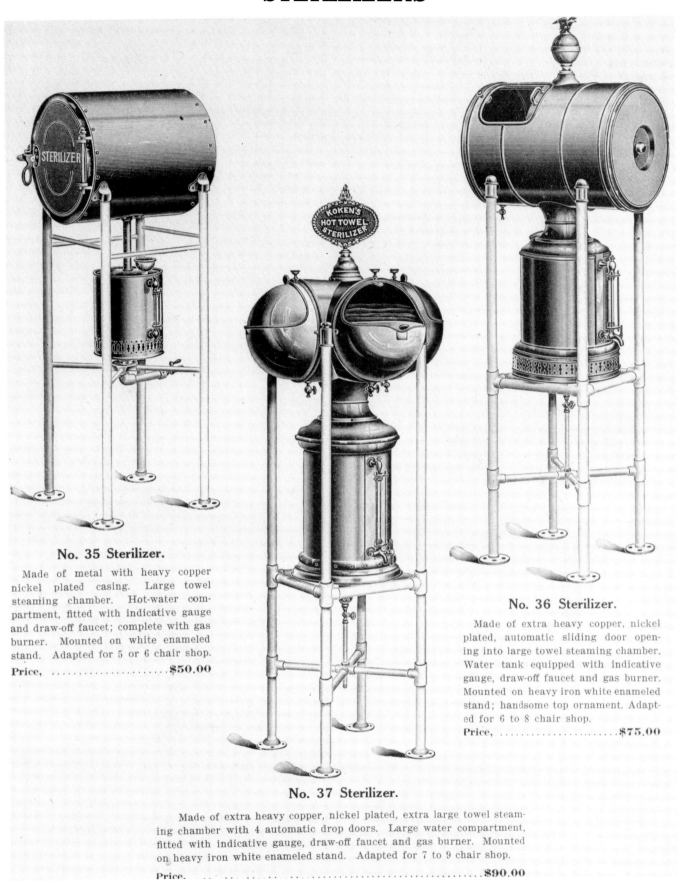

No. 35 Sterilizer.

Made of metal with heavy copper nickel plated casing. Large towel steaming chamber. Hot-water compartment, fitted with indicative gauge and draw-off faucet; complete with gas burner. Mounted on white enameled stand. Adapted for 5 or 6 chair shop.
Price, ...$50.00

No. 36 Sterilizer.

Made of extra heavy copper, nickel plated, automatic sliding door opening into large towel steaming chamber. Water tank equipped with indicative gauge, draw-off faucet and gas burner. Mounted on heavy iron white enameled stand; handsome top ornament. Adapted for 6 to 8 chair shop.
Price, ...$75.00

No. 37 Sterilizer.

Made of extra heavy copper, nickel plated, extra large towel steaming chamber with 4 automatic drop doors. Large water compartment, fitted with indicative gauge, draw-off faucet and gas burner. Mounted on heavy iron white enameled stand. Adapted for 7 to 9 chair shop.
Price, ...$90.00

Koken Supply Co., 1910 catalog page.

STERILIZERS

No. 30 Cabinet Sterilizer.

Frame made of polished oak, with glass all around; white enameled trays, metal trimmings. Formaldehyde is used for sterilizing.

Price, ... $7.50

No. 31 Bystrom Heater and Sterilizer.

Polished copper tank on metal brackets. Sterilizing compartment has capacity for several dozen towels. Holds 6 gallons of water. Fitted with gasoline burner, flame spreader and tank.

Price, ... $9.00

No. 32—Nickel plated tank. Otherwise same as No. 31.

Price, ... $10.00

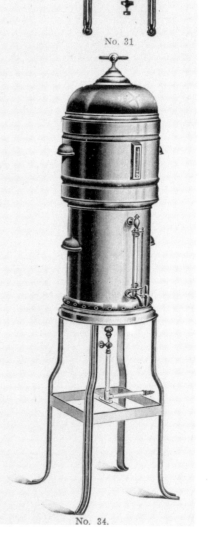

No. 33 Sterilizer.

Made of heavy copper, nickel plated. Has horizontal towel steaming chamber, fitted with rolling door; has vertical body for hot water, with draw-off faucet, indicative gauge and gas burner. The sterilizing chamber has a steam channel with copper perforated disks resting on same with steam outlet. Mounted on iron white enameled stand, fancy glass sign on top. Adapted for a 3 or 4 chair shop.

Price, ... $50.00

No. 34 Sterilizer.

Made of heavy copper, nickel plated. Has sterilizing compartment for steaming towels; noiseless revolving top (no hinges), indicative gauge, draw-off faucet, thermometer and gas burner. Mounted on iron white enameled stand. Adapted for a 2 or 3 chair shop.

Price, ... $35.00

Gasoline burner and tank for Nos. 33 and 34 sterilizers, extra 6.00

Koken Supply Co., 1910 catalog page.

STERILIZERS

THE ANTISEPTIC RAZOR STERILIZER

A simple and effective method of sterilizing razors.

FORMULA FOR STERILIZING LIQUID

Dissolve ½ ounce boracic acid in one gallon of boiling water.

The urn should be refilled once a week. It is provided with a hinged cover and it is made of white metal, nickel-plated, so that there is no danger of rust or of the formation of verdigris.

Price of the sterilizer............$1.50

THE LITTLE DAISY STERILIZER

These sterilizers are made of heavy copper, finely nickel-plated, and hold four to six turkish towels. Equipped with porcelain tray, which prevents the towels from rusting. Fitted with hinged cover and a very fine brass faucet with wooden handle. Water capacity, two gallons. This is an ideal sterilizer for shops where not too many hot towels are in constant use.

Price, complete, with gas burner $10.00

FORMALDEHYDE CABINET STERILIZER

Finely enameled in white. Size, 10½ x 13 x 13. Fitted with four perforated enameled steel trays, which are adjustable; glass paneled back and sides. Door fitted with nickel-plated brass hinges and lock. Rubber strips on door, rendering same air-tight. This cabinet provides an up-to-date method for sterilizing razors, tools and brushes without heat by steam or hot water. The sterilizing is done by formaldehyde, which is placed in a receptacle for this purpose in the bottom of the cabinet. One of the trays is fitted with racks for holding the razors.

Price, complete $10.00

No. 436. GASOLINE VAPOR LAMP

The most economical heater in the market. For use under hot-water urns or copper boilers.

Each ....65c.

No. 845. HOT-WATER URN

Capacity, 3 gallons. Made of heavy copper, nickel-plated. Brass faucet. Nickel-plated stand.

Price, complete, with vapor lamp $6.50

No. 357. No. 356. INVINCIBLE GAS BURNERS

No. 357. For natural or artificial gas. Used under hot-water urns or copper boilers. Height, 4 inches.
Each ....35c.

No. 356. Same burner as No. 357, but with stand.
Each ....60c.

THE MONITOR CASH REGISTER

This cash register is operated by checks which, when inserted into the register, open the cash drawer and ring a bell. The check then moves back, making room for the next to cover it, being thus kept in the order in which sales are made. Seven different colored checks are supplied, also checks to record "No Sale," amounts "Paid Out" and "Rec'd on Acc't." The colors of Monitor checks are bronze, black, blue, green, red, yellow and white, in the following denominations: 5c, 10c, 15c, 20c, 25c, 30c, 35c, 40c, 45c, 50c, 55c, 60c, 65c, 70c, 75c, 80c, 85c, 90c, 95c, $1.00; in blue, red and yellow, the following: $1.05, $1.10, $1.15, $1.20, $1.25, bath. We list this cash register without checks, as the number and assortment vary according to the number of chairs and the price charged for work. About ninety checks make up an ample supply for a day's work for each chair.

Price, without checks............$12.50
Checks, 2 cents each; in lots of 100.. 1.50
Racks to hold twelve denominations.. .25
Check holders, each................. .03
Fillers for check holders, per 1,000... .30
Springs, per dozen.................. .20

COPPER BOILERS

Capacity, 7 quarts.

No. 12. Round, polished $2.50
No. 23. Round, nickel-plated 3.00
No. 34. Crescent shape, polished .. 2.50
No. 48. Crescent shape, nickel-plated 3.00
No. 59. Round, nickel-plated. Capacity, 3 gallons 3.50

No. 714. CASH DRAWER

Fitted with alarm and a combination susceptible of 32 changes.

Price $1.75

John Rieder & Co., 1912 catalog page.

STERILIZERS

BARBERS' STERILIZERS

THE HANDY WATER HEATER AND STERILIZER
Economical and convenient.
Always ready for instant use.

This sterilizer and water heater will give perfect satisfaction in barber shops where not too large a number of hot towels are in constant use. It is the most practical outfit devised for the purpose. The tank holds about six gallons of water and is made of 14-ounce copper. It is fitted with a copper lid and a substantial brass faucet with wooden handle. A copper wire tray provides a compartment for hot steam towels. Furnished complete with brackets, iron grate casting and gasoline fixture or gas burner as desired.

PRICES

No. 615.	Polished copper, complete with gasoline fixture	$ 9.00
No. 616.	Copper, nickel-plated, complete with gasoline fixture	10.00
No. 619.	Polished copper, complete with gas burner	6.35
No. 620.	Copper, nickel-plated, with gas burner	7.35
No. 625.	Water tank only, copper polished	5.50
No. 626.	Water tank only, copper, nickel-plated	6.50

BUFFALO SANITARY STERILIZERS

Made of copper, nickel-plated, with two hinged covers and mounted on white enameled iron stand. Large towel compartment for five to ten chairs with porcelain tray. Equipped with water gauge and brass faucet. Water capacity, four gallons.

No. 10. Complete, with gas burner.....................$21.75
No. 11. Complete, with gasoline tank and burner......... 24.75

BUFFALO SANITARY STERILIZERS

Made of copper, nickel-plated, with two hinged covers. Large towel compartment for five to ten chairs with porcelain tray. Equipped with water gauge and brass faucet. Water capacity, four gallons.

No. 20. Complete, with gas burner.$18.50
No. 21. Complete, with gasoline tank and burner 21.50

CABINET STERILIZERS

Made of copper, nickel-plated, mounted on 18-inch nickel-plated brass legs. Two towel compartments with removable porcelain trays. Door fitted with heavy beveled plate glass. Equipped with water gauge, thermometer, brass faucets and dome with ruby glass. Holds enough towels for ten to twenty chairs.

No. 30. Complete, with gas burner........................$45.00
No. 31. Complete, with gasoline tank and burner......... 48.00

John Rieder & Co., 1912 catalog page.

John Rieder & Co., 1912 catalog page.

ATOMIZERS

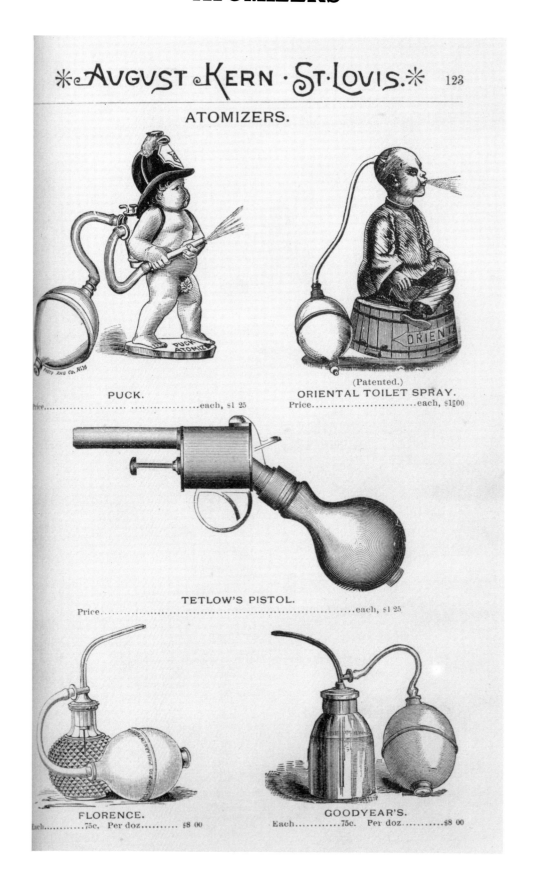

August Kern Co., 1888 catalog page.

CUSPIDORS

Cuspidors

Two Styles. Solid brown. Also blue mottled outside, white-lined inside.

6" Diameter .... $4.05 Doz.
7" Diameter .... 4.32 Doz.

Weight per dozen, 24 lbs.—6".
Weight per dozen, 36 lbs.—7".

Flat Bottom Hotel Cuspidor

Solid light brown or dark blue glaze.

List price, per dozen $5.40

Weight, 48 lbs. doz.

Both top pictures are from Buerger Bros. Supply Co., 1935 catalog page. (authorized Koken dealer)

—LEYDEN— ENAMELED WARE

Best quality sheet steel triple coated with enamel. Outside neatly marbleized a light blue and white, inside a pure white porcelain enamel, acid proof and free from poisonous substance. Black enameled rim.

SPITTOONS
Seamless; two-piece; sunk top with opening; rolled rim.

Nos.	12L	13L
Diam, ins	9⅝	11¼
Depth, ins	3¼	3¾
Doz in case	1	1
Wt case, lbs	90	100
Per Doz	$28 50	33 00

CUSPIDORS
Seamed at breast and neck; smooth rim.
Per Doz
No. 18L—Diam 7 ins; depth 4 ins.. $15 00
Six doz in case; wt case 95 lbs.

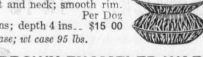

BROWN ENAMELED WARE
LOOSE TOP SPITTOONS

Seamless; two-piece flaring top with wide opening.

Nos.	HB12	HB13
Diam, ins	9⅛	10⅞
Depth, ins	3⅝	4⅝
Wt doz, lbs	24	38½
Less carton, Per Doz	$24 00	31 50
Full cartons, Per Doz	22 50	30 00

Half doz in carton.

CUSPIDORS
BRASS
Self-righting weighted bottom.

Per Doz
No. 1—Height 12 ins; diam top 8 ins; diam body 9 ins $118 50
One in box; wt doz 96 lbs.

BRASS
Self-righting weighted bottom.

Per Doz
No. 25—Height 7½ ins; diam. top 7½ ins; diam body 7 ins $44 25
One in carton; wt doz 36 lbs

Sanitary Two Piece.
Sheet steel pan, white enameled interior, dark green enameled exterior, polished brass top.

Per Doz
No. 28—Height 5 ins; diam bottom 9½ ins; diam top 8½ ins $90 00
One in carton; wt doz 36 lbs.

CUSPIDOR MATS
Black rubber, for use under cuspidors, slop jars, etc.

No.	HR15
Diam, ins	15
Wt doz, lbs	9
Per Doz	$6 30

Two doz in carton.

The two bottom pictures shown above are from a Winchester/Keen Kutter, 1937 catalog.

CUSPIDORS

148 THEO. A. KOCHS & SON, NEW YORK CITY.

CUSPIDOR, No. 889.
Metal, nickel-plated, self-righting.
Each .... 25c.

CUSPIDOR, No. 888.
Made of heavy brass, highly nickel-plated, self-righting.
Each $1.00

CUSPIDOR, No. 886.
Glazed earthenware, green color.
Each .... 35c.

CUSPIDOR, No. 891.
9½ inches in diameter.
Made of indurated fiber with heavy solid spun brass top. Neat and substantial.
Each .... 80c.

CUSPIDOR, No. 880.
Iron, enameled, self-righting.
Each .... 60c.

WOOD FIBER SPITTOONS.
The cleanest and most durable spittoon ever made. Far better than rubber.
No. 908. 13½ inches in diam., each ... 75c.
No. 911. 9½ inches in diam., each .... 50c.

SHAVING PAPER BOX, No. 763.
Highly nickel-plated on brass. A very ornamental article.
Each $1.00

CUSPIDOR, No. 890.
Urn shape, made of heavy brass, self-righting. Height, 12 inches.
Price, each $2.75

SHAVING PAPER HOLDER, No. 776.
Made of solid brass, highly nickel-plated.
Each $1.00

Theo. A. Kochs & Son, 1903 catalog page.

CUSPIDORS

No. 705 Fiber Cuspidor.
Strong, durable and light.
Each $0.60

No. 703 Cuspidor.
Brass, nickel plated......each, $1.00
No. 704—Steel, nickel
plated..............each, .60

**No. 702
Enameled Iron Cuspidor.**
Large, heavy and substantial.
Each $0.75

No. 534 Sanitary Cuspidor.
Not a nook or corner for germs to lurk in. Polished brass outside, inner receptacle made of enameled steel; it will stand abuse; is easy to clean.
Each $2.25

No. 710 Cuspidor.
Solid brass, urn shape.
Each $1.75

No. 708 Cuspidor.
Made of heavy brass; height, 4¼ inches; diameter, 10½ inches.
Each $2.25

No. 701 Cuspidor.
Heavy brass. 8x9 self-righting.
Each $2.00

No. 700 Cuspidor.
Heavy brass, urn shape.
9x12 self-righting.
Each $2.50

No. 535 Cuspidor.
Solid brass. Extra large and heavy.
Each $2.25

Koken Supply Co., 1910 catalog page.

HAIR CLIPPERS

PATENT HAIR CLIPPING MACHINES,
FOR ONE HAND.

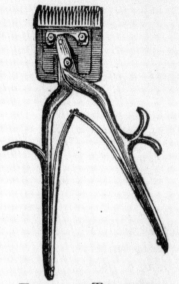

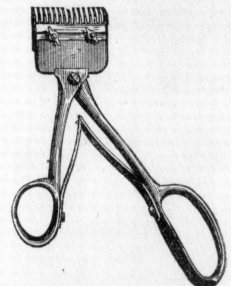

Coates' Adjust.
Price $6.00.

French Toilet.
Price $5.00.

X-L-N-T.—Price $4.50.

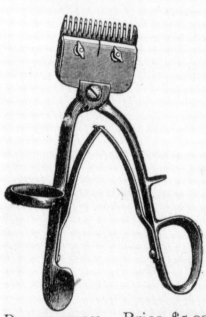

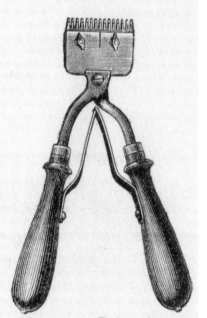

Perfection.—Price $5.00

Clark's No. 2.—$5.00.

Handy.—Price $4.50.

Coates' Adjustable will cut hair any length required, from $\frac{1}{8}$ to $\frac{3}{4}$ inches; it is very simple in its construction, and is operated same as Clark's No. 2.

The Clark's Clipper has been universally introduced, and everyone knows its superior qualities.

The French Toilet is same pattern as Clark's No. 2, only it is lighter in weight.

The "X-L-N-T", "Perfection" and "Handy" are manufactured in this country, and have proved satisfactory wherever used. They are Nickle plated.

Theo. A. Kochs & Son, 1898 catalog page.

HAIR CLIPPERS

The "Model" Clipper.

This is a first-class clipper in every respect and every pair is fully guaranteed. These clippers are specially made for us by the American Shearer Manufacturing Company. The blades are made of the highest grade tool steel, tempered in a manner to leave the teeth very hard, which is necessary to insure a keen cutting edge. Every clipper is carefully inspected and tested, and none better can be had at any price.

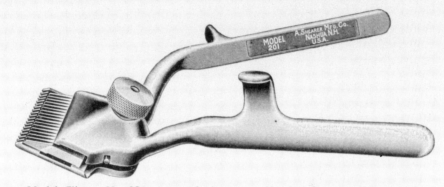

Model Clipper No. 201, commonly known as No. 1. Cuts the hair ⅛ inch.
Price, each $2.25

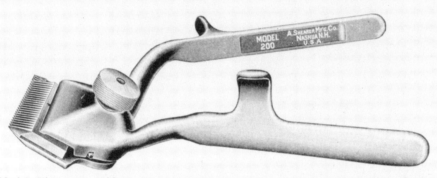

Model Clipper No. 200, commonly known as No. 0. Cuts the hair equal to shaving.
Price, each $2.25

Model Clipper No. 2000, commonly known as No. 00. Cuts the hair equal to shaving, but narrower than No. 200.
Price, each $2.25

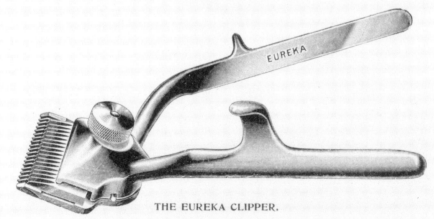

THE EUREKA CLIPPER.
Made in one size only. To cut the hair ⅛ inch long.
Price, each ....85c.

We carry in stock Coates' Left=Hand Clippers.
Size No. 1 only, price, each $2.75

Theo. A. Kochs & Son, 1903 catalog page.

HAIR CLIPPERS

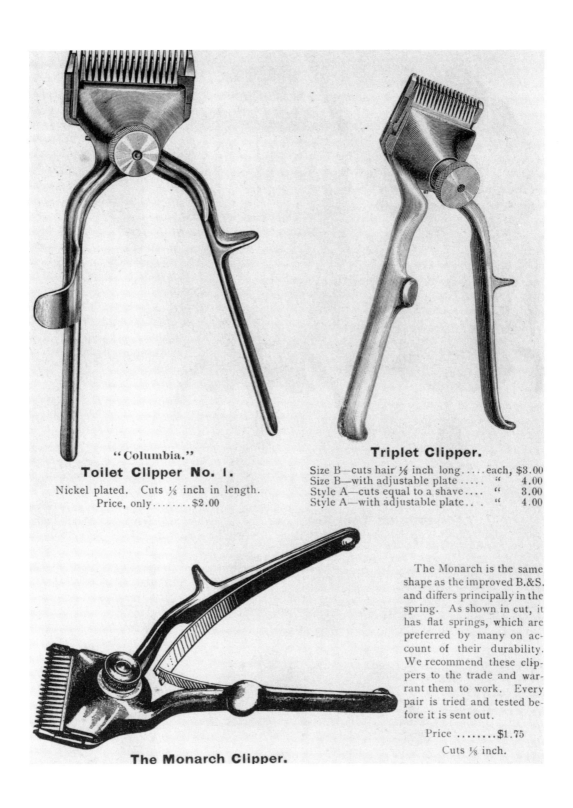

"Columbia."
Toilet Clipper No. 1.
Nickel plated. Cuts ⅛ inch in length.
Price, only........$2.00

Triplet Clipper.
Size B—cuts hair ⅛ inch long.....each, $3.00
Size B—with adjustable plate..... " 4.00
Style A—cuts equal to a shave.... " 3.00
Style A—with adjustable plate... " 4.00

The Monarch Clipper.

The Monarch is the same shape as the improved B.&S. and differs principally in the spring. As shown in cut, it has flat springs, which are preferred by many on account of their durability. We recommend these clippers to the trade and warrant them to work. Every pair is tried and tested before it is sent out.

Price........$1.75
Cuts ⅛ inch.

Fred Dolle Inc., 1914 catalog page.

HAIR CLIPPERS

"BRESSANT"—BROWN & SHARPE CLIPPER

No. 0. To cut the hair nearly equal to shaving.........$2.50
No. 1. To cut the hair 1/8 inch long...................... 2.50
No. 2. To cut the hair 1/4 inch long...................... 3.00
No. 3. To cut the hair 5-16 inch long.................... 3.50

"FIGARO"—BROWN & SHARPE CLIPPER

These clippers are durable, powerful, clean-cutting and unusually comfortable to the hand. The simplicity of construction is a feature which is readily appreciated by every barber. In taking these clippers apart, no wrench, screw-driver or other tool is necessary. The spring, owing to its shape and form, is practically indestructible. These clippers are somewhat lighter than those of earlier design. The lower plates of the Nos. 0 and 1 clippers are grooved on the bottom.

No. 0 ....:$2.50
No. 1 .... 2.50

No. 1. COATES' BAY STATE CLIPPER

To cut the hair 1/8 inch long. A perfect barber's clipper. Simply constructed and easy to adjust. Light weight and provided with an almost unbreakable spring.
Each $2.25

THE SHAVER CLIPPER — FRENCH MODEL

A small clipper of neat and very light pattern. To cut closer than No. 00 size and especially made for trimming the beard and close neck clipping.
Each $2.25

"IMPROVED"—BROWN & SHARPE CLIPPER

No. 1. To cut hair 1/8 inch long......................$2.50
No. 0. To cut the hair nearly equal to shaving.......... 2.50
No. 00. A small and narrow clipper to cut hair very short. 2.50
No. 000. A light toilet clipper to use about the neck or for trimming the beard. It is the same in general construction as the Improved Clippers, with the exception that it has a nut with wings for the adjustment of the plates. The bottom of the lower plate is grooved.
Each 2.50

THE MODEL CLIPPER

No. 201. Cuts the hair 1/8 of an inch....................$2.25

THE EUREKA CLIPPER

Made in one size only. To cut the hair 1/8 inch long. Although this clipper is sold at a very low price, we can recommend it as a first-class article and one which will give good satisfaction.
Each .... 85c.

THE EAGLE CLIPPER

Made in one size only. To cut the hair 1/8 inch long. This is a ball-bearing clipper, made of best material and carefully adjusted. It is a very easy-running clipper and a smooth cutter.
Each $1.50

Fred Bender Co., 1909 catalog page.

SHEARS

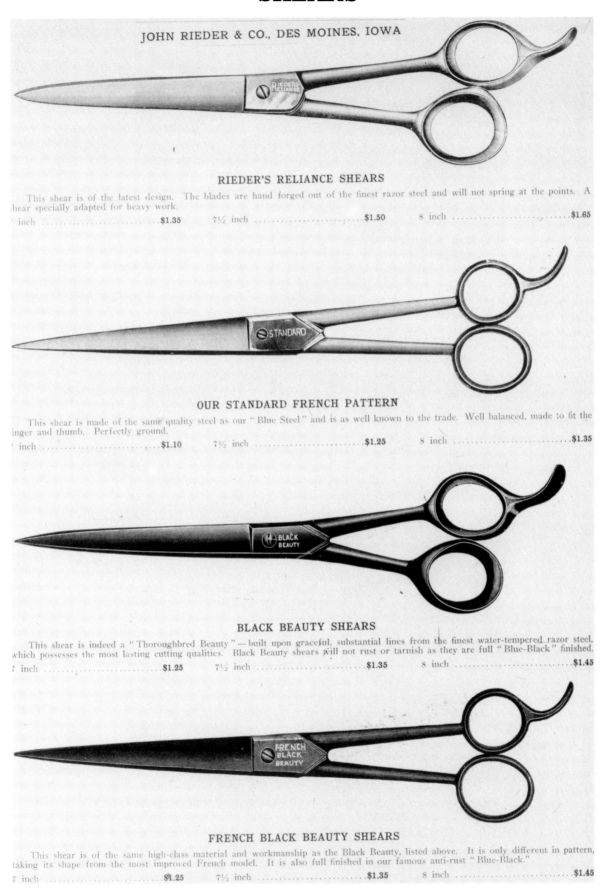

JOHN RIEDER & CO., DES MOINES, IOWA

RIEDER'S RELIANCE SHEARS

This shear is of the latest design. The blades are hand forged out of the finest razor steel and will not spring at the points. A shear specially adapted for heavy work.

  inch ....$1.35   7½ inch ....$1.50   8 inch $1.65

OUR STANDARD FRENCH PATTERN

This shear is made of the same quality steel as our "Blue Steel" and is as well known to the trade. Well balanced, made to fit the finger and thumb. Perfectly ground.

  inch ....$1.10   7½ inch ....$1.25   8 inch $1.35

BLACK BEAUTY SHEARS

This shear is indeed a "Thoroughbred Beauty"—built upon graceful, substantial lines from the finest water-tempered razor steel, which possesses the most lasting cutting qualities. Black Beauty shears will not rust or tarnish as they are full "Blue-Black" finished.

  inch ....$1.25   7½ inch ....$1.35   8 inch $1.45

FRENCH BLACK BEAUTY SHEARS

This shear is of the same high-class material and workmanship as the Black Beauty, listed above. It is only different in pattern, taking its shape from the most improved French model. It is also full finished in our famous anti-rust "Blue-Black."

  inch ....$1.25   7½ inch ....$1.35   8 inch $1.45

John Rieder & Co., 1912 catalog page.

SHEARS

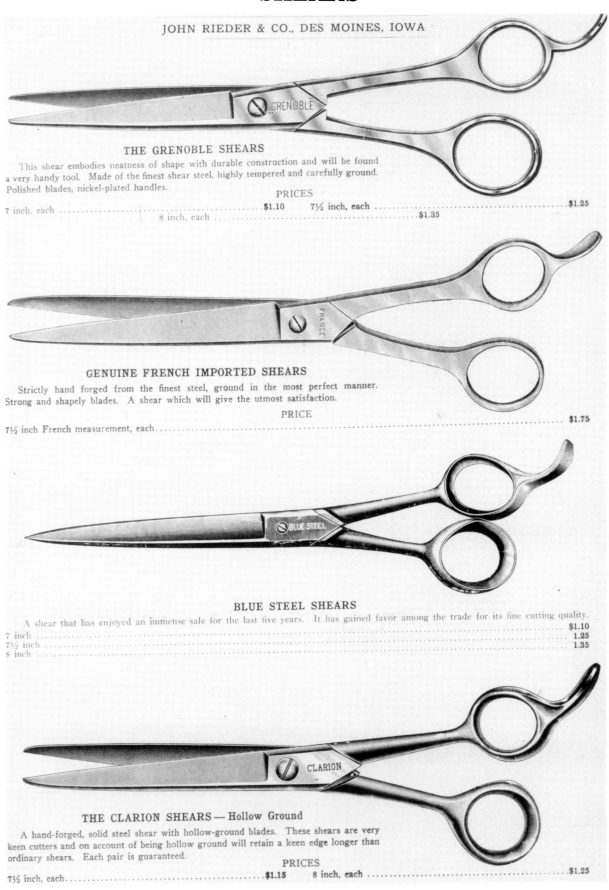

JOHN RIEDER & CO., DES MOINES, IOWA

THE GRENOBLE SHEARS
This shear embodies neatness of shape with durable construction and will be found a very handy tool. Made of the finest shear steel, highly tempered and carefully ground. Polished blades, nickel-plated handles.

PRICES

7 inch, each ....$1.10 7½ inch, each $1.25
8 inch, each $1.35

GENUINE FRENCH IMPORTED SHEARS
Strictly hand forged from the finest steel, ground in the most perfect manner. Strong and shapely blades. A shear which will give the utmost satisfaction.

PRICE

7½ inch French measurement, each.................................$1.75

BLUE STEEL SHEARS
A shear that has enjoyed an immense sale for the last five years. It has gained favor among the trade for its fine cutting quality.

7 inch $1.10
7½ inch 1.25
8 inch 1.35

THE CLARION SHEARS — Hollow Ground
A hand-forged, solid steel shear with hollow-ground blades. These shears are very keen cutters and on account of being hollow ground will retain a keen edge longer than ordinary shears. Each pair is guaranteed.

PRICES

7½ inch, each.................................$1.15 8 inch, each.................................$1.25

John Rieder & Co., 1912 catalog page.

SHEARS

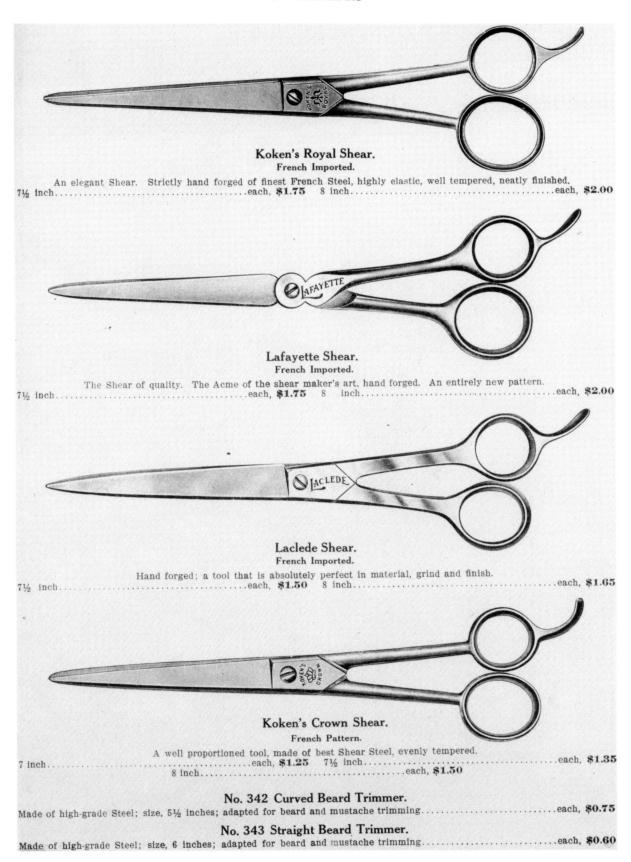

Koken's Royal Shear.
French Imported.

An elegant Shear. Strictly hand forged of finest French Steel, highly elastic, well tempered, neatly finished.
7½ inch..................................each, **$1.75**   8 inch..................................each, **$2.00**

Lafayette Shear.
French Imported.

The Shear of quality. The Acme of the shear maker's art, hand forged. An entirely new pattern.
7½ inch..................................each, **$1.75**   8 inch..................................each, **$2.00**

Laclede Shear.
French Imported.

Hand forged; a tool that is absolutely perfect in material, grind and finish.
7½ inch..................................each, **$1.50**   8 inch..................................each, **$1.65**

Koken's Crown Shear.
French Pattern.

A well proportioned tool, made of best Shear Steel, evenly tempered.
7 inch..................................each, **$1.25**   7½ inch..................................each, **$1.35**
8 inch..................................each, **$1.50**

No. 342 Curved Beard Trimmer.
Made of high-grade Steel; size, 5½ inches; adapted for beard and mustache trimming..................................each, **$0.75**

No. 343 Straight Beard Trimmer.
Made of high-grade Steel; size, 6 inches; adapted for beard and mustache trimming..................................each, **$0.60**

Koken Supply Co., 1910 catalog page.

SHEARS

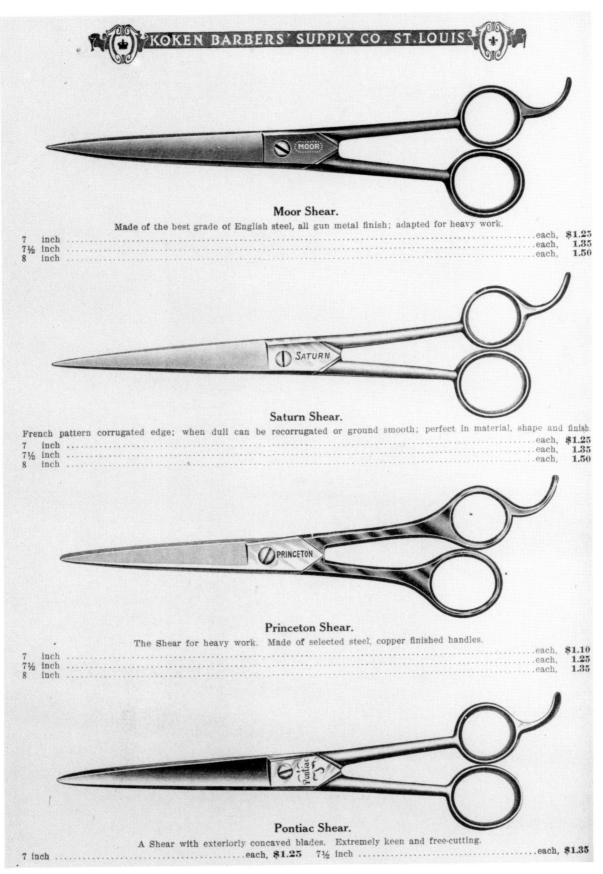

Moor Shear.
Made of the best grade of English steel, all gun metal finish; adapted for heavy work.

7 inch	each,	$1.25
7½ inch	each,	1.35
8 inch	each,	1.50

Saturn Shear.
French pattern corrugated edge; when dull can be recorrugated or ground smooth; perfect in material, shape and finish.

7 inch	each,	$1.25
7½ inch	each,	1.35
8 inch	each,	1.50

Princeton Shear.
The Shear for heavy work. Made of selected steel, copper finished handles.

7 inch	each,	$1.10
7½ inch	each,	1.25
8 inch	each,	1.35

Pontiac Shear.
A Shear with exteriorly concaved blades. Extremely keen and free-cutting.

7 inch ......each, **$1.25**   7½ inch ......each, **$1.35**

Koken Supply Co., 1910 catalog page.

NECK & HAIR BRUSHES

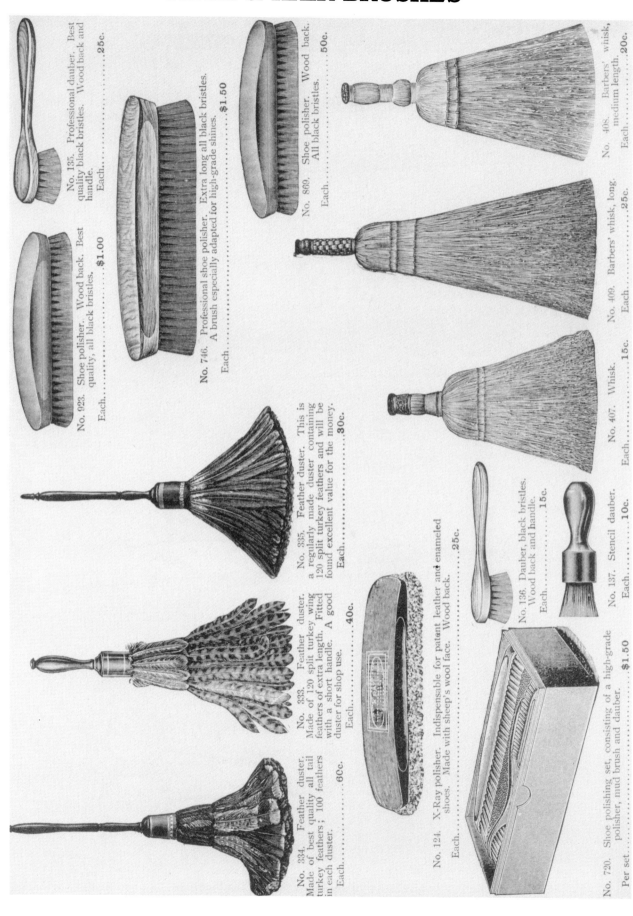

Theo. A. Kochs & Son, 1903 catalog page.

NECK & HAIR BRUSHES

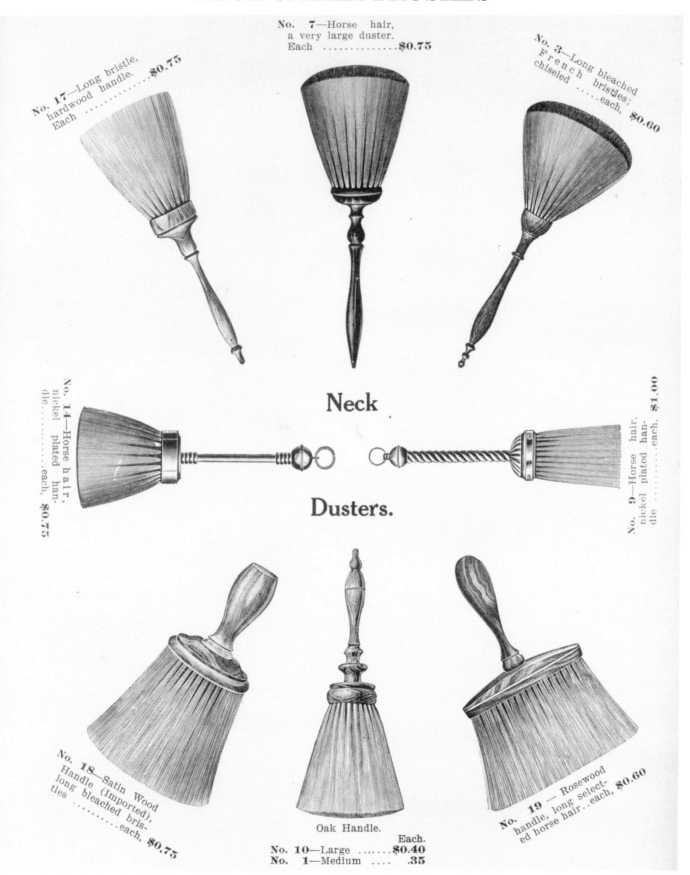

Koken Supply Co., 1910 catalog page.

NECK & HAIR BRUSHES

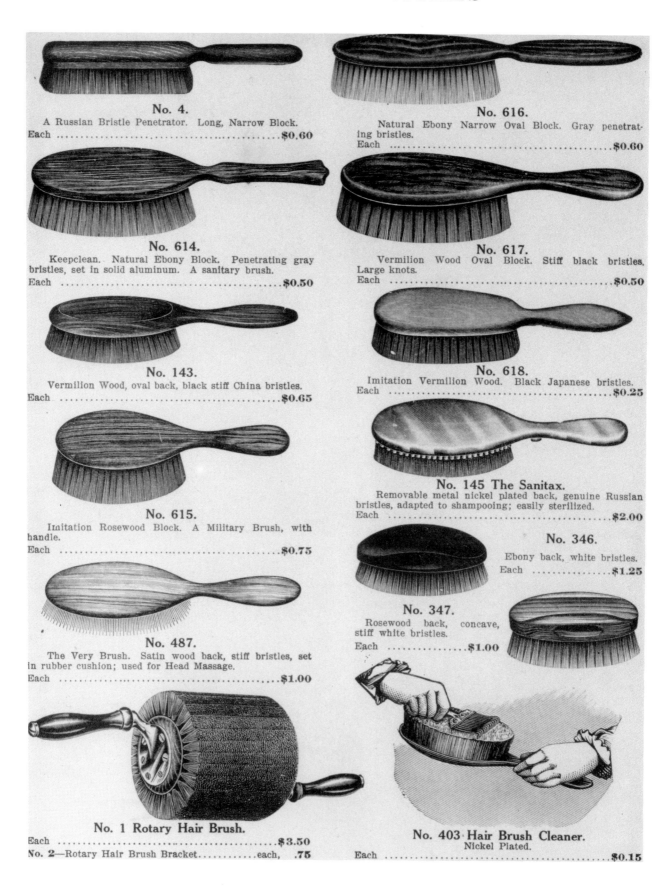

No. 4.
A Russian Bristle Penetrator. Long, Narrow Block.
Each $0.60

No. 616.
Natural Ebony Narrow Oval Block. Gray penetrating bristles.
Each $0.60

No. 614.
Keepclean. Natural Ebony Block. Penetrating gray bristles, set in solid aluminum. A sanitary brush.
Each $0.50

No. 617.
Vermilion Wood Oval Block. Stiff black bristles. Large knots.
Each $0.50

No. 143.
Vermilion Wood, oval back, black stiff China bristles.
Each $0.65

No. 618.
Imitation Vermilion Wood. Black Japanese bristles.
Each $0.25

No. 615.
Imitation Rosewood Block. A Military Brush, with handle.
Each $0.75

No. 145 The Sanitax.
Removable metal nickel plated back, genuine Russian bristles, adapted to shampooing; easily sterilized.
Each $2.00

No. 346.
Ebony back, white bristles.
Each $1.25

No. 487.
The Very Brush. Satin wood back, stiff bristles, set in rubber cushion; used for Head Massage.
Each $1.00

No. 347.
Rosewood back, concave, stiff white bristles.
Each $1.00

No. 1 Rotary Hair Brush.
Each $3.50
No. 2—Rotary Hair Brush Bracket .... each, .75

No. 403 Hair Brush Cleaner.
Nickel Plated.
Each $0.15

Koken Supply Co., 1910 catalog page.

LATHER BRUSHES

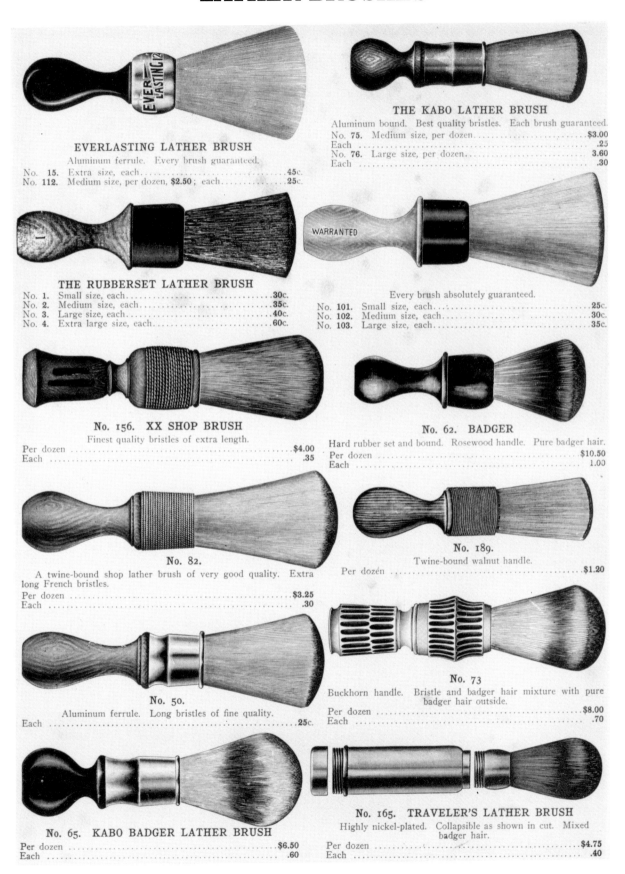

EVERLASTING LATHER BRUSH
Aluminum ferrule. Every brush guaranteed.
No. 15. Extra size, each............................45c.
No. 112. Medium size, per dozen, $2.50; each............25c.

THE KABO LATHER BRUSH
Aluminum bound. Best quality bristles. Each brush guaranteed.
No. 75. Medium size, per dozen........................$3.00
Each.. .25
No. 76. Large size, per dozen......................... 3.60
Each.. .30

THE RUBBERSET LATHER BRUSH
No. 1. Small size, each............................30c.
No. 2. Medium size, each...........................35c.
No. 3. Large size, each............................40c.
No. 4. Extra large size, each......................60c.

Every brush absolutely guaranteed.
No. 101. Small size, each..........................25c.
No. 102. Medium size, each.........................30c.
No. 103. Large size, each..........................35c.

No. 156. XX SHOP BRUSH
Finest quality bristles of extra length.
Per dozen..$4.00
Each... .35

No. 62. BADGER
Hard rubber set and bound. Rosewood handle. Pure badger hair.
Per dozen......................................$10.50
Each... 1.00

No. 82.
A twine-bound shop lather brush of very good quality. Extra long French bristles.
Per dozen..$3.25
Each... .30

No. 189.
Twine-bound walnut handle.
Per dozen..$1.20

No. 50.
Aluminum ferrule. Long bristles of fine quality.
Each...25c.

No. 73
Buckhorn handle. Bristle and badger hair mixture with pure badger hair outside.
Per dozen..$8.00
Each... .70

No. 65. KABO BADGER LATHER BRUSH
Per dozen..$6.50
Each... .60

No. 165. TRAVELER'S LATHER BRUSH
Highly nickel-plated. Collapsible as shown in cut. Mixed badger hair.
Per dozen..$4.75
Each... .40

Fred Bender Co., 1909 catalog page.

LATHER BRUSHES

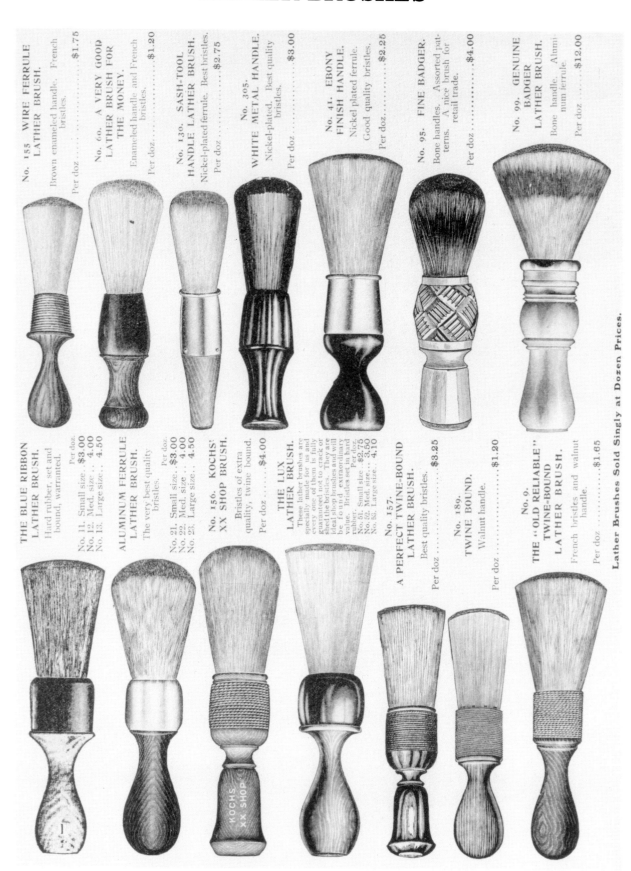

Theo. A. Kochs & Son, 1903 catalog page.

COMBS

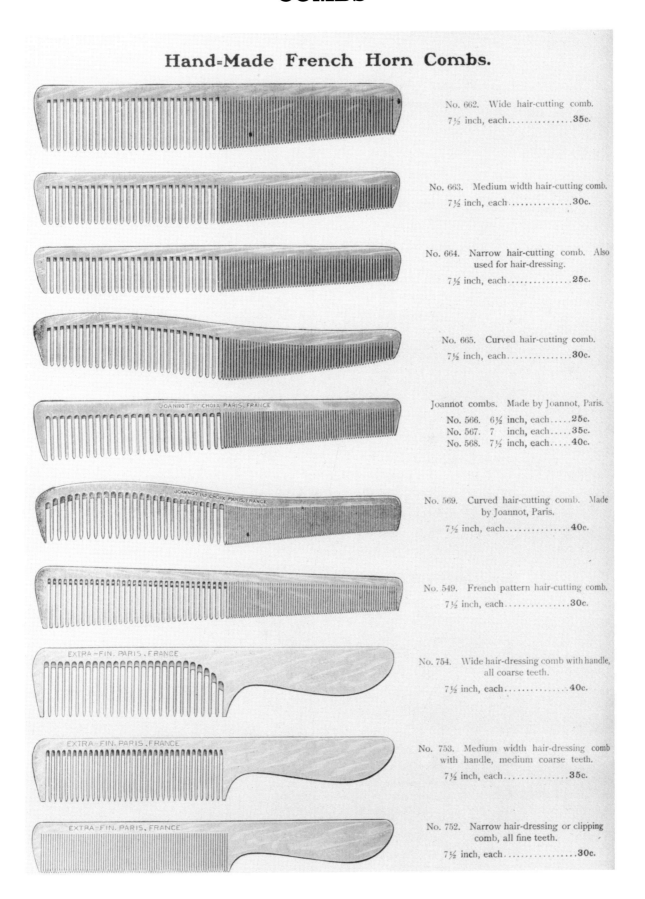

Hand-Made French Horn Combs.

No. 662. Wide hair-cutting comb.
7½ inch, each..............35c.

No. 663. Medium width hair-cutting comb.
7½ inch, each..............30c.

No. 664. Narrow hair-cutting comb. Also used for hair-dressing.
7½ inch, each..............25c.

No. 665. Curved hair-cutting comb.
7½ inch, each..............30c.

Joannot combs. Made by Joannot, Paris.
No. 566.   6½ inch, each.....25c.
No. 567.   7 inch, each.....35c.
No. 568.   7½ inch, each.....40c.

No. 569. Curved hair-cutting comb. Made by Joannot, Paris.
7½ inch, each..............40c.

No. 549. French pattern hair-cutting comb.
7½ inch, each..............30c.

No. 754. Wide hair-dressing comb with handle, all coarse teeth.
7½ inch, each..............40c.

No. 753. Medium width hair-dressing comb with handle, medium coarse teeth.
7½ inch, each..............35c.

No. 752. Narrow hair-dressing or clipping comb, all fine teeth.
7½ inch, each..............30c.

Theo. A. Kochs & Son, 1903 catalog page.

COMBS

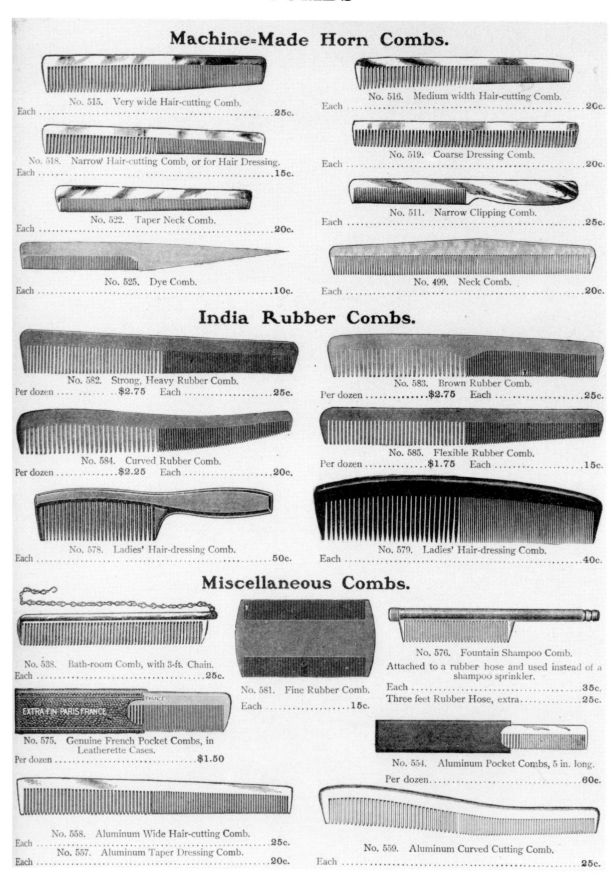

Theo. A. Kochs & Son, 1903 catalog page.

BARBERS' JACKETS

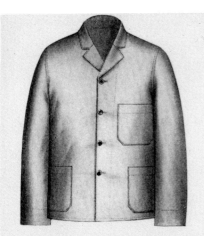

No. 40—Coat, made of light white Drill, 3 pockets, black buttons.

Price, each................. $0.75

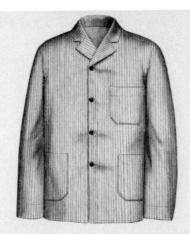

No. 41—Coat, made of white, black striped heavy Drill, black buttons, 3 pockets.

Price, each.................. $1.00

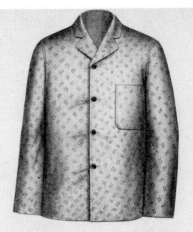

No. 42—A new pattern of figured white and black Drill, 4 buttons, 1 pocket.

Price, each.................. $1.25

No. 43—Made of heavy, special white, very fine black stripe Drill, collar and pockets trimmed with white Duck.

Price, each............. $1.10

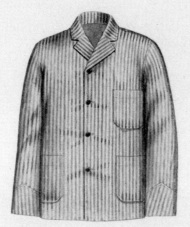

No. 44—Made of white, strong, blue striped classics, a well finished coat, 4 buttons, 3 pockets.

Price, each................. $0.75

No. 45—Vest, made of high grade white Drill, collar and cuffs trimmed with white and black striped Drill, very neat.

Price, each................. $1.25

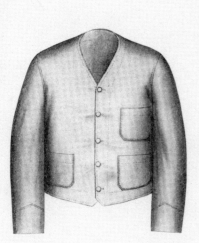

No. 46—Vest, light white Duck, collarless, white buttons.

Price, each $1.00

No. 47—Vest, fine white Duck, small gilt or white buttons, very attractive.

Price, each... $1.50

Oversleeves.
Rubber, good quality.....Per pr., 35c
Gingham, black or figured, " 20c

Koken Supply Co., 1904 catalog page.

BARBERS' JACKETS

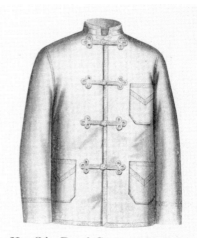

No. 31—Royal Coat, made of finest Army Duck, trimmed with silk loops and braid. The best made.
Price, each $2.50

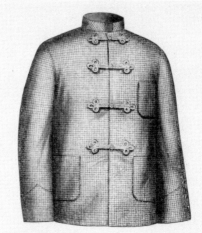

No. 32—Royal Coat, made of fine black and white checked Sateen, silk loops.
Price, each $2.00

No. 33—Royal Coat, made of fancy figured Drill; very neat; loop trimmings.
Price, each $1.40

No. 34—Royal Coat, made of fine white Drill, pockets and cuffs trimmed with fine striped material, black or brass buttons.
Price, each $1.25

No. 35—Coat, made of superior black Sateen. A very serviceable coat.
Price, each $1.35

No. 26—Royal Coat, made of choice Army Duck, invisible buttons, fine linen braid trimmings.
Price, each $1.75

No. 37—Royal Vest, made of fine Army Duck, invisible buttons, silk braid, two pockets.
Price, each $2.00

No. 38—Coat, made of very fine white, black striped Duck; neat pattern; black buttons.
Price, each $1.25

No. 39—Royal Vest, made of fine white Pique, silk braid, invisible buttons, four pockets.
Price, each $2.25

Koken Supply Co., 1904 catalog page.

BARBERS' JACKETS

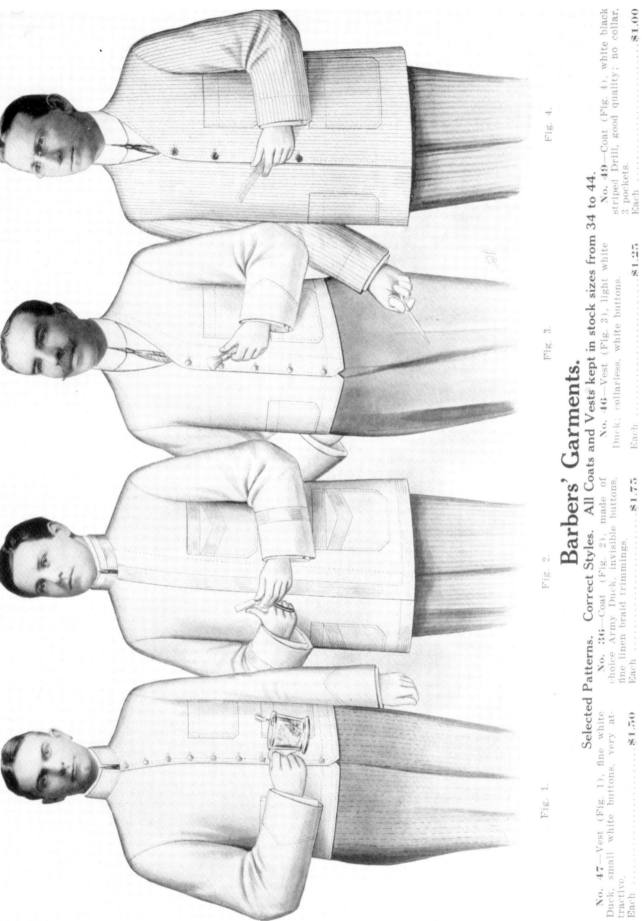

Barbers' Garments.

Selected Patterns. Correct Styles. All Coats and Vests kept in stock sizes from 34 to 44.

No. 47—Vest (Fig. 1), fine white Duck, small white buttons, very attractive. Each $1.50

No. 36—Coat (Fig. 2), made of choice Army Duck, invisible buttons, fine linen braid trimmings. Each $1.75

No. 46—Vest (Fig. 3), light white Duck; collarless, white buttons. Each $1.25

No. 49—Coat (Fig. 4), white black striped Drill, good quality; no collar, 3 pockets. Each $1.00

Koken Supply Co., 1910 catalog page.

BARBERS' JACKETS

No. 267. Coat. White drill. Pockets, collar and sleeves trimmed with black-striped duck. Black buttons.
Each $1.00

No. 242. Coat. Made of heavy white duck. Black buttons. 34 inches long.
Each $1.50

No. 266. Coat. White drill. The standard plain white coat. Black buttons.
Each .... 75c.

No. 232. Coat. White drill, with black stripes. Black buttons.
Each $1.00

No. 301. Trousers. Made of heavy white washable duck with belt loops and side buckles.
Per pair $1.75

No. 241. Coat. White drill, black stripes, black buttons. 34 inches long.
Each $1.25

No. 275. Vest. Best quality white duck.
Each $1.25

No. 276. Vest. Best quality white duck, with black stripes. Six brass buttons.
Each $1.25

John Rieder & Co., 1912 catalog page.

BARBERS' SIGNS & POLES INTRODUCTION

The barbershop pole is the uniform symbol of barbers. Originally consisting of a striped pole from which a basin was suspended, centuries later the basin was removed as the bloodletting services of a barber waned. The fillet around the pole symbolized a bandage twisted around the arm prior to bloodletting. Another interpretation has been offered that describes each color of the pole as representing something different- red for blood, blue to symbolize the veins, and white for the bandage.

In earlier times, the pole was used to hang and dry bandages. As they would blow and twist in the wind, they formed reddish pink patterns on the poles like the paint on modern barber poles.

Although the candy-striped pole is still recognized as a barbershop symbol today, many barbershops preferred a sign or a painted front window for their establishment as well, to offset the similarity between the shop they are proud to operate and the competition down the street.

The advent of printing technology also led to hundreds of advertising signs, catered to the products and customers of barbershops in addition to all businesses which relied on bright colors and gimmickry to lure potential patronage. These signs alone are tell-tale reminders of days past, advertising the newest sea foam, soaps, and any paraphernalia of the sort a barber and his clientele could appreciate.

Haircuts and beards in fashion during the 19th Century

Haircuts and beards in fashion at the onset of the 20th Century

BARBERS' SIGNS & POLES

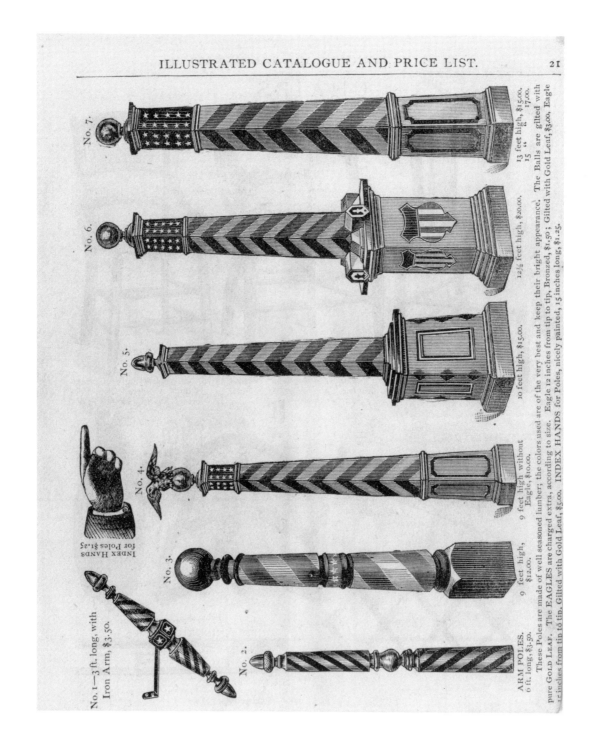

Eugene Berninghaus, 1882 catalog page.

BARBERS' SIGNS & POLES

Theo. A. Kochs Co., 1897 catalog page.

BARBERS' SIGNS & POLES

Theo. A. Kochs Co., 1897 catalog page.

BARBERS' SIGNS & POLES

Theo. A Kochs Co., 1897 catalog page.

BARBERS' SIGNS & POLES

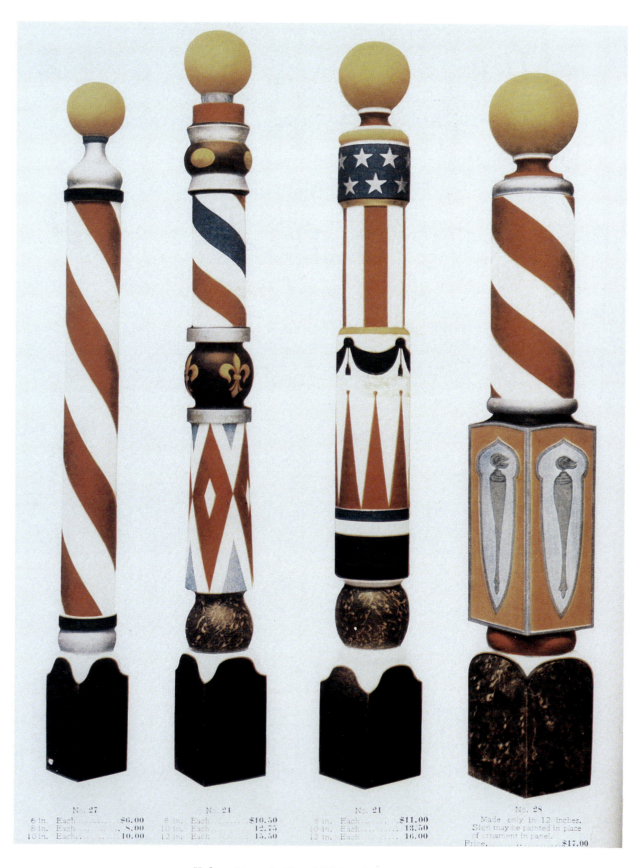

Koken Supply Co., 1904 catalog page.
(The two end poles on page are 8' in height with the two in middle standing at 9'.)

BARBERS' SIGNS & POLES

No. 45
This pole is made to be fastened to the front of the building with iron brackets. Suitable for shops where barbers' poles are not permitted on the sidewalk. Length, 4 feet 8 inches; diameter 8 inches. Furnished complete with brackets. 10-inch glass globe and electric light attachments, same as furnished on pole No. 30.
Price $18.50

No. 46
This pole is made to fasten to the wall in front of the shop and is well adapted for upstairs or interior shops. Length, 4 feet. Diameter, 8 inches.
Price, complete with iron brackets $12.75

No. 30
A handsome display pole; very attractive at night. Furnished with 12-inch ground glass globe with raised and baked enameled letters in translucent colors, electric light socket, flash-light plug and 10 feet of heavy rubber-covered wire. Globes with lettering "Barber Shop" carried in stock. Other lettering, such as "Baths," "Massage" and "Manicuring," furnished on short notice. Lettering on two sides. Height of pole, 8 feet.
Price, 10 in. $22.50
Price, 12 in. 27.50

No. 31
Price, 10 in. $16.00
Price, 12 in. 19.50

No. 32
Price, 12 in. $21.00
Price, 14 in. 25.50

Fred Bender Co., 1909 catalog page. (The square based poles are 8' in height.)

BARBERS' SIGNS & POLES

No. 39—IRON
Price $27.00

No. 40—IRON
Price $30.00

No. 44—IRON
Price $27.00

The No. 39, No. 40 and No. 44 poles illustrated above are made of iron and are a new departure in the construction of barbers' poles. The ornamental parts and base are made of hollow cast iron and the straight sections of steel tubing. The ball is made of spun copper, perfectly smooth and round, and covered with pure gold leaf. The ball on the iron poles is detachable and if desired we can furnish the glass globe and electric light connection shown and described on preceding page in place of the copper ball. There is no difference in the price whether the copper ball, gilded, or the glass globe is furnished. These poles are attractive in design and very durable. They are 8 feet high and 12 inches in diameter. They are painted with the finest and most durable colors and coated with extra quality exterior varnish.

Fred Bender Co., 1909 catalog page.

BARBERS' SIGNS & POLES

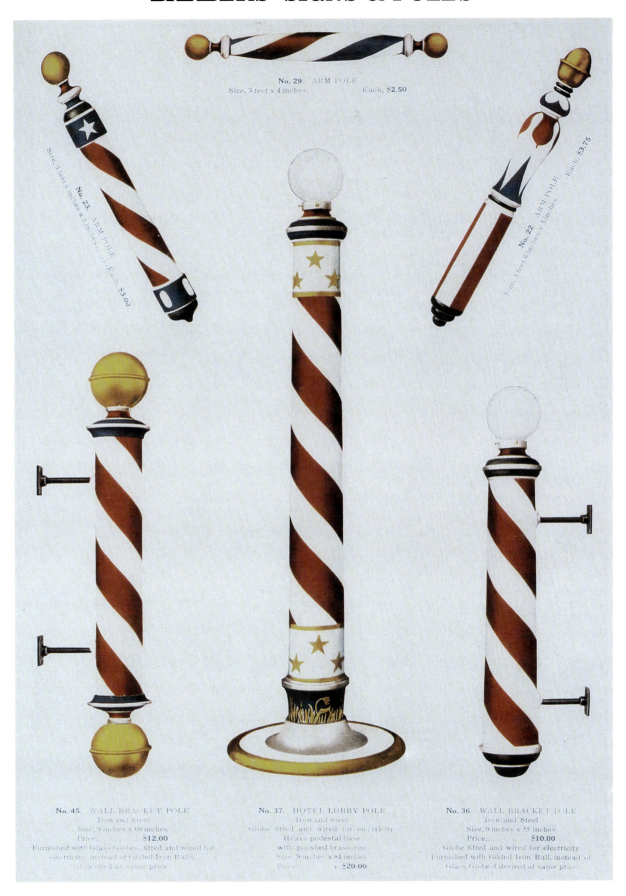

Koken Supply Co., 1910 catalog page.

Koken Supply Co., 1910 catalog page.

BARBERS' SIGNS & POLES
IRON BARBERS' POLES

No. 67
Height, 8 feet. Diameter, 12 inches. Fitted with 12-inch glass globe, rubber-covered electric feed wire and electric light socket.
Price $29.00

No. 71 WALL BRACKET POLE
Black and Gold. Height, 56 inches. Diameter, 10 inches. Fitted with 10-inch glass globe with "burnt-in" lettering "Barber Shop" on two sides. Furnished complete with rubber-covered electric feed wire, flash-light electric light socket and wall brackets.
Price $23.50

No. 69
Height, 7 feet 6 inches. Diameter, 10 inches. Fitted with 10-inch glass globe, rubber-covered electric feed wire and electric light socket.
Price $25.00

No. 70
Same pole as No. 69, but striped red and white.
Price $25.00

No. 72 WALL BRACKET POLE
Height, 56 inches. Diameter, 10 inches. Fitted with 10-inch glass globe and furnished complete with rubber-covered feed wire, electric light socket and wall brackets.
Price $14.50

No. 73
Same pole as No. 72, but striped red and white.
Price $14.50

No. 68
Red and Gold. Height, 8 feet. Diameter, 12 inches. The most attractive iron barbers' pole made. Fitted with 12-inch glass globe with "burnt-in" lettering "Barber Shop" on two sides. Furnished complete with rubber-covered electric feed wire and flash-light electric light socket.
Price $45.00

These poles are made completely of iron and steel. The bases and molded parts are made of hollow cast iron and the straight sections of steel tubing. They are painted with the finest and most durable colors and coated with extra quality exterior varnish. The gold stripes and decoration are not bronzed, but made of genuine gold-leaf and will not tarnish, but retain their luster. For the Nos. 68 and 71 poles globes lettered "Barber Shop" are carried in stock. Other lettering furnished on short notice.

John Rieder & Co., 1912 catalog page.

BARBERS' SIGNS & POLES

John Rieder & Co., 1912 catalog page. (All poles are 8' in height.)

BARBERS' SIGNS & POLES

No. 15.
Height 12½ feet, price $30.00.

No. 8 Black and Gold.
Price, 12 in. diameter .. $21.00
" 14 " " 24.00
Red, White and Blue.
Price, 10 in. diameter.... 13.00
" 12 " " 15.00

Style A.
Price, 10 inch pole..... $12.00
" 12 " " 15.00

No. 16.
Height 12½ feet.
Price $35.0
Illuminated Barber Pole.
See description.

Fred Dolle Inc., 1914 catalog page

BARBERS' SIGNS & POLES

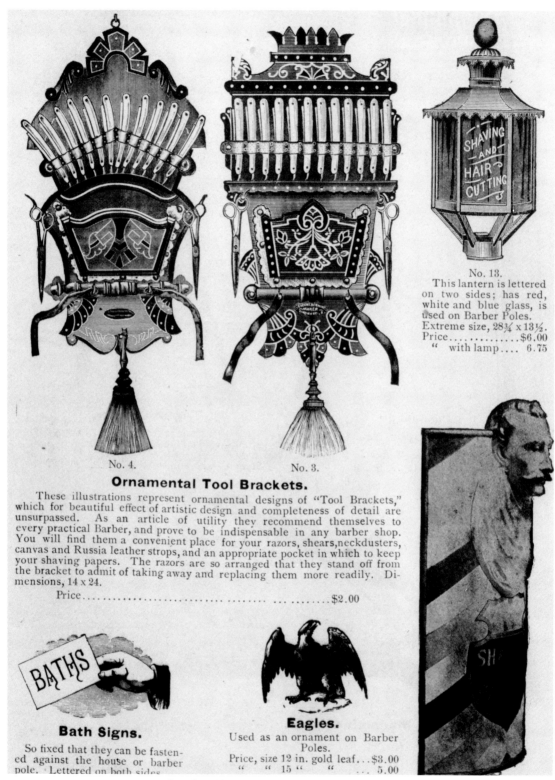

No. 13.
This lantern is lettered on two sides; has red, white and blue glass, is used on Barber Poles. Extreme size, 28¾ x 13½.
Price.............$6.00
" with lamp.... 6.75

No. 4. No. 3.

Ornamental Tool Brackets.

These illustrations represent ornamental designs of "Tool Brackets," which for beautiful effect of artistic design and completeness of detail are unsurpassed. As an article of utility they recommend themselves to every practical Barber, and prove to be indispensable in any barber shop. You will find them a convenient place for your razors, shears, neckdusters, canvas and Russia leather strops, and an appropriate pocket in which to keep your shaving papers. The razors are so arranged that they stand off from the bracket to admit of taking away and replacing them more readily. Dimensions, 14 x 24.
Price...$2.00

Bath Signs.
So fixed that they can be fastened against the house or barber pole. Lettered on both sides

Eagles.
Used as an ornament on Barber Poles.
Price, size 12 in. gold leaf...$3.00
"   "   15 "   "   ... 5.00

Fred Dolle Inc., 1914 catalog page.

BARBERS' SIGNS & POLES

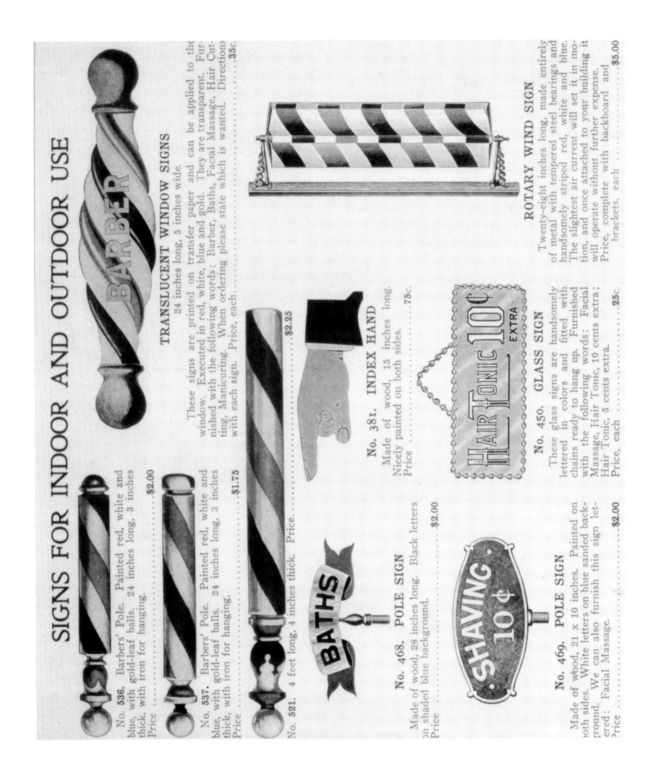

Fred Bender Co., 1909 catalog page.

BARBERS' SIGNS & POLES

No. 484

Pleasingly shaped, this pole is constructed of heavy metal. It is striped with care and best of materials. Then varnished and thoroughly dried. Ready to put up. Wired and with lamp for illuminating glass globe.

Dimensions: 42 inches high, 15¼ inches from wall.

Diameter of pole, 7¼ inches, of white glass globe, 8 inches.

No. 9

No. 9

Finished entirely in porcelain enamel. Cylinder sections enameled blue and white. Base blue and white except red and white striped steel section.

Paper cylinder red, white and blue. A handsome and strong pole for side-walk display where plenty of space is available.

Height: 7 feet 5 inches.
Diameter of base: 17 inches.
Shipping weight (crated): 300 lbs.

No. 14 Non-Revolving Pedestal Pole

The cylinders are striped red and white porcelain enamel on iron. All castings are blue porcelain enamel. Top has electric light with round white globe.

The workmanship and finish of this pole are of the same high quality as No. 9 (revolving) pole.

Height (with globe): 7 feet 1 inch.
Shipping weight: 100 lbs.

Poles Nos. 9, 13, 5, 12 and 15 are operated by clock-motors. A single winding is all that is required to keep poles running 15 to 20 hours.

The winding crank and motor gears are case hardened and of the best steel, thus insuring the greatest length of service, and reducing the cost of frequently replacing worn parts.

Poles are wired and equipped with two electric lamps—one inside globe, the other inside cylinder.

Each pole and motor are carefully tested, and NO POLE IS SHIPPED UNTIL IT HAS BEEN OPERATING PERFECTLY IN OUR SHOP.

No. 14

No. 15

This is a very neat and attractive pole for side-walk display.

Cylinder sections blue and white porcelain enamel. Base finished in black enamel. Paper cylinder red, white and blue stripes.

Height: 7 feet 3 inches.
Diameter of base plate: 13 inches.

Shipping weight (crated): 200 lbs.

No. 12

"Baby" Pole (Revolving)

Top and bottom castings white, middle casting blue porcelain enamel. Paper cylinder red, white and blue.

This beautifully finished little pole is a gem, mechanically perfect.

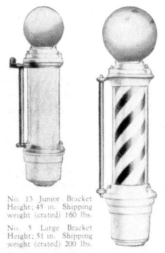

No. 13 Junior Bracket Height; 45 in. Shipping weight (crated) 160 lbs.

No. 5 Large Bracket Height; 51 in. Shipping weight (crated) 200 lbs.

Finished entirely in blue and white porcelain enamel.
Paper cylinder striped red, white and blue.

No. 5 is designed for outside use where plenty of space is available.

No. 13 is designed for interior hallways or outside if space is limited.

Eugene Berninghaus, 1924 catalog page.

BARBERS' SIGNS & POLES

No. 487—STRAIGHT SIGN

Made of sheet steel porcelain enameled and very attractive. An economical and lasting method of advertising your business.

No. 486—CORNER SIGN

This attractive corner sign is porcelain enameled sheet steel, curved. It is 24 inches high and 16 inches wide. Built to give years of service.

No. 480—BARBER POLE

All porcelain enameled, beautifully finished barber pole. Non-revolving. It is 40 inches high. Top is of white porcelain and bottom of blue porcelain enamel. 8-inch steel porcelain cylinder. Cylinder is striped red and white. Height, 40 inches over all. Wired with lamp and 10-inch illuminated globe. Ready to install.

ILLUMINATED GLOBES

Flat side white glass with red lettering, 16-inch globe with 6-inch opening. Completely wired ready to install.

Illuminated Globe, with bracket No. 493—Barber Shop.
Illuminated Globe, with bracket, No. 498—Beauty Shop.
Illuminated Globe on counter stand, No. 492—Barber Shop.
Illuminated Globe on counter stand, No. 497—Beauty Shop.

Eugene Berninghaus, 1924 catalog page.

BARBERS' SIGNS & POLES

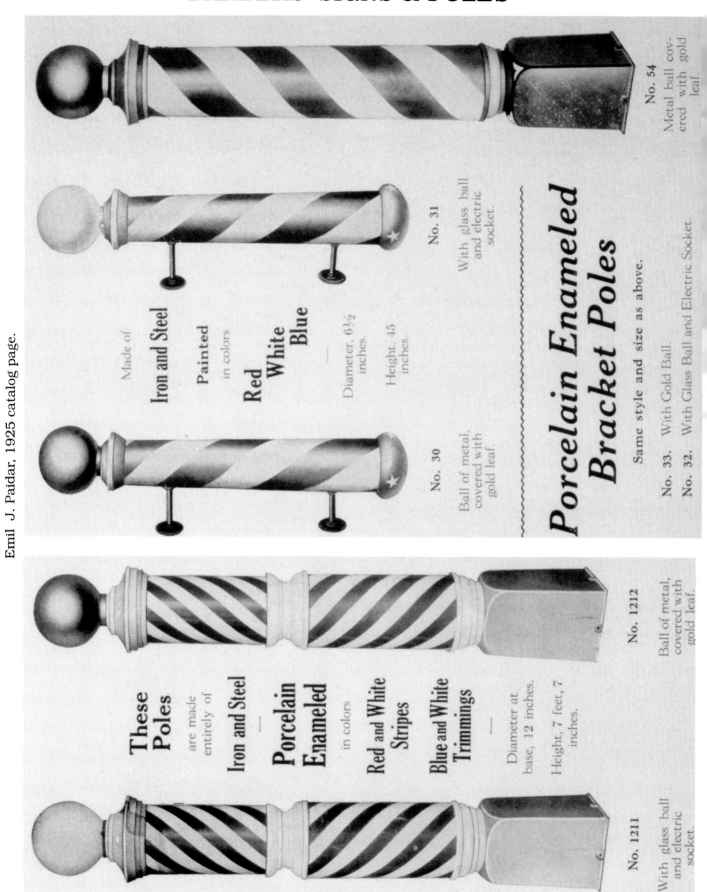

Emil J. Paidar, 1925 catalog page.

BARBERS' SIGNS & POLES

**JUNIOR BRACKET POLE,
No. 23**

Height, 45 inches.
Finished in blue and white porcelain enamel.

No. 84. SIGN

Porcelain enameled sign, 12x 24 inches. Both sides alike. Fitted with flange to fasten to wall or can be hung. Decorated in red, white and blue.

**No. 94
BEAUTY PARLOR SIGN**

Porcelain enameled, 12 x 24 inches. Both sides alike; fitted with flange to fasten to wall. Letters are blue. Background is white.

91

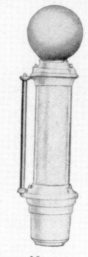

No. 25

BRACKET POLE, No. 25

Height, 51 inches.
Finished in blue and white porcelain enamel.

No. 74

PORCELAIN ENAMELED SIGN

18x24 inches. Oval or bent, to fit on corner. Hanger furnished. Beautifully decorated in red, white and blue.

No. 26

Height, 7 feet 8 inches.
Finished entirely in white enamel, including pedestal. Revolving cylinder, red and white.

No. 27

Same style as above; pedestal is painted in bright colors. Height, 7 feet 3 inches.

Emil J. Paidar Co., 1925 catalog page.

BARBERS' SIGNS & POLES

No. 7 REVOLVING BARBER POLE

KOKEN'S exclusive, illuminated, Electric Clock Barber Pole. Bottom Bowl of heavy spun copper, chrome plated. Cylinder Rings of non-corrosive White Metal Alloy. All other castings, wrinkled finished.
Electric motor revolves Sparkler Cylinder. Glass Cylinder — size 8 x 20 inches. Overall height — 42 inches.
A substantial light-weight Pole, easy to install.

No. 8 REVOLVING BARBER POLE

Same as No. 7, but with double face Electric Clock.

No. 9 REVOLVING BARBER POLE

A large 8-inch Revolving Pole, equipped with Sparkler Cylinder. Electric motor revolves cylinder. Large opal glass Dome. Overall height — 42 inches.

No. 10 PEDESTAL POLE

A beautiful sidewalk Pole, topped by a 10-inch Electric Clock. Electric motor revolves Sparkler Cylinder. Glass Cylinder 8 x 24 inches. Porcelain enameled Base. Height of Pole — 7 feet 1 inch. A real business-getter.

No. 11 PEDESTAL POLE

Same as No. 10, but with double face Clock.

No. 277 REVOLVING BARBER POLE

Dome and Bowl of Chrome Plated Copper — all other castings, Porcelain Enameled. Glass Cylinder, size 6 x 16 inches, fitted with Sparkler Cylinder. Clockwork Mechanism. Height — 33½ inches.

No. 278 REVOLVING BARBER POLE

Same as No. 277, but with Electric Motor.

No. 742 REVOLVING BARBER POLE

Bowl and Dome of non-corrosive White Metal Alloy, highly polished. Glass Cylinder, size 6 x 16 inches, equipped with Sparkler Cylinder. Height overall — 27 inches. Supplied with Electric Motor only.

KOKEN COMPANIES, Inc., ST. LOUIS, U.S.A.

Buerger Bros. Supply Co., 1935 catalog page. (authorized Koken dealer)

BARBERS' SIGNS & POLES

Paidar Electric Barbers' Poles

NO SPRINGS   NO WINDING

Turn on the Switch Inside the Shop

REVOLVING

Unsurpassed for real beauty and convenience. All colors are very bright and attractive. Electric Light in Globe and Cylinder.

These Revolving Poles will operate indefinitely provided the motor is serviced occasionally; we suggest at least once each year the motor be removed and cleaned.

Service Can Be Had at Any General Electric Station.

PORCELAIN ENAMEL

These Poles are made entirely of iron and steel and are fully enameled in porcelain in the colors as shown on illustrations. Any combination of these colors may be had when so ordered.

CURRENT

These Motors will operate only on Alternating Current

110 Volts   50 to 60 Cycles

Ask Your Electric Company What Current You Have

No. 378
Electric Revolving Pole
Height over all 7' 4"
Diameter at Base 17"
Glass Cylinder 8x22"
Paper Cylinder 6¾x22"

No. 377
Electric Revolving Pole
Height over all 6' 8½"
Diameter at Base 17"
Glass Cylinder 8x19"
Paper Cylinder 6¾x19"

No. 376
Electric Revolving Pole
Height over all 7' 10"
Diameter at Base 17"
Glass Cylinder 8 x 22"
Paper Cylinder 6¾x22"

Emil J. Paidar Co., 1932 catalog page.

BARBERS' SIGNS & POLES

Emil J. Paidar Co., 1932 catalog page.

Paidar Electric Barbers' Poles

Fitted with General Electric Motor — Recognized as the Best

BUILT SPECIAL FOR BARBERS' POLES

Simple in Design — Sturdy in Construction — Quiet in Operation

The motors in these poles are manufactured by the General Electric Company, and are known as induction disc motors. They were developed to replace the spring motor or clock-work mechanism in the regular revolving pole. The principal features of these electric motors are as follows:

1st—Require a minimum amount of attention—making it most convenient and dependable type of mechanism for a revolving pole.

2nd—No winding or adjusting of springs is necessary to control this motor. A simple switch with the off and on position will operate the motor.

3rd—The cost of operating a motor of this kind is about three-fifths the cost of burning a plain 25-watt lamp.

4th—Individual fusing of the motor circuit requires only a 1/2 ampere fuse.

No. 374
Electric Revolving Pole
Height over all 49″
Glass Cylinder 8x22″
Paper Cylinder 6¾x22″

For **Alternating Current**
110 Volts—50 to 60 Cycles

FULLY GUARANTEED

No. 373
Electric Revolving Pole
Height over all 42″
Glass Cylinder 8x19″
Paper Cylinder 6¾x19″

No. 372
Electric Revolving Pole
Height over all 38″
Glass Cylinder 6x17″
Paper Cylinder 5¼x17″

No. 371
Electric Revolving Pole
Height over all 48″
Glass Cylinder 8x19″
Paper Cylinder 6¾x19″

Motor Built in a Motor Factory by
The World's Largest Builder

A **GENERAL ELECTRIC PRODUCT**

RAZORS, STROPS, AND HONES INTRODUCTION

In order to maintain a cache of keen razors and a professional reputation, an assortment of razor hones and strops were needed on hand by every barber who took his trade seriously.

A hone is a rectangular block of abrasive material which is harder than steel.

Clean hone with water and a pumice stone. Wipe dry, do not let drip dry (or tiny metal shavings will cling to any razors honed). Test honed razors on a moist thumbnail- if it leaves a direct, very smooth, easy cut it should be keen enough. A smooth yet forceful cut indicates a semi-sharp edge. A jagged, forceful cut shows that this dull razor needs more honing.

NATURAL HONES- Derived from natural rock deposits, usually used wet with water or lather.
  <u>Water Hone</u>- Usually imported from Germany. Comes with a small piece of slate (called the "rubber") which gives proper cutting surfaces. Comes in brown and grey, with brown being the better grade.
  <u>Belgian Hone</u>- Light yellowish rock glued to dark red slate.

SYNTHETIC HONES- Mostly made from Carborundum (silicon carbide, fused alumina, and other materials creating a abrasive, dense material.) Also referred to as "swaty hones".

COMBINATION HONES- Carborundum glued to a natural hone.

CANVAS STROPS- High quality linen or silk woven into a fine or coarse texture (fine textured linen strops are the most desirable).

COWHIDE/RUSSIAN STROPS- Durable leather strops, needs worked and worn slightly before day-to-day usage. "Russian" strops refer to those constructed of horse hide.
  <u>Ordinary</u>- Medium grade and fine grain, very smooth.
  <u>Shell/Russian Shell</u>- Taken from rump area of horse, very good yet expensive.

MAIN PARTS OF A STRAIGHT RAZOR

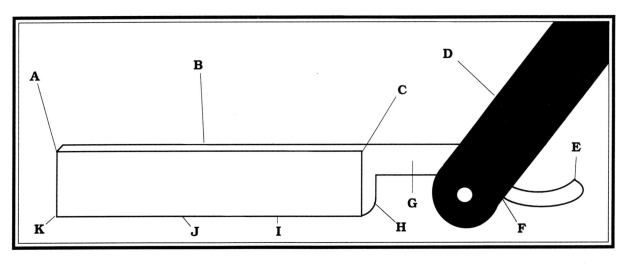

A- Head
B- Back
C- Shoulder
D- Handle
E- Tong
F- Pivot
G- Shank
H- Heel
I- Blade
J- Edge
K- Point

RAZORS

August Kern color catalog ad, depicting the different departments of razor manufacturing. Circa 1888.

RAZORS

August Kern, 1888 catalog page.

RAZORS

THE DAMASCUS RAZOR.

A very good razor and very highly spoken of by those who have used it. Imitation tortoise shell handle.

Sizes $\frac{4}{8}$, $\frac{5}{8}$ and $\frac{6}{8}$.

| Each | $1.25 | Per ½ doz | $6.50 |
| Per ¼ doz | 3.50 | Per doz | 12.00 |

THE DIAMOND STEEL RAZOR.

This is a popular brand and one that gives general satisfaction. Plain black handle.

Sizes $\frac{4}{8}$, $\frac{5}{8}$ and $\frac{6}{8}$.

| Each | $1.25 | Per ½ doz | $6.50 |
| Per ¼ doz | 3.50 | Per doz | 12.00 |

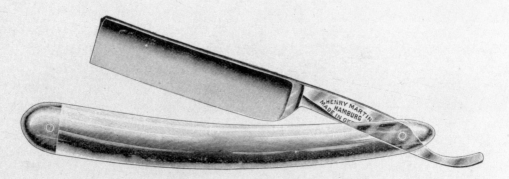

THE HENRY MARTIN RAZOR.

Almost any barber in America can tell you of the excellence of this razor. We have sold thousands of them, and as the sale increases from year to year we take it for granted they are giving satisfaction. They ought to, for they are made by expert workmen from the best material obtainable. Yellow horn handle. Sizes $\frac{4}{8}$, $\frac{5}{8}$ and $\frac{6}{8}$.

Each ....$1.25   Per ¼ doz..........$3.50   Per ½ doz..........$6.50   Per doz............$12.00

THE BESSEMER RAZOR.

One of our oldest brands and a good one. Every blade is carefully ground and finished, and the satisfaction expressed by our customers has proven that the work is conscientiously done. White bone handle. Sizes $\frac{4}{8}$, $\frac{5}{8}$ and $\frac{6}{8}$.

| Each | $1.25 | Per ½ doz | $6.50 |
| Per ¼ doz | 3.50 | Per doz | 12.00 |

THE SILVER KING RAZOR.

Never before has such a razor been offered at the price. The blade is highly finished and the file shank permits of a firm grip. The handle is black and of the best quality.

Sizes $\frac{4}{8}$, $\frac{5}{8}$ and $\frac{6}{8}$.

Each ....$1.00   Per doz $12.00

Our razors are made from the very best material obtainable, and strict attention is given to the shaping and tempering of the blades. Our concavers are experts in their line and the greatest possible care is exercised to obtain perfect results in this department. We have established a world-wide reputation for excellent concaving and we fully guarantee every razor that we quote above. If the razor you buy does not exactly suit you, send it back to us and we will cheerfully exchange it for another, if it is returned to us promptly, **free of charge and in good order.**

Loeffler & Sykes Co., 1902 catalog page.

RAZORS

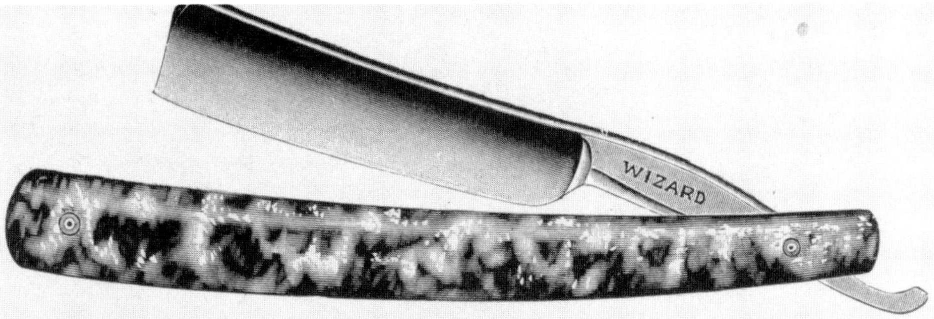

THE WIZARD RAZOR.

A general favorite with the profession. Best shell handle of very neat shape, and blade made of carefully selected steel. Sizes, $\frac{4}{8}$, $\frac{5}{8}$ and

Price, each..................................$1.50 Per dozen..$18.00

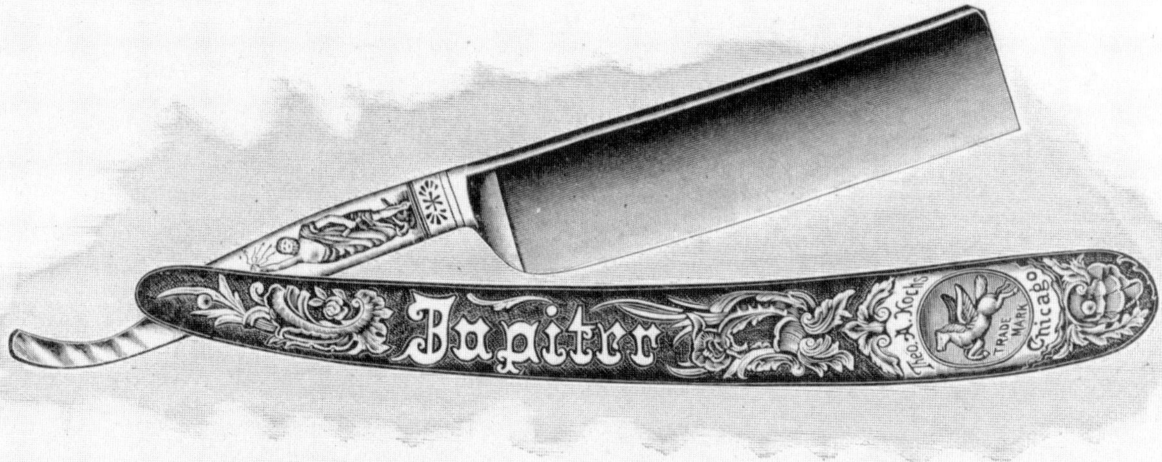

THE JUPITER RAZOR. FANCY ALUMINUM HANDLE.

The handle of this razor is made of aluminum and stamped with a beautiful design on both sides. The blade is made of the finest tool steel, and in its selection and grinding extraordinary care has been exercised. Sizes, $\frac{4}{8}$ and $\frac{5}{8}$ only.

Price, each..$2.00

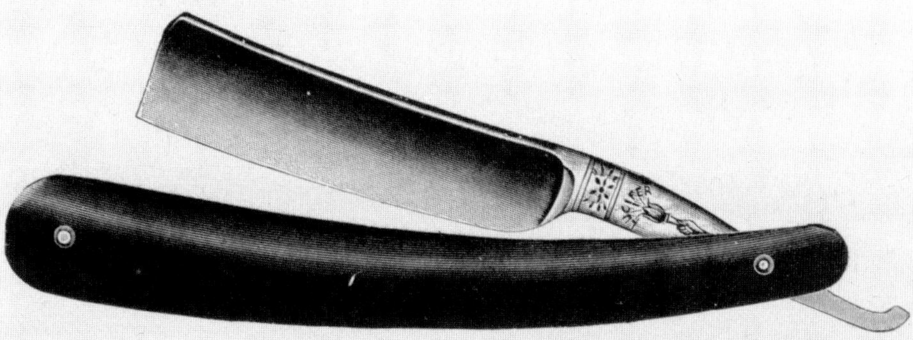

THE LUCIFER RAZOR.

Our Old Reliable brand, made of the best material obtainable and ground by only expert concavers. Best quality black handle. Sizes, $\frac{4}{8}$, $\frac{5}{8}$, $\frac{6}{8}$ and $\frac{7}{8}$.

Price, each..$1.75 Per dozen ... $21.00

Theo. A. Kochs Co., 1897 catalog page.

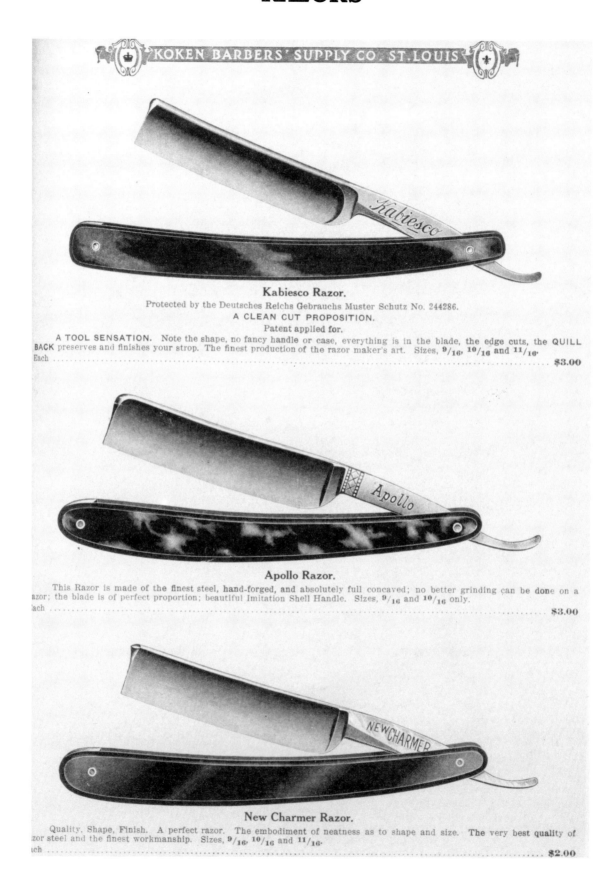

Koken Supply Co., 1910 catalog page.

RAZORS

HIBBARD, SPENCER, BARTLETT & CO'S WARRANTED.

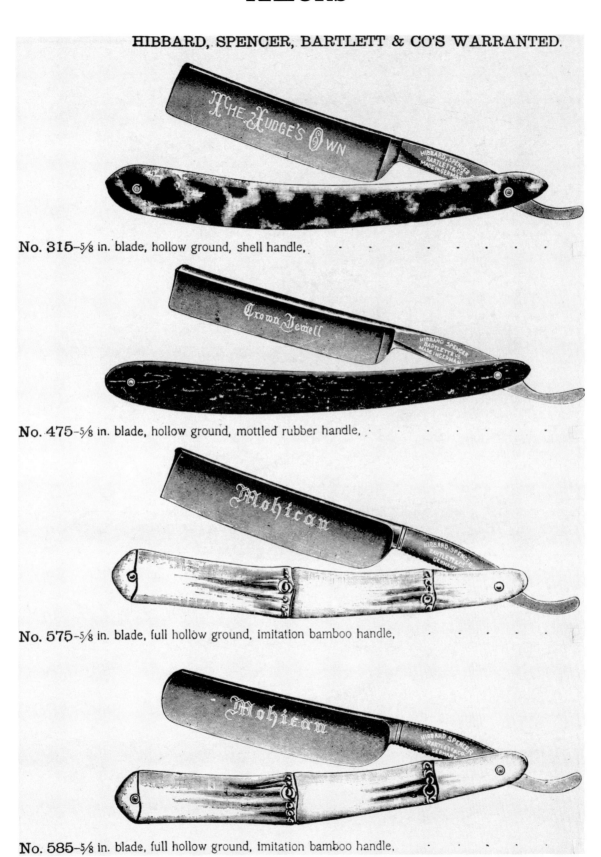

No. 315–5/8 in. blade, hollow ground, shell handle,

No. 475–5/8 in. blade, hollow ground, mottled rubber handle,

No. 575–5/8 in. blade, full hollow ground, imitation bamboo handle,

No. 585–5/8 in. blade, full hollow ground, imitation bamboo handle,

Keen Kutter Co., 1899 catalog page.

RAZORS

GEORGE WOSTENHOLM & SON'S CELEBRATED I✶XL.

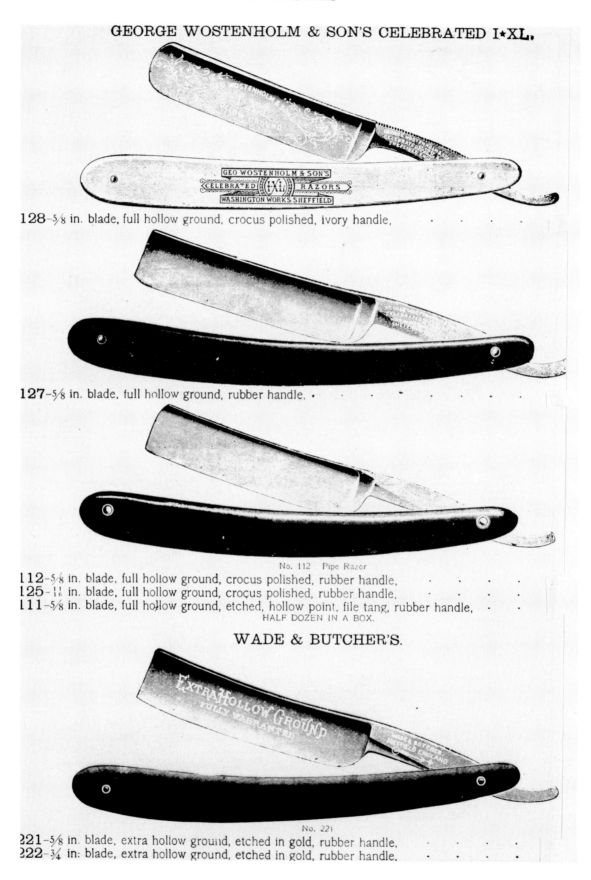

128—5/8 in. blade, full hollow ground, crocus polished, ivory handle,

127—5/8 in. blade, full hollow ground, rubber handle,

No. 112 Pipe Razor

112—5/8 in. blade, full hollow ground, crocus polished, rubber handle,
125—11/16 in. blade, full hollow ground, crocus polished, rubber handle,
111—5/8 in. blade, full hollow ground, etched, hollow point, file tang, rubber handle,
HALF DOZEN IN A BOX.

WADE & BUTCHER'S.

No. 221

221—5/8 in. blade, extra hollow ground, etched in gold, rubber handle,
222—3/4 in. blade, extra hollow ground, etched in gold, rubber handle,

Keen Kutter Co., 1899 catalog page.

RAZORS

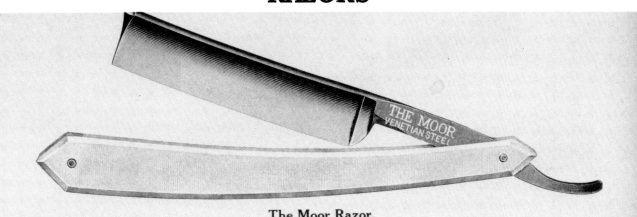

The Moor Razor.

A Razor of merit, made of selected steel, hand-forged and fine workmanship; full concaved; gun metal finished tang; white handle. Two sizes only, 9/16 and 10/16.

Each $2.00

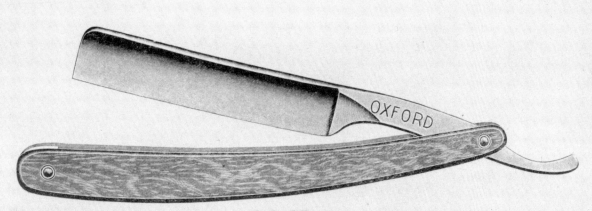

Oxford Razor.

Made of Boehler steel, recognized as the best. The tempering and grinding show expert workmanship. Has a composition handle in imitation of Circassian Walnut. Two sizes only, 9/16 and 10/16.

Each $2.00

New Congress Razor.

"Best in the World." A well ground razor; full concaved; handsomely mounted in German Silver tipped handle. Sizes 9/16, 10/16 and 11/16.

Each $2.00

Koken Supply Co., 1910 catalog page.

RAZORS

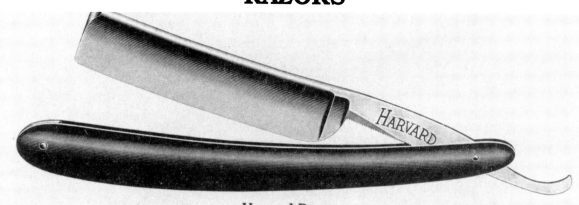

Harvard Razor.

The finest Boehler steel. There is none better than is used in this razor. Has a full hollow ground blade, set in an Oval Hard Rubber Handle. Two sizes only, $9/16$ and $10/16$.

Each $2.00

Gazelle Razor.

THAT SHORT BLADE razor; perfect temper, perfect grind and perfect shape; requires little honing, and is a noiseless shaver. Imitation Shell Handle. One size only, $10/16$.

Each $1.75

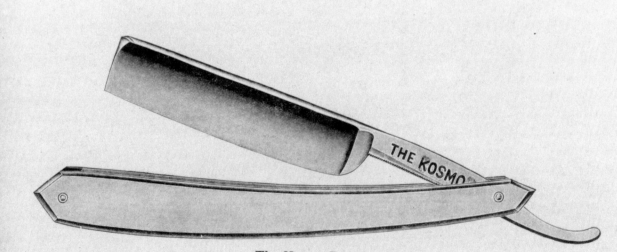

The Kosmo Razor.

This razor shows an entirely new style of grinding, is strictly full concaved, and still retains that often wanted stiff blade. Is set in White Flat Bone Handle. Two sizes only, $9/16$ and $10/16$.

Each $1.75

Koken Supply Co., 1910 catalog page.

RAZORS

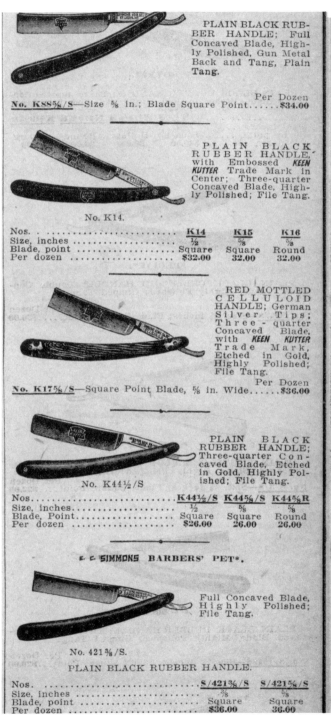

PLAIN BLACK RUBBER HANDLE; Full Concaved Blade, Highly Polished, Gun Metal Back and Tang, Plain Tang.

Per Dozen
No. K88⅝/S—Size ⅝ in.; Blade Square Point......$34.00

PLAIN BLACK RUBBER HANDLE, with Embossed KEEN KUTTER Trade Mark in Center; Three-quarter Concaved Blade, Highly Polished; File Tang.

No. K14.

Nos.	K14	K15	K16
Size, inches	½	⅝	⅝
Blade, point	Square	Square	Round
Per dozen	$32.00	32.00	32.00

RED MOTTLED CELLULOID HANDLE; German Silver Tips; Three-quarter Concaved Blade, with KEEN KUTTER Trade Mark, Etched in Gold, Highly Polished; File Tang.

Per Dozen
No. K17⅝/S—Square Point Blade, ⅝ in. Wide......$36.00

PLAIN BLACK RUBBER HANDLE; Three-quarter Concaved Blade, Etched in Gold, Highly Polished; File Tang.

No. K44½/S.

Nos.	K44½/S	K44⅝/S	K44⅝R
Size, inches	½	⅝	⅝
Blade, Point	Square	Square	Round
Per dozen	$26.00	26.00	26.00

E. C. SIMMONS BARBERS' PET*.

Full Concaved Blade, Highly Polished; File Tang.

No. 421⅜/S.

PLAIN BLACK RUBBER HANDLE.

Nos.	S/421⅜/S	S/421⅝/S
Size, inches	⅜	⅝
Blade, point	Square	Square
Per dozen	$36.00	36.00

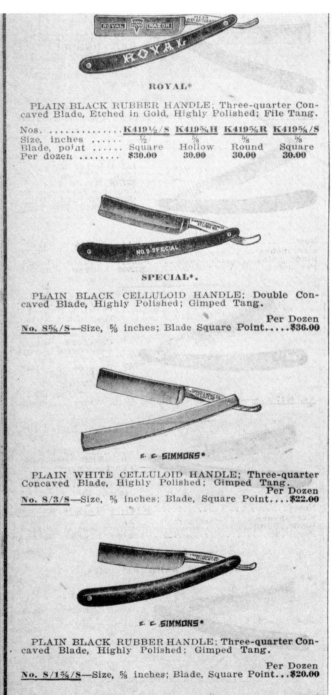

ROYAL*

PLAIN BLACK RUBBER HANDLE; Three-quarter Concaved Blade, Etched in Gold, Highly Polished; File Tang.

Nos.	K419½/S	K419⅝H	K419⅝R	K419⅝/S
Size, inches	½	⅝	⅝	⅝
Blade, point	Square	Hollow	Round	Square
Per dozen	$30.00	30.00	30.00	30.00

SPECIAL*.

PLAIN BLACK CELLULOID HANDLE; Double Concaved Blade, Highly Polished; Gimped Tang.

Per Dozen
No. 8⅝/S—Size, ⅝ inches; Blade Square Point......$36.00

PLAIN WHITE CELLULOID HANDLE; Three-quarter Concaved Blade, Highly Polished; Gimped Tang.

Per Dozen
No. 8/3/S—Size, ⅝ inches; Blade, Square Point......$22.00

PLAIN BLACK RUBBER HANDLE; Three-quarter Concaved Blade, Highly Polished; Gimped Tang.

Per Dozen
No. S/1⅝/S—Size, ⅝ inches; Blade, Square Point......$20.00

Keen Kutter Co., 1927 catalog page.

RAZORS

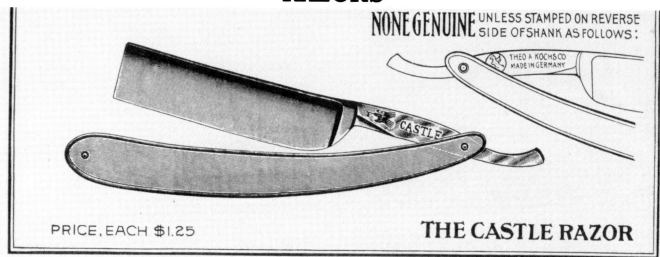

The best quality of steel is used in the manufacture of this razor. The blade is full concaved and perfectly proportioned. Fitted with a flat yellow horn handle and kept in stock in 4/8 and 5/8 sizes.

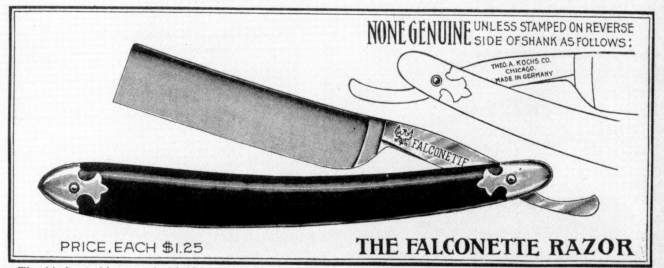

The blade of this razor is highly tempered, of neat shape and full hollow ground by expert grinders. Fitted with black handle, metal tipped. Sizes 4/8 and 5/8.

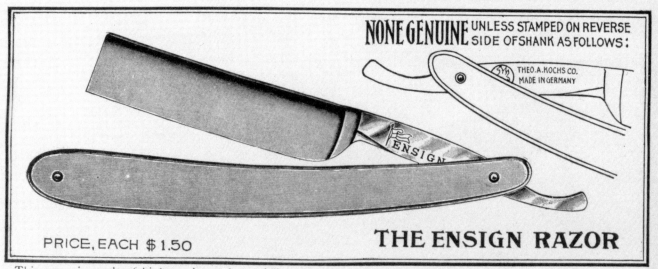

This razor is made of high-grade steel, specially selected as to its fitness for razor-making. It is full concaved and fitted with a flat white bone handle. Kept in 4/8 and 5/8 sizes only.

Theo. A. Kochs & Son Co., 1903 catalog page.

RAZORS

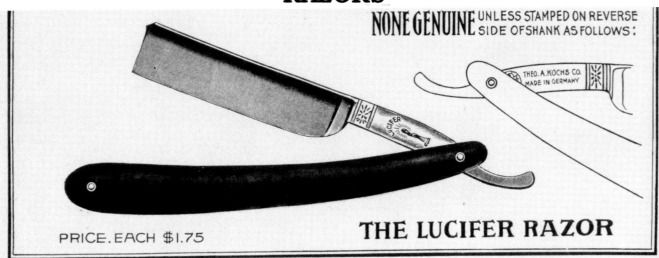

This is one of our old reliable brands and well known to barbers all over the country. The finest quality of steel is used for this razor and it is ground only by expert concavers. It is full concaved and fitted with best quality black rubber handle. Sizes, 4/8, 5/8 and 6/8.

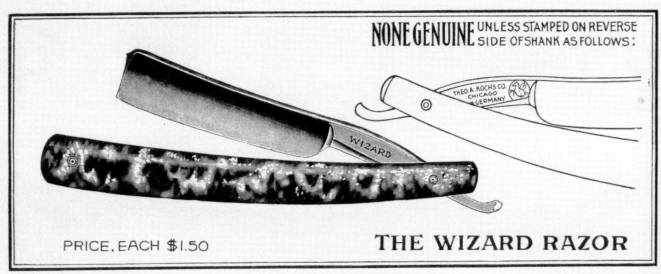

This is another favorite among the profession. The Wizard razor has been in the market for a number of years and has gained great popularity. It is made of the best steel, full concaved and fitted with mock shell handle. Sizes, 4/8, 5/8 and 6/8.

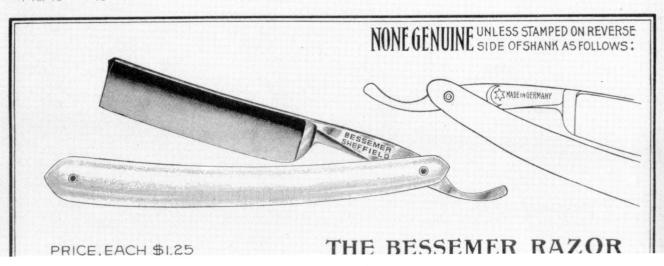

Theo. A. Kochs & Son, 1903 catalog page.

RAZORS

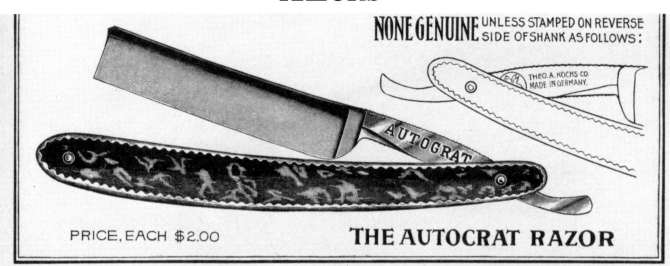

A beautiful razor, full hollow ground and finished in the most perfect manner possible. The handle is made of mock shell, lined with aluminum, and with aluminum edge. File shank on thumb side and fluted on top, allowing firm grip. Kept in 4/8 and 5/8 sizes only.

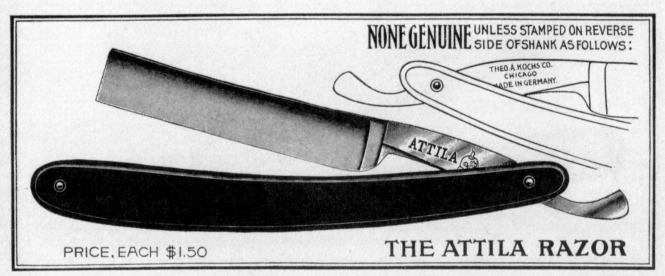

Made of the finest razor steel, full concaved and fitted with best quality flat black handle. File shank on thumb side. Kept in following sizes: 4/8, 5/8 and 6/8.

Theo. A. Kochs & Son, 1903 catalog page.

STROPS

No. 598. Turkish Brand Linen Hose. Size, 2½ x 24. The finest in canvas..Each, $1.00
No. 599. Same as No. 598. Size, 2¼ x 24................Each, .75
No. 525. Buffalo Brand, choice Shell Cordovan. Size, 2½ x 24. Will always draw...........................Each, 1.25
No. 526. Same as No. 525. Size, 2¼ x 24................Each, 1.00
No. 500. Gun Metal Shell, velvet finish back. Size, 2¼ x 24. Has fine drawing quality...................Each, $1.00
No. 501. Same as No. 500. Size, 2½ x 24................Each, 1.25
No. 542. Select, extra heavy, Eagle Russia, buff finish. Size, 2½ x 24................................Each, 1.50
No. 563. Same as No. 542, with broke in, natural finish. Size 2½ x 24................................Each, 2.00

Koken Supply Co., 1910 catalog page.

STROPS

Koken Supply Co., 1904 catalog page.

STROPS

Kolen Supply Co., 1904 catalog page.

STROPS

—1364—

RAZOR STROPS.
*KEEN KUTTER**

PROFESSIONAL COMBINATION.

Both Sides Leather; Finishing Side Mahogany Color Heavy Selected Shell Horsehide, with Red Russia Finish Back; Sharpening Side White Whale Finish Horsehide; Embossed in Gold; Heavy Nickel Plated Tip, Swivel and Snap Hanger; Length over all 24 in.; Width 2½ in.

Per Dozen
No. K94—KEEN KUTTER*; Double Swing................$52.00

PROFESSIONAL COMBINATION.

Finishing Side Mahogany Color Heavy Selected Shell Horsehide; Sharpening Side Genuine Linen Tubular Hose, Ready for use; Embossed in Gold; Heavy Nickel Plated Tip, Swivel and Snap Hanger; Length over all 24 in.; Width 2½ in.

Per Dozen
No. K25—KEEN KUTTER*; Double Swing................$54.00

PROFESSIONAL COMBINATION.

Finishing Side Oxford and Natural Suede Selected Shell Horsehide; Sharpening Side Solid Woven Linen Canvas, Ready for use; Embossed in Gold; Gilt Metal Tip, Swivel and Snap Hanger; Length over all 25 in.; Width 2½ in.

Per Dozen
No. K85—KEEN KUTTER*; Double Swing................$40.00

PROFESSIONAL COMBINATION.

Finishing Side Amber Tan Heavy Horsehide; Sharpening Side Amber Finish Solid Woven Linen Canvas, Ready for use; Heavy Nickel Plated Tip, Swivel and Snap Hanger; Length over all 25 in.; Width 2½ in.

Per Dozen
No. K82—KEEN KUTTER*; Double Swing................$34.50

Finishing Side Mahogany Color and Natural Suede Selected Shell Horsehide; Sharpening Side Brown Heavy Solid Woven Canvas; Stitched Fashioned Black Leather Handles and Tip, Embossed in Gold; Gilt Clincher Swivel; Length over all 26 in.; Width 2½ in.

Per Dozen
No. K81—KEEN KUTTER*; Double Swing................$30.00

PROFESSIONAL SINGLE.

Finishing Side Black Silk Shell Horsehide; Sharpening Side Gray Suede; Embossed in Gold; Gilt Eyelet, with Cord; Length over all 24 in.; Width 2½ in.

Per Dozen
No. K711—KEEN KUTTER*; Single Swing................$22.50

One-half Dozen in a Cardboard Box; Weight per Dozen about 6 lbs.

RAZOR STROPS.
*KEEN KUTTER**

Both Sides Leather; Finishing Side Gray Buff Finish Horsehide; Sharpening Side Black Leather, London Grain Finish; Embossed Natural Buff Stitched Fashioned Leather Handles; Nickel Plated Tip and Swivel; Length over all 24 in.; Width 2¼ in.

Per Dozen
No. K503—KEEN KUTTER*; Double Swing................$21.?

Both Sides Leather; Finishing Side Black Heavy Horsehide; Sharpening Side Maroon Color, Oil Hone, Heavy Horsehide; Stitched Leather Tips; Embossed Full Fashioned Cut-Out Handles; Black Japanned Clutch Swivel; Length over all 24 in.; Width 2¼ in.

Per Dozen
No. K67—KEEN KUTTER*; Double Swing................$25.?

Both Sides Leather; Finishing Side Maroon Color, Heavy Horsehide; Sharpening Side Black Heavy Horsehide, London Grain Finish; Full Fashioned Cut-Out Leather Handles; Heavy Black Japanned Tip and Swivel; Length over all 24 in.; Width 2¼ in.

Per Dozen
No. K80—KEEN KUTTER*; Double Swing................$25.0?

Both Sides Leather; Finishing Side Dark Oak Color, Heavy Horsehide; Sharpening Side Black Heavy Leather, London Grain Finish; Stitched Fashioned Brown Leather Handles and Tip; Embossed in Silver; Nickel Plated Army Hook Swivel; Length over all 24 in.; Width 2¼ in.

Per Dozen
No. K502—KEEN KUTTER*; Double Swing................$17.?

DOUBLE REVERSIBLE.

Finishing Side Brown Shell Horsehide; Sharpening Side Brown Solid Woven Web, Dry Hone; Stitched Leather Tips; Nickel Plated Cavalry Style Handles; Nickel Plated Reversible Swivel; Length over all 21 in.; Width 2 in.

Per Dozen
No. K5—KEEN KUTTER*; Cavalry, Double Swing........$16.0?

Finishing Side Light Tan Heavy Shell Horsehide; For Sharpening, Grain Side can be used; Stitched Fashioned Red Leather Handle and Tip, Embossed in Silver; Nickel Plated Eyelet and 6 in. Cord; Length over all 22 in.; Width 2¼ in.

Per Dozen
No. K83—KEEN KUTTER*; Single Swing................$17.0?

One-half Dozen in a Cardboard Box; Weight per Dozen about 6 lbs.

Keen Kutter Co., 1927 catalog page.

HONES

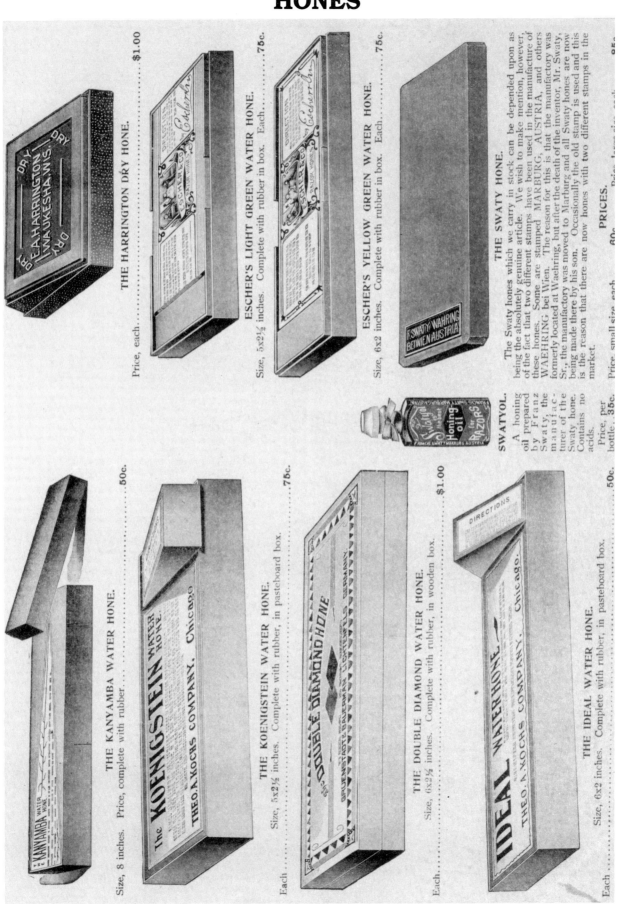

Theo. A. Kochs & Son, 1903 catalog page.

HONES

Koken's Moor.
A Black Hone equally adapted to dry and wet honing; medium fast cutter. Size, 2x3⅞ inches.

Each $0.75

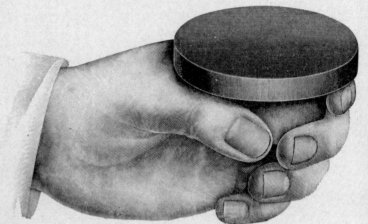

Koken's Risco.
The Round Brown Hone with a hand hold. Size, 3 inches in diameter. Has a texture that is different; rapid edge maker. Use dry or wet.

Each $1.00

Koken's Cosmos.
The White Hone of soft texture; fast cutter; a keen edge maker. Size, 2x5½ inches. Use dry or wet.

Each $0.60

Koken's Royal Blue.
The Original Blue Hone. The result of scientific hone building; it makes a soft, penetrating edge. Size 2x5½ inches. Use dry or wet.

Each $0.75

Koken Supply Co., 1910 catalog page.

Shaving Mugs

Barber Bottles

Urns & Vases

STERLING AND PLATED SHAVING SETS

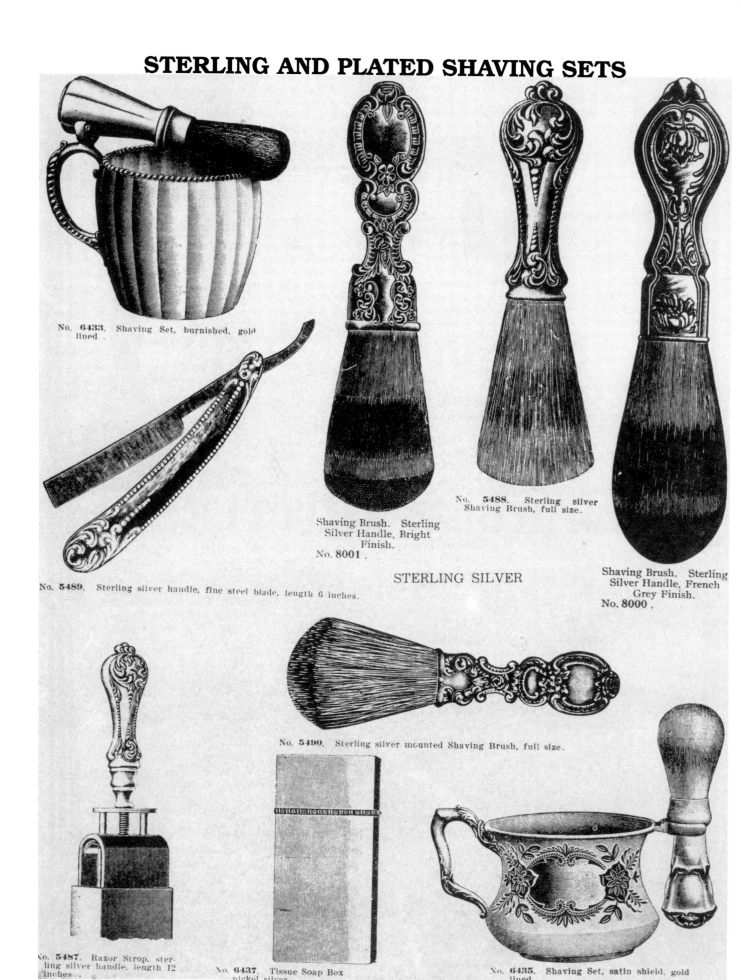

Sears Roebuck & Co., 1903 catalog page.

STERLING AND PLATED SHAVING SETS

Sears Roebuck & Co., 1903 catalog page.

Sears Roebuck & Co., 1903 catalog page.

STERLING AND PLATED SHAVING SETS

Sears Roebuck & Co., 1903 catalog page.

STERLING AND PLATED SHAVING SETS

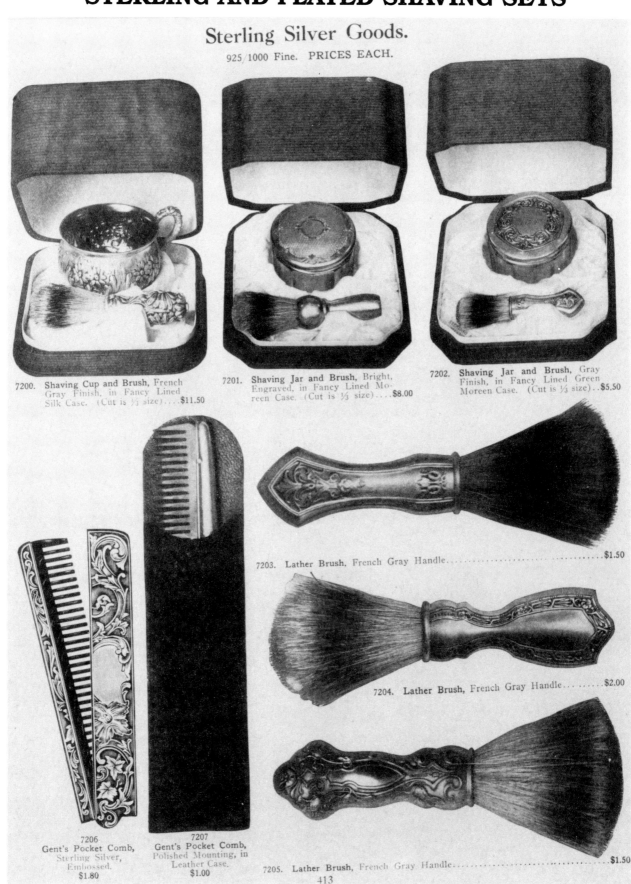

Sears Roebuck & Co., 1903 catalog page.

DECORATED SHAVING MUGS

THEO. A. KOCHS, CHICAGO.

DECORATED SHAVING MUGS.
PRICES TO BARBERS ONLY.

Prices are *Net Cash*, and not subject to any discount except on orders of $20.00 or over. Gold lettering on all mugs, unless otherwise mentioned below.

Please be careful to state in each order whether medium or large size mugs are wanted. If no size is given, medium mugs will be sent.

No.		Medium Size.	Large Size.
1	Gold stroke and bands	$0.40	$0.50
2	Gold wreath and bands	.50	.60
4	Flower decoration, blue background	.85	1.00
6	Gold wreath, blue letters with gold shading	.60	.70
7	Gold band, with flower wreath	.70	.90
8	Gold strokes and blue bands	.45	.55
10	Flower decoration on sides of name	.85	1.00
17	Monogram style, blue band at top	1.00	1.25
18	Carel mug, flower decoration with buff-colored background	.90	1.05
19	Green band at top, bouquet in center	1.00	1.15
20	Maroon foot, black letters with gold shading	.60	.85
22	Rich flower decoration and gold lace work, blue scalloped top	1.10	1.25
24	Scroll with white ribbon having black folds and red ends	.60	.70
25	Colored band and gold leaves	.75	.90
26	Tulip cups, pink ribbon, buff-colored band	.85	1.00
27	Beautiful bouquet	.75	.90
28	Buff scalloped top with gold decoration, black foot	.65	.80
29	Red, white and blue bands with gilt lines	.60	.70
30	Narrow blue band between black lines, with the scroll work at top	.90	1.05
31	Fancy gold border top, buff band bottom, scroll through name	1.00	1.15
32	Forget-me-nots at top, maroon foot	.70	.85
33	Rye flowers and ears of rye on sides of name, gold foot	.85	1.00
34	Broad pink band with bunch of pansies at top	1.00	1.15
35	Rich flower decoration, maroon background, name on white ribbon	1.10	1.25
36	Red and white clover, bright colored butterfly, and gold foot	1.10	1.25
37	Bird of bright plumage perched on a sprig of berries and leaves, extending around name	1.25	1.50
39	Blue band at top, strawberries and gold scalloped decoration	1.00	1.20
40	Antique pitcher with moss and forget-me-nots around name	.85	1.05
41	Flying bird holding gold ribbon in bill, light green background	1.10	1.30
42	Flower decorations at side of name	.50	.60
43	Name on white center framed with morning glories and leaves on pink ground	1.00	1.15
44	Name on ribbon crossing a blue diamond, buds and leaves	.65	.75
47	Rich flower and gilt decoration	.70	.80
48	Purple curtain and flowers at top, gold foot	.75	.90
49	Landscape design	.85	1.00
50	Blue ornament with flower decoration at top	.85	1.00
51	Banner on light green decorated background	.85	1.00
52	White ribbon running through fancy ornament	.90	1.05
53	Mosaic pattern, in five colors	.90	1.05
54	Antique column entwined by vines, buff-colored background	$0.40	$1.10
55	Fancy blue band at top	1.00	1.20
56	Antique vase with flowers on gold background, blue foot	1.00	1.20
57	Deep fancy border in blue and gold at top	1.00	1.20
58	Sprig of cherries and leaves	1.00	1.25
59	White ribbon decoration decorated green background	.85	1.00
60	Gold band and ivy wreath at top, gold foot	1.25	1.50
61	Hand holding a bunch of flowers, pink background	1.00	1.20
62	Fan on maroon background	1.00	1.75
63	Two birds perched on branch, light green background	.70	
64	Heavy gold bands top and bottom, with two wreaths	1.15	1.40
65	Design of frog smoking and fishing	1.00	1.25
66	Buff-colored background with fancy floral border, gold foot	1.25	1.50
67	Floral designs between blue bands	1.25	1.50
68	Light green background with gold band and floral design	1.00	1.20
69	Horse's head in horseshoe with floral design	.90	1.10
70	Bridge scene and landscape	.95	1.10
71	Blue background, fancy white band with floral decoration	1.50	1.70
72	Ocean scene showing fish, gold foot	1.25	1.45
73	Maroon band at top with floral design and landscape panel	.85	1.00
74	Black band at top with scroll and floral panels	1.25	1.50
75	Beautiful colored butterfly and fuchsias, white ribbon	.85	1.05
76	Winter Indian scene, gold foot	.50	.60
77	Bouquet of roses with white ribbon through center	1.50	1.75
78	Black and gold letters, gold decoration	.60	.70
79	Nude child sitting on a bed of flowers, fancy base	1.25	1.50
80	Character design of rabbit, with gold stripped base	.85	1.00
81	Water scene, showing water lilies, gold stripped base	.90	1.05
82	Moonlight scene, showing owl seated on branch	.85	
83	Red berries on pink background, gold band on base	1.05	1.25
84	Name on card, surrounded by flowers, with beautiful bird	.65	.80
85	Peacock feathers in beautiful colors	1.25	1.50
86	Black background, gold base and band at top	.65	.75
87	Frogs roasting on bicycles	.75	.90
88	Red band and gilt decoration	.85	1.00
89	Frogs seated on pipe smoking	.80	.95
91	Fancy scroll and flower design	.90	1.05
92	Carl on mug, with leaves decoration	.85	1.15
93	Carl design in holly berries and leaves, yellow background	1.00	1.20
94	Beautiful design of landscape and autumn leaves, gold base	.60	.70
95	Comic design	1.50	1.75
96	Black background, with flower decoration, gold base		

EXTRA CHARGES.

For monograms of two letters there will be an additional charge of $0.25
For fac-similes there will be an additional charge of .... .25
For script letters there will be an additional charge of .... .10

For monograms of three letters there will be an additional charge of $0.35
For cups and saucers we charge from 35c. to 60c. more than for mugs. according to design.

For black and gold letters on mugs not so specified, there will be an extra charge of 10 cents.

Prices for mugs quoted above are for the mugs as they are described, and extra charges will be made for any additional decoration that is wanted.

NUMBERED MUGS.

	Medium	Large
Gold Striped, per doz	$4.00	$5.00
Gold Banded, per doz	5.00	6.00
Gold Banded, per doz., with gold wreath	5.50	6.50

PLAIN MUGS.

	Medium	Large
Plain French China Mugs	$2.50	$3.00
Plain Gold Band at Top	3.50	4.00

Shown on page 270, is a descriptive price quote on Theo. A. Kochs shaving mugs. (circa. 1897)

DECORATED SHAVING MUGS

Shown on page is a descriptive price quote on Theo. A. Kochs shaving mugs. (circa. 1897)

THEO. A. KOCHS, CHICAGO.

DESIGNS FOR MUGS.

We can place upon a Shaving Mug any design, drawing or lettering desired, and from our large selection of sketches can usually fill an order for anything desired; but if we should not have the especial design wanted, we can copy it on a shaving mug, reduced in size or enlarged, if a drawing or sketch is furnished. The No. 1 Mug, large size, is the best style to use for designs. We quote below prices for some of our trade designs, and these prices are to be added to the price of the mug on which the design is placed.

Accordion	$0.50
Anchor	.50
Anvil and Hammer	.25
A. O. U. W. Emblem	.50
Architect's Emblem	.50
Arc Light	.50
Baker at Work	1.00
Baker's Emblem (two lions and pretzel)	.75
Barber Shop	1.00
Barber's Tools, (razor and shears)	.35
Base Ball and Bats	.35
Bass Violin	.50
Bear	.75
Beer Glass	.25
Beer Wagon, Horses and Driver	1.00
Bicycle	.75
Bicycle and Rider	1.00
Billiard Table, Balls and Cues	.75
Billiard Players at Table	1.25
Bill Poster Posting Bills	1.00
Bird, any kind	.50
Blacksmith Shoeing Horse	1.00
Bookbinder at Work	1.00
Boilermaker at Work	1.00
Boot and Shoe	.35
Bottle Blower at Work	1.15
Bricklayer's Emblem (trowel and square)	.35
Bricklayer at Work	1.00
Brotherhood of Railroad Trainmen	.75
Brushmaker's Store	1.00
Buggy	.75
Buggy, Two Horses and Driver	1.00
Bull's Head and Tools	.50
Butcher Shop	1.00
Butcher Killing Steer	1.00
Butcher Chopping Meat	1.00
Butcher Standing by Steer	1.00
Butcher's Emblem (knife, saw, cleaver and steel)	.25
Caboose	.75
Calf	.50
Calipers and Hammer	.60
Camera with Stand	.50
Carpenter at Work	1.00
Carpenter's Tools (saw, plane and square)	.50
Carriage	.75
China Store	1.00
Cigar	.15
Cigar Box	.50
Cigars, bunch	.35
Cigar Store	.50
Clarionet	.50
Clerk at Desk	.75
Clock	.50
Clothing Store	1.00
Coal Cart	.75
Coal Cart, Horse and Driver	1.00
Coal Miner at Work	1.00
Coal Pick and Scoop	.50
Coffin or Casket	.50
Conductor's Punch	.50
Confectionery Store	.75
Cooper at Work	1.00
Cornet	.50
Cow	.75
Cowboy Lassoing Steer	2.00
Cylinder Press	.75
Deer	.50
Deer Head	.75
Dentist Drawing Teeth	1.00
Dentist's Emblem (set of teeth)	.50
Dog	.50
Dray	.75
Dray, Two Horses and Driver	1.00
Drove of Cattle	1.00
Drug Store	.75
Druggist's Mortar and Pestle	.35
Druid Emblem	.50
Drum	.75
Dry Goods Store and Clerk	1.00
Eagle	.75
Eagle, Shield and Flags	1.00
Eagle with Two Flags	.75
Express Wagon	.50
Express Wagon, Horses and Driver	1.00
Farmer Plowing, with Two Horses	1.00
Fire Engine (steam)	1.25
Fire Engine with Two Horses	1.00
Fireman's Hat	.35
Fish	.50
Flag of any Nation	.50
Flags, Two of any Nation, Crossed	1.00
Flag, Sword and Cannon	1.00
Flour and Feed Store	1.00
Flute	.50
Forester's Emblem	.75
Freight Car	1.00
Freight Elevator	1.00
Furniture Emblem (sofa and chairs)	.75
Furniture Store	1.00
Fruit Stand	1.00
Gambrinus and Keg	1.00
Gas Fitter's Emblem	.75
Grain Elevator	1.00
Grand Army Republic Emblem	1.00
Grocery Store	1.00
Guitar	.50
Hand Car	.75
Hand and Pen	.25
Hands Clasped	.50
Hand Holding Card	.50
Hardware Store	1.00
Hare or Rabbit	.50
Harp and Shamrock	.50
Harp	.50
Harness Maker at Work	1.25
Hearse, Horses and Driver	1.00
Hod	.35
Hod Carrier at Work	1.00
Hog	.50
Hog's Head, Knife and Steel	.75
Horn	1.00
Horse	50c. to 1.00
Horse's Head	.75
Horse Shoe	1.00
Hook and Ladder Truck, Horses and Driver	1.00
Hose Cart, Horses and Driver	1.00
Ice Wagon, Horses and Driver	1.25
Incandescent Electric Lamp	.50
Iron Moulder at Work	1.25
Jockey Emblem (cap and whip)	.40
Jockey Driving Horse	1.00
Jockey Riding Horse	1.00
Jug	.35
Key-Stone (Masonic)	.25
Keg of Beer	.50
Knights of Golden Eagle Emblem	.75
Knights of Honor Emblem	.50
Knights of Labor Emblem	.50
Knights of Pythias Emblem (uniform rank)	.75
Lantern	.50
League of American Wheelmen Emblem	.75
Ledger	.50
Leopard	1.00
Letter Carrier in Uniform	.75
Livery Stable	$1.25
Locomotive and Tender	1.50
Locomotive and Cars	.35
Lumberman's Rule	.35
Lumber Yard	1.00
Lyre	.50
Machinist at Work	1.25
Mail Pouch	.50
Maltese Cross	.25
Man on Horseback	1.00
Man Shearing Sheep	1.50
Marble Cutter at Work	1.00
Masonic Emblem (square and compass)	.25
Mechanic's Emblem (hand and hammer)	.35
Milk Can	.35
Mill Stone	.60
Miller Dressing Burr	1.00
Miller's Roller	1.00
Miner's Design (two picks crossed)	.35
Moulder's Emblem	.50
Moulder at Work	1.00
Mule	.50
Ocean Steamer	1.00
Oil Derrick	2.00
Oil Derrick with Fine Scenery	1.00
Omnibus, Horses and Driver	1.00
Organ, Parlor	.50
Owl	.50
Ox	.75
Oyster	.35
Painter's Palette	.35
Paint Pot and Brush	.35
Paper Hanger at Work	1.00
Passenger Coach	.75
Passenger Elevator	1.00
Patriotic Order Sons of America Emblem	.75
Photographer at Camera	1.00
Piano or Organ	.75
Pistol or Revolver	.50
Plasterer's Trowel and Hook	.50
Plow	.50
Plumber's Emblem	.60
Policeman in Uniform	1.00
Portable Engine	1.00
Printer at Case	1.00
Printer's Stick	.25
Red Men's Emblem	.75
Restaurant	.50
Roller Skate	.75
Royal League Emblem	1.00
Saddle	.50c. to $1.00
Safety Bicycle	.75
Satchel	.50
Saloon (bartender and customers)	1.00
Saw Mill	1.00
Schooner Sailing	1.00
Scotch Thistle	.35
Sewing Machine	.75
Sheaf of Wheat	.50
Sheep or Sheep's Head	.50
Shingles, bunch	.60
Shirt and Collar	.25
Shoemaker at Work	1.25
Sign Painter at Work	1.25
Skull and Cross Bones	.35
Sportsman and Dog	1.25
Stage Coach, Four or Six Horses	1.50
Star and Crescent	.30
Stationary Engine	1.00
Steamboat	1.00
Stone Cutter at Work	1.00
Stove	.50
Street Car, Horses, Driver and Conductor	1.50
Surveyor's Transit	1.00
Switchman's Emblem	.75
Tailor at Work	1.00
Tailor's Shears	.35
Tanner's Emblem	.75
Telegraph Key	.40
Telegraph Key and Hand	.75
Telegraph Operator	1.00
Telephone	.75
Ten Pin Alley	.10
Three Links	1.25
Tinsmith at Work	.35
Tinsmith's Furnace, Iron and Shears	.75
Trunk	.50
Tug Boat	1.00
Umbrella, open	.65
U. S. Flags, crossed	.50
Violin and Bow	.50
Wagon, One or Two Horses and Driver	1.00
Watch	.70
Whisker Barrel	.50
Wind Mill	1.00
Wood Turner at Work	1.25
Yacht Sailing	1.00

DECORATED SHAVING MUGS

August Kern color catalog ad depicting the different departments of shaving mug manu. Circa 1888.

DECORATED SHAVING MUGS

August Kern, 1888 catalog page.

DECORATED SHAVING MUGS

August Kern, 1888 catalog page.

DECORATED SHAVING MUGS

August Kern, 1888 catalog page.

DECORATED SHAVING MUGS

August Kern, 1888 catalog page.

DECORATED SHAVING MUGS

August Kern, 1888 catalog page.

DECORATED SHAVING MUGS

August Kern, 1888 catalog page.

DECORATED SHAVING MUGS

August Kern, 1888 catalog page.

DECORATED SHAVING MUGS

August Kern, 1888 catalog page.

DECORATED SHAVING MUGS

August Kern, 1888 catalog page.

DECORATED SHAVING MUGS

August Kern, 1888 catalog page.

DECORATED SHAVING MUGS

No. 301

No. 321

No. 322

No. 431

No. 571

Theo. A. Kochs Co., 1897 catalog page

DECORATED SHAVING MUGS

NO. 572

NO. 592

NO. 831

Theo. A. Kochs Co., 1897 catalog page.

DECORATED SHAVING MUGS

Theo. A. Kochs Co., 1897 catalog page.

DECORATED SHAVING MUGS

Theo. A. Kochs Co., 1897 catalog page.

DECORATED SHAVING MUGS

Theo. A. Kochs Co., 1897 catalog page.

DECORATED SHAVING MUGS

Theo. A. Kochs & Son, 1898 catalog page.

DECORATED SHAVING MUGS

Theo. A. Kochs & Son, 1898 catalog page.

DECORATED SHAVING MUGS

Theo. A. Kochs & Son, 1898 catalog page.

DECORATED SHAVING MUGS

Prices quoted below are the prices to barbers only, are net cash, and are not subject to any discount, except the usual discount of 5 per cent on orders of $10.00 or over. Please be careful always to state whether medium or large mugs are wanted. If no size is given, medium sized mugs will be sent.

LIST OF MUGS WITH FANCY DECORATION.

No.		Medium.	Large.
109	Pretty flower decoration running through name	$0.50	$0.60
114	Beautiful design, in rich colors, of bird and fly and scenery	1.50	1.75
119	Name on white ribbon running through bouquet of roses	.70	.85
120	Name running through bunch of violets	.65	.80
123	Name in script in wreath of roses	.85	1.00
127	Landscape in rustic panel, with flower decoration	1.25	1.50
130	Two children seated on a wall	1.50	1.75
135	Gold decoration	.45	.55
136	Name on card in script letters	.60	.70
137	Gold scroll and decoration	.65	.75
139	Butterfly and flowers in beautiful colors, green background	1.15	1.25
140	Landscape design, with floral decoration	.90	1.00
141	Beautiful bouquet, blue background	1.25	1.35
145	Gilt scroll	.50	.60
146	Rustic scroll and gilt decoration	.55	.65
147	Neat design in red and gold; light green base	.60	.70
148	Blue band and floral decoration	.65	.75
150	Landscape panel and floral design	.75	.85
151	Floral wreath in bright colors and gilt leaves	.75	.85
152	Wide blue band at top and floral decoration	.85	.95
153	Marine scene in panel and design of daisies	.90	1.00
154	Robin's eggs and nest	1.00	1.10
155	Beautiful design, child and basket of roses	1.25	1.35
156	Daisies in bold relief on solid black background	1.50	1.60
157	Bicycle rider on country road	1.10	1.20
158	Sportsman's design, very elaborate	1.25	1.35
159	Humorous blacksmith design	1.50	1.60
160	Jockey design, showing race course	1.75	1.85
161	Beautiful flower decoration, blue background, gold base	1.10	1.20
162	Fern decoration, very neat	.45	.55
163	Gold bands at top and bottom	.40	.50
164	Wreath in red and gold around name	.40	.50
165	Birds and scenery in bright colors	.70	.80
166	Gold decoration running through name	.50	.60
167	Gold decoration	.35	.45
168	Scotch thistle and gold decoration	.35	.45
169	Beautiful decoration of scroll and drapery, gold base	.90	1.00
170	Festoons of flowers and scrolls	.65	.75
171	Grapevine wreath of green and gold, name in black letters	.60	.70
172	Beautiful flower decoration, name on scroll	.70	.80
173	Golden-rod decoration on bright red background, gold base	1.50	1.60
174	Flower decoration, gold base	.95	1.05
175	Spray of flowers, name on scroll	.60	.70
176	Beautiful drapery and basket of flowers, gold base	.85	.95
177	Field flower decoration	.65	.75
178	Hand holding card	.45	.55
179	Name on scroll with red ends, flower decoration	.55	.65
180	Name in letters of black and gold on scroll, flower decoration	.55	.65
181	Photograph mug, gold decoration	2.00	2.10
184	Name in black letters, floral decoration	.45	.55
185	Flower decoration on black panel	.85	.95
193	Tiger lily decoration, name on scroll	.65	.75
911	Gold decoration	.45	.55
912	Landscape design with floral decoration	.90	1.00
913	Beautiful bouquet, blue background	1.25	1.35
914	Blue band and floral decoration	.65	.75
917	Gold bands at top and bottom	.40	.50
918	Beautiful drapery and basket of flowers, gold base	.85	.95
919	Name in scroll across scene on palette, in beautiful colors	1.00	1.10
920	Unique decoration in brown and gold, gold base	1.10	1.20
921	Flower decorations, with name in fancy scroll	.90	1.00
922	Beautiful landscape in bright colors, gold base	1.25	1.35
923	Owl perched on tree, with moon in background	1.00	1.10
924	Panel decoration in maroon, green and gold effect, gold base	1.50	1.60
925	Butterfly and flowers, gold base	.70	.80
926	Name in black and white	.40	.50
927	Green decoration	.35	.45
928	Bunch of wild flowers	.65	.75
929	Design of horseshoe and four-leaf clover	.75	.85
930	Spray of lilies of the valley	.60	.70
931	Patriotic design of eagle perched upon the globe, red, white and blue base	1.25	1.35
932	Name in black letters in fancy panel of green and gold	.55	.65
933	Holly wreath with name in scroll	.45	.55
934	Beautiful winter scene, blue background, gold base	1.35	1.45
935	Spray of carnations	.50	.60
937	Name in black letters, floral decoration	.45	.55
938	The man in the moon	.80	.90
939	Beautiful festoon of violets, with gold decoration	.75	.85
940	Exquisite decoration of moss roses, name in black and white letters, gold base	1.50	1.60
941	Name in black letters, with neat decoration	.40	.50
942	Design of scarf pin	.45	.55
943	Spray of forget-me-nots	.50	.60
944	Floral design, name on ribbon	.60	.70
945	Name on card, with flower decoration, blue background	.65	.75
946	Flower decoration	.65	.75
947	Name in black letters on scroll, flower decoration	.70	.80
948	Bird with beautiful plumage	.75	.85
949	Water lilies	.75	.85
950	Spider and web, with flower decoration	.80	.90
951	Blue band, with scenic panel	.85	.95
952	Scroll decoration, with scenic panel, gold base	.90	1.00
953	Design of wild roses, name in black letters, gold base	1.10	1.20
954	Beautiful design of lilies on dark background, gold base	1.25	1.35
955	Exquisite decoration of apple blossoms, with name in panel, gold base	1.35	1.45
956	Unique panel decoration in blue and gold, gold handle	1.50	1.60
957	Gold decoration	.40	.50
958	Fan and bird in gold	.45	.55
959	Country scene	.50	.60
960	Decoration of daisies	.55	.65
961	Spray of apple blossoms	.60	.70
962	Sweet peas in beautiful colors	.65	.75
963	Birds in winter scene	.75	.85
964	Name on scroll, beautiful flower decoration	.75	.85
965	Colored panel decoration	.85	.95
966	Beautiful flower decoration, with gold band on base	.85	.95
967	Name in panel on floral background	.90	1.00
968	Floral panels in maroon and gold background	1.15	1.25
969	Exquisite floral decoration, gold base	1.25	1.35
970	Handsome decoration of currants and leaves, maroon base	1.35	1.45
971	Floral and scenic panels	1.50	1.60
972	Summer and winter scene in panels upon beautifully decorated background	1.75	1.85
973	Name in gold letters with scrolls (see colored pages)	.40	.50
974	Lily and leaves in gold, with name on panel (see colored pages)	.45	.55
975	Clover leaf and horseshoe (see colored pages)	.50	.60
976	Flowers in gold, green base (see colored pages)	.55	.65
977	Name in gold on fancy panel (see colored pages)	.60	.70
978	Tulips in various colors (see colored pages)	.65	.75
979	Geraniums and leaves, name on panel (see colored pages)	.70	.80
980	Red flowers with leaves (see colored pages)	.70	.80
981	Narcissus, purple base (see colored pages)	.75	.85
982	Bird on sprig (see colored pages)	.75	.85
983	Pansy decoration (see colored pages)	.80	.90
984	Blackberries and leaves (see colored pages)	.90	1.00
985	Name in white on blue background, heavy gold bands (see colored pages)	1.00	1.10
986	Morning glories (see colored pages)	1.10	1.20
987	Scene of wrecked sailing vessel, gold base (see colored pages)	1.15	1.25
988	Bouquet of flowers, black background, gold base (see colored pages)	1.25	1.35
989	Wreath of daisies on green background, name in gold on white panel (see colored pages)	1.35	1.45
990	Water scene and floral decoration (see colored pages)	1.50	1.60
991	Bouquets of flowers in white panels on purple background (see colored pages)	1.75	1.85

Please note that prices quoted above are for complete Mugs, with name and decoration.

EXTRA CHARGES.

For monograms of two letters there will be an additional charge of............20c.
For monograms of three letters there will be an additional charge of............30c.
For facsimiles there will be an additional charge of............20c.
For cups and saucers we charge from **35c.** to **60c.** more than for mugs, according to design.
For black and gold letters on mugs not so specified, there will be an extra charge of **10c.**

Prices for mugs quoted are for the mugs as they are described, and extra charges will be made for any additional decoration that is wanted.

NUMBERED MUGS.

	Medium.	Large.
Gold striped, per dozen	$3.50	$4.50
Gold banded, per dozen	4.00	5.00
Gold banded, per dozen, with gold wreath	5.00	6.00

PLAIN MUGS.

	Medium.	Large.
Plain Mugs, per dozen	$1.75	$2.50
With gold band at top, per dozen	3.00	3.50

We can make any Mug shown in other catalogues or mug sheets at the prices quoted therein.

Shown on page is a descriptive price quote on Theo. A. Kochs & Son shaving mugs. (circa 1903)

DECORATED SHAVING MUGS

No. 621

No. 973

No. 974

No. 975

Theo. A. Kochs & Son, 1903 catalog page.

DECORATED SHAVING MUGS

No. 976

No. 977

No. 978

No. 979

Theo. A. Kochs & Son, 1903 catalog page.

DECORATED SHAVING MUGS

Theo. A. Kochs & Son, 1903 catalog page.

DECORATED SHAVING MUGS

Theo. A. Kochs & Son, 1903 catalog page.

DECORATED SHAVING MUGS

Koken Supply Co., 1904 catalog page.

DECORATED SHAVING MUGS

Koken Supply Co., 1904 catalog page.

DECORATED SHAVING MUGS

749

750

751

752

753

754

Koken Supply Co., 1904 catalog page.

DECORATED SHAVING MUGS

Koken Supply Co., 1904 catalog page.

DECORATED SHAVING MUGS

Fred Bender Co., 1908 catalog page.

DECORATED SHAVING MUGS

Fred Bender Co., 1908 catalog page.

DECORATED SHAVING MUGS

Fred Bender Co., 1908 catalog page.

DECORATED SHAVING MUGS

Fred Bender Co., 1908 catalog page.

DECORATED SHAVING MUGS

209

973

203

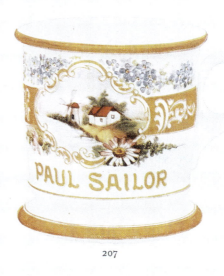

207

206

201

Fred Bender Co., 1908 catalog page.

DECORATED SHAVING MUGS

No. 757

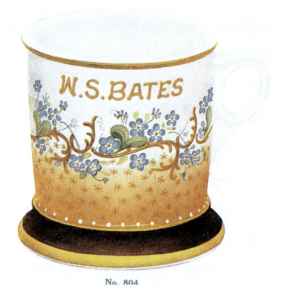

No. 804

No. 805

No. 806

No. 807

Koken Supply Co., 1910 catalog page.

DECORATED SHAVING MUGS

Koken Supply Co., 1910 catalog page.

DECORATED SHAVING MUGS

Koken Supply Co., 1910 catalog page.

DECORATED SHAVING MUGS

John Rieder & Co., 1912 catalog page.

DECORATED SHAVING MUGS

252

253

255

256

John Rieder & Co., 1912 catalog page.

DECORATED SHAVING MUGS

258

310

336

780

John Rieder & Co., 1912 catalog page.

BARBERS' BOTTLES

(PLEASE KEEP IN MIND THAT THE GLASS BOTTLES ON THE NEXT FEW PAGES ARE OF AN UNKNOWN MANUFACTURER. BECAUSE OF THIS, PRICES ARE AT THEIR LOWER DOLLAR AMOUNT.)

August Kern, 1888 catalog page

BARBERS' BOTTLES

August Kern, 1888 catalog page

BARBERS' BOTTLES

August Kern, 1888 catalog page.

BARBERS' BOTTLES

August Kern, 1888 catalog page.

BARBERS' BOTTLES

August Kern, 1888 catalog page.

BARBERS' BOTTLES

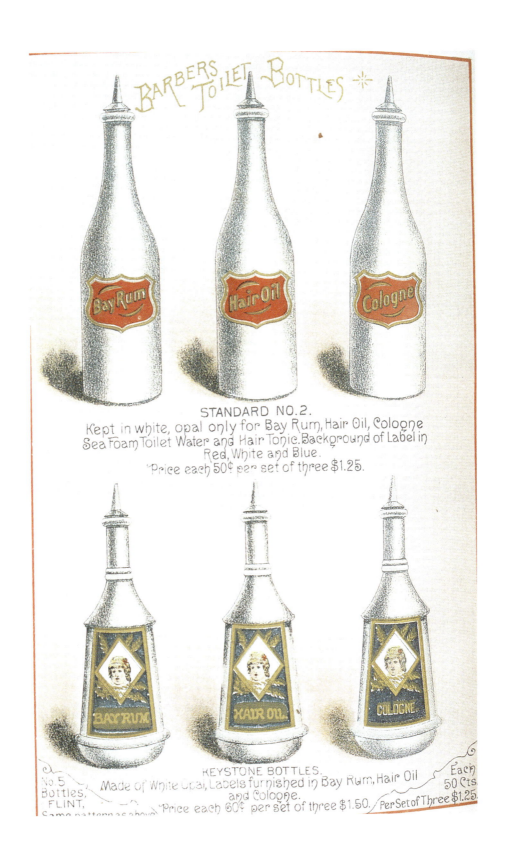

August Kern, 1888 catalog page.

BARBERS' BOTTLES

Theo. A. Kochs Co., 1891 catalog page.

Theo. A. Kochs Co., 1891 catalog page.

BARBERS' BOTTLES

THE IMPERIAL GLASSWARE.
Bohemian glassware, with decoration in gold and silver, thoroughly burned so that it cannot be effaced. Colors— Dark blue, light blue or green.

PRICES:
Bottles, each .... 60c.
Bowls, each .... 60c.
Bottles hold 13 oz., and are furnished with improved valve tubes.

GLASSWARE, No. 726
Bohemian glassware. Bottles hold 14 oz., and are furnished with valve tube. Colors—Light green, blue or purple.

PRICES:
Bottles, each .... 45c.
Bowls, each .... 45c.

Theo. A. Kochs Co., 1897 catalog page.

BARBERS' BOTTLES

Theo. A. Kochs Co., 1897 catalog page.

BARBERS' BOTTLES

BOHEMIAN GLASSWARE, No. 5.

This line of glassware is rich in gold decoration, with white flowers in bold relief. Nothing richer has ever been offered, and the general effect is highly artistic.

PRICES.

No. 5 STAND BOTTLES, holding 12 ounces, green, blue or purple, each	$0.65
No. 5 SHAVING PAPER VASE, about 7 inches high, blue color, each	1.50
No. 5 SMALL BOTTLE, for brilliantine or shampoo liquor, purple color, each	.40
No. 5 POMADE JAR, green color, each	.40
No. 5 BOWL, blue color, each	.65

Theo. A. Kochs Co., 1897 catalog page.

BARBERS' BOTTLES

Theo. A. Kochs & Son, 1898 catalog page.

BARBERS' BOTTLES

Theo. A. Kochs & Son, 1903 catalog page.

BARBERS' BOTTLES

Theo. A. Kochs & Son, 1903 catalog page.

BARBERS' BOTTLES

Theo. A. Kochs & Son, 1903 catalog page.

BARBERS' BOTTLES

325

Koken Supply Co., 1904 catalog page.

Fred Bender Co., 1908 catalog page.

BARBERS' BOTTLES

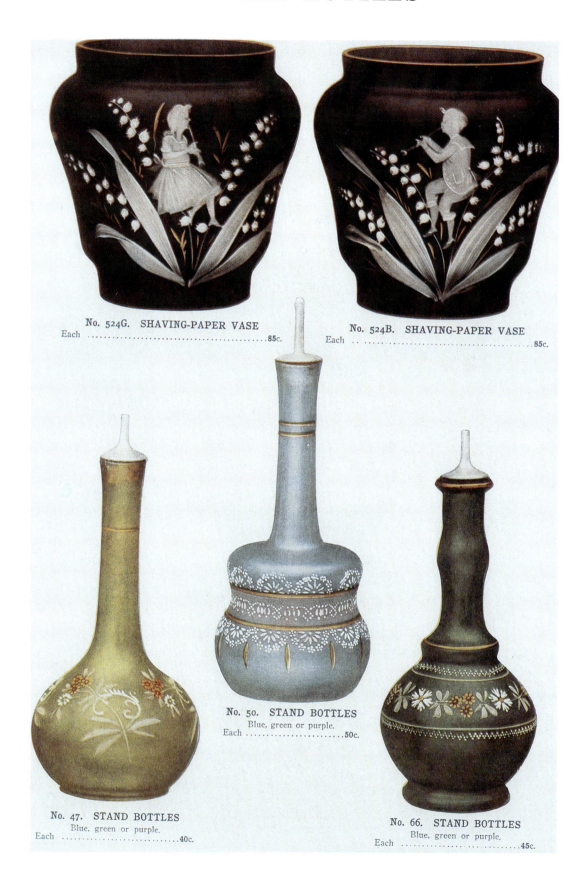

No. 524G. SHAVING-PAPER VASE
Each .... 85c.

No. 524B. SHAVING-PAPER VASE
Each .... 85c.

No. 47. STAND BOTTLES
Blue, green or purple.
Each .... 40c.

No. 50. STAND BOTTLES
Blue, green or purple.
Each .... 50c.

No. 66. STAND BOTTLES
Blue, green or purple.
Each .... 45c.

Fred Bender Co., 1908 catalog page.

BARBERS' BOTTLES

Fred Bender Co., 1908 catalog page.

BARBERS' BOTTLES

No. 19. BOHEMIAN GLASSWARE — Design Patented

This glassware is blue in color, the figures being in white enamel relief. The figure upon the bottle is different so that the contents can be distinguished.

PRICES

No. 19. Stand bottles, with tubes as shown, each	45c.
No. 19. Bowls, each	45c.
No. 19. Shaving-paper vases, 7 inches high, each	90c.

Fred Bender Co., 1908 catalog page.

BARBERS' BOTTLES

No. 17. STAND BOTTLES, Blue, Green or Purple. DESIGN PATENTED
Each .... 35c.

No. 29. STAND BOTTLES
Decorated in satin-finish gold. Blue, green or purple.
Each .... 60c.

No. 35. STAND BOTTLES
Iridescent colors. Flint, blue or amber.
Each .... 50c.

No. 20. STAND BOTTLES
Silver decorated. Blue, green or purple.
Each .... 55c.

Fred Bender Co., 1909 catalog page.

BARBERS' BOTTLES

Our Exclusive Designs

Koken Supply Co., 1910 catalog page.

BARBERS' BOTTLES

Koken Supply Co., 1910 catalog page.

BARBERS' BOTTLES

No. 20. STAND BOTTLES
Silver decorated. Blue, green or purple.
Each .... 55c.

No. 7. ANTISEPTIC VASE
For holding sterilizing liquid for razors and tools.
Each $1.00

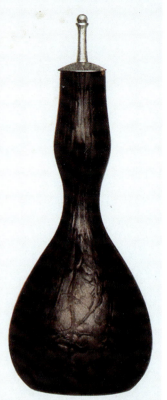

No. 35. STAND BOTTLES
Iridescent colors. Flint, blue or amber.
Each .... 50c.

No. 524. SHAVING-PAPER VASE
Each .... 85c.

No. 31. SHAVING-PAPER VASE
Each $1.10

John Rieder & Co., 1912 catalog page.

BARBERS' BOTTLES

No. 53. STAND BOTTLES, Sky-blue, Golden-luster or Eleonor-green.
Each .... 45c.

No. 61. STAND BOTTLES, Eleonor-green, Roman-gold or Sky-blue.
Each .... 65c.

John Rieder & Co., 1912 catalog page.

BARBERS' BOTTLES

No. 27. STAND BOTTLES. Purple, Green or Blue
Each .... 40c.

No. 8. BOWL
Each .... 50c.

No. 24. BOWL
Each .... 65c.

No. 8. STAND BOTTLES
Each .... 50c.

No. 24. STAND BOTTLES
Each .... 65c.

John Rieder & Co., 1912 catalog page.

COMMERCIAL BOTTLES

Theo. A. Kochs & Son, 1898 catalog page.

Theo. A Kochs & Son, 1898 catalog page.

COMMERCIAL BOTTLES

Theo. A Kochs & Son, 1898 catalog page.

Theo. A. Kochs & Son, 1898 catalog page.

COMMERCIAL BOTTLES

Theo. A Kochs & Son, 1903 catalog page.

COMMERCIAL BOTTLES

Koken Supply Co., 1904 catalog page.

Koken Supply Co., 1904 catalog page.

COMMERCIAL BOTTLES

Both pictures from Koken Supply Co., 1904 catalog.

COMMERCIAL BOTTLES

Koken Supply Co., 1910 catalog page.

COMMERCIAL BOTTLES

Koken Supply Co., 1910 catalog page.

COMMERCIAL BOTTLES

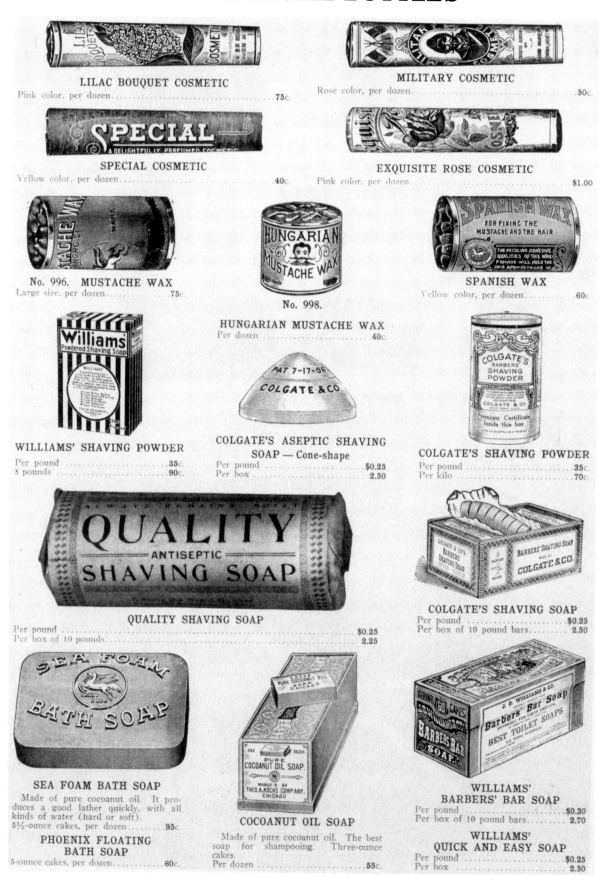

LILAC BOUQUET COSMETIC
Pink color, per dozen.................................75c.

MILITARY COSMETIC
Rose color, per dozen.................................50c.

SPECIAL COSMETIC
Yellow color, per dozen...............................40c.

EXQUISITE ROSE COSMETIC
Pink color, per dozen...............................$1.00

No. 996. MUSTACHE WAX
Large size, per dozen................................75c.

No. 998. HUNGARIAN MUSTACHE WAX
Per dozen..40c.

SPANISH WAX
Yellow color, per dozen..............................60c.

WILLIAMS' SHAVING POWDER
Per pound..35c.
3 pounds...90c.

COLGATE'S ASEPTIC SHAVING SOAP — Cone-shape
Per pound..$0.25
Per box...2.50

COLGATE'S SHAVING POWDER
Per pound..35c.
Per kilo...70c.

QUALITY SHAVING SOAP
Per pound..$0.25
Per box of 10 pounds................................2.25

COLGATE'S SHAVING SOAP
Per pound..$0.25
Per box of 10 pound bars............................2.50

SEA FOAM BATH SOAP
Made of pure cocoanut oil. It produces a good lather quickly, with all kinds of water (hard or soft).
5½-ounce cakes, per dozen............................95c.

PHOENIX FLOATING BATH SOAP
5-ounce cakes, per dozen.............................60c.

COCOANUT OIL SOAP
Made of pure cocoanut oil. The best soap for shampooing. Three-ounce cakes.
Per dozen..55c.

WILLIAMS' BARBERS' BAR SOAP
Per pound..$0.30
Per box of 10 pound bars............................2.70

WILLIAMS' QUICK AND EASY SOAP
Per pound..$0.25
Per box...2.50

John Rieder & Co., 1912 catalog page

URNS & VASES

Powder Stands

"NOBBY"
Kept in Assorted Colors price 50¢ each.

Twist Spone or Powder Bowl.
price 50¢ each
Assorted Colors.

Silvered Powder Stand.
Price. Small 50¢ each.
Med. 65¢ "
Large 75¢ "

(PLEASE KEEP IN MIND THAT THE POTTERY ON THE NEXT FEW PAGES ARE OF AN UNKNOWN MANUFACTURER. BECAUSE OF THIS, PRICES ARE AT THEIR LOWER DOLLAR AMOUNT.)

August Kern Co., 1888 catalog page.

URNS & VASES

Theo. A. Kochs & Son, 1903 catalog page.

URNS & VASES
Art Towel Urns
Our Exclusive Designs

No. 25. Height 17 inches .... Each, $2.00
  Shaving Paper Urn to match
No. 155 .... Each, .50

No. 26. Height 15 inches ..... Each, $2.50

No. 27. Height 19 inches ...... Each, $2.50
  Shaving Paper Urn to match
No. 156 .... Each, .50

No. 28. As shown. Height 16 inches
  Each $4.00
No. 38. Same Pattern. Ivory
  Each $4.00

No. 29. Height 20 inches ..... Each, $3.00
  Shaving Paper Urn to match
No. 157 .... Each, .60

No. 30. Height 16 inches ...... Each, $4.50

Koken Supply Co., 1904 catalog page.

URNS & VASES

SHAVING PAPER URNS.

No. 45.
Height, 8½ inches. Each, $1.35

No. 50.
Height, 7 inches. Each, 50c

No. 55.
Height, 9 inches. Each, 85c

COMBINED ART AND UTILITY.

No. 60.
Height, 9½ inches. Each, $1.10

No. 65.
Height, 7½ inches. Each, 75c

No. 70.
Height, 9½ inches. Each, $1.00

Koken Supply Co., 1904 catalog page.

URNS & VASES

TOWEL URNS
FINE MOTTLE UNDERGLAZED EARTHEN WARE

No. 1. Each............$4.00

No. 2. Each............$3.00

No. 3. Each............$2.25

No. 4. Each............$3.50

No. 5. Each............$3.00

Just out, Patent applied for.

No. 6. Each............$2.50

In No. 6 we show a New Feature in the construction of Towel Urns, the practicability is apparent on sight. It is far ahead of all other Urns for the purpose. We stock other designs having this feature.

Koken Supply Co., 1904 catalog page.

URNS & VASES

Koken Supply Co., 1910 catalog page.

URNS & VASES
Art Shaving Paper Urns
Our Exclusive Designs

No. 145 . . . . Each, $0.50
To Match Urn No. 26

No. 146 . . . . Each, $0.90
To Match Urn No. 38
No. 147. Ivory Blue Tint . . . . . Each, $0.90
To Match Urn No. 28

No. 148 . . . . Each, $1.25
To Match Urn No. 14
No. 158. Ivory . . . . Each, $1.25
To Match Urn No. 34

No. 149 . . . . Each, $1.25
To Match Urn No. 35

No. 150 . . . . Each, $1.50
To Match Urn No. 32

No. 151 . . . . Each, $1.25
To Match Urn No. 17

No. 152 . . . . Each, $1.10
To Match Urn No. 31

No. 153 . . . . Each, $1.00
To Match Urn No. 39

No. 154 . . . . Each, $1.50
To Match Urn No. 33

Koken Supply Co., 1910 catalog page.

URNS & VASES

No. 31. SHAVING-PAPER VASE
Each $1.10

No. 29. SHAVING-PAPER VASE
Each $1.35

No. 762. SHAVING-PAPER VASE
Each $1.50

No. 656. SHAVING-PAPER VASE
Each $2.00

Koken Supply Co., 1910 catalog page.

John Rieder & Co., 1912 catalog page.

URNS & VASES

No. 517. SHAVING-PAPER VASE
Each $1.50

No. 518. SHAVING-PAPER VASE
Each $1.25

This line of Pottery for use as Shaving-paper Vases and Towel Urns is very beautiful.

The decoration on this ware is very artistic.

Finished in dull ivory.

Attractive Shaving-paper Vases and Towel Urns add greatly to the appearance of the modern barber shop.

We recommend this ware as being particularly adapted for the purpose.

No. 512. SHAVING-PAPER VASE
Each $1.90

No. 731. TOWEL URN
Each $6.50

No. 733. TOWEL URN
Each $5.50

John Rieder & Co., 1912 catalog page.

PHOTOS AND POSTCARDS INTRODUCTION

Postcards, as well as delivering a heartfelt greeting to the recipient, have depicted every major aspect of the American lifestyle whether in the form of a photograph, painting, or sketch. Barbers and barbershops are no exception. Old photo enthusiasts and paper collectors fawn over stacks of postmarked cards and dated pictures, many of which directly or indirectly include barbershops as the subject. Therefore, as is the focus of this chapter, we investigate the realm of barbershop advertising cards, photographs, and postcards.

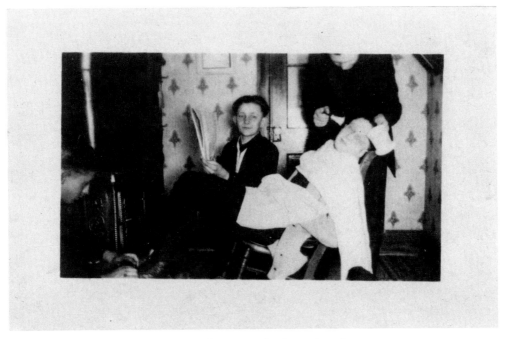

Interior photographed postcard.

Exterior photographed postcard.

ADVERTISING CARDS

Woolson Spice Co., advertising card Copyright 1894.

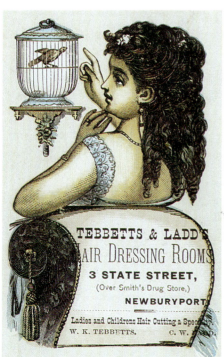

Business card for Tebbetts & Ladd's Hair Dressing Rooms (year of card unknown)

ADVERTISING CARDS

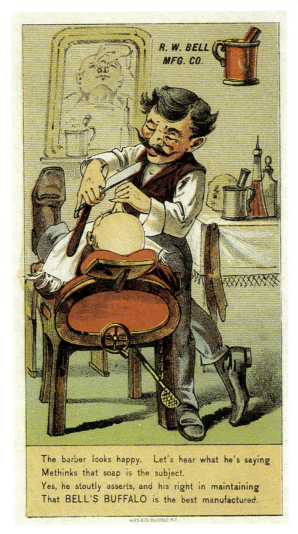

This card is from a set of 24, showing various occupations in humorous ways (Compliments of R.W. Bell Mfg. Co.)

Nursery rhyme trade card for L. Cook & Co., Rhyme on back reads as follows: Barber barber, shave a pig. How many hairs will make a wig? Four and twenty that's enough. Give the barber a pinch of snuff.

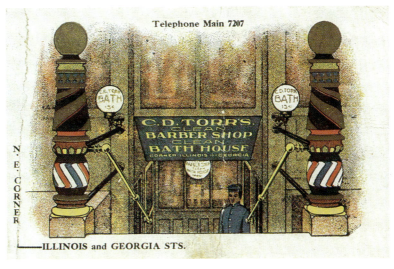

C.D. Torr's. Barber shop trade card.

ADVERTISING CARDS

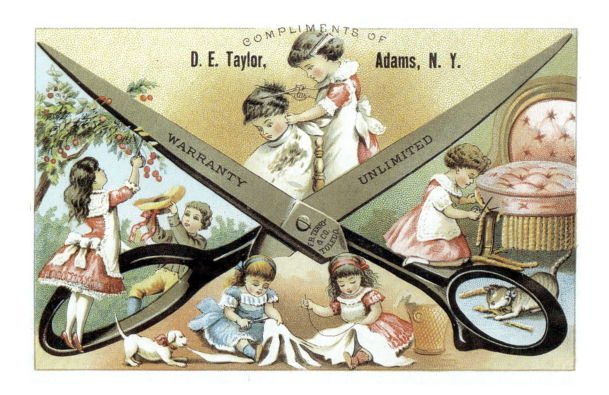

Trade card for F.B. Terry & Co. (shear advertisement)

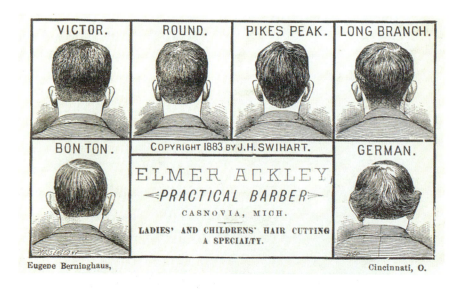

Trade card for Elmer Ackley "Practical Barber"

ADVERTISING CARDS

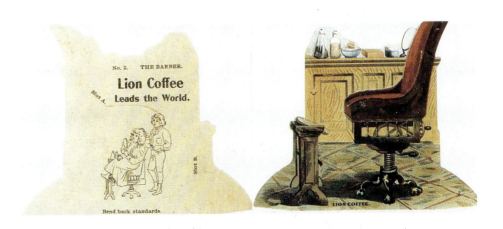

Lion Coffee - "Occupation Series" advertising cards. Each series of 16, shows lithographed prints of subjects in various occupational fields. Shown above are 3 of 4 pictures in the No. 2 "BARBER" series.

ADVERTISING CARDS

This sign, lithographed on metal, furnished free to purchasers of VEGEDERMA.
Theo. A. Kochs & Son, 1903 catalog page.

POSTCARDS

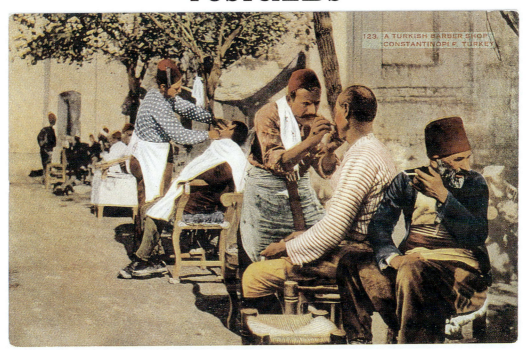

Turkish barber shop scene, details unknown.

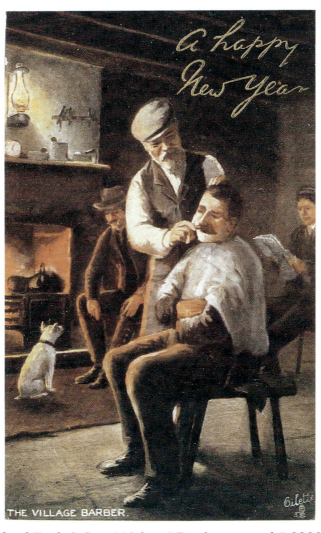

Raphael Tuck & Sons' "Oilette" Regd. post card # 9236

POSTCARDS

Busy street scene.
(Note: Barber shop and poles on left side of street)

Published by Michigan Litho. Co., Grand Rapids, Mich. and Chicago, Ill.

POSTCARDS

Interior photo of large barber shop.

Interior photo of large barber shop.

POSTCARDS

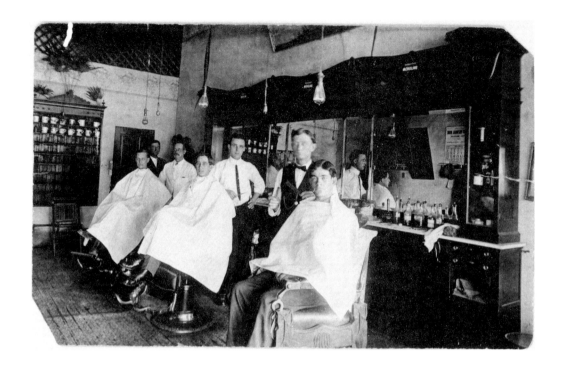

Three chaired barber shop. Location unknown.

C.P. Johnson Co., printed postcard.

POSTCARDS

Interior photo of barber shop postcard. Location unknown.

Exterior photo of barber shop postcard. Location unknown.

POSTCARDS

Enlargement of regular sized postcard. Other details unknown.

Exterior photo of barber shop postcard. Country or location unknown.

POSTCARDS

Interior photo of barber shop postcard. Location unknown

John Schultz's barber shop. Location unknown.

POSTCARDS

Calender on postcard reads: May, 1916.

Interior photo of barber shop postcard. Location unknown.

POSTCARDS

Enlargement of actual postcard.

Postcard of Lumberman getting hair cut. Location unknown.

COMICAL POSTCARDS

Barber shop valentine card.

Comical card is by Jess Meltsner. Other details unknown.

COMICAL POSTCARDS

Comical postcard is actual size. Other details unknown.

Actual size comical postcard.

COMICAL POSTCARDS

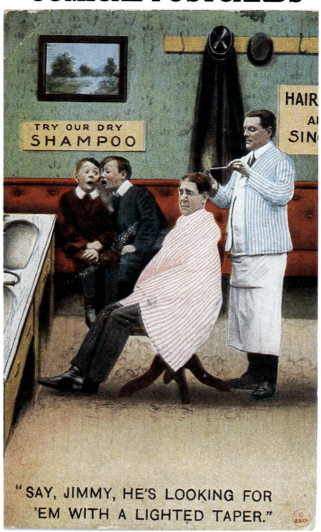

Colorized actual size postcard.

Actual size postcard. Other details unknown.

COMICAL POSTCARDS

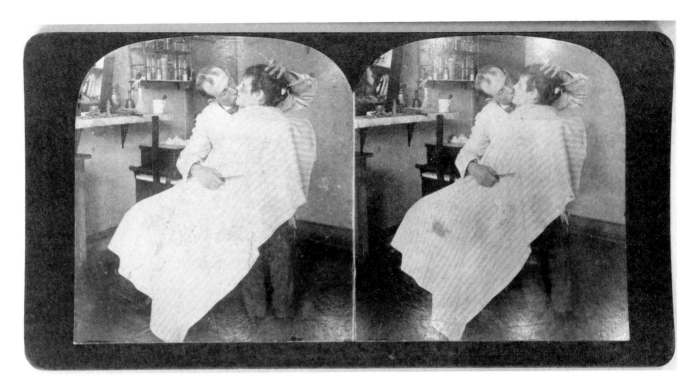

Keystone View Company manufacturers & publishers. Copyright 1897 by B.L. Singleys.
Caption under picture reads: "GETTING HER HAIR BANGED."

Caption under picture reads: "GETTING HIS HAIR BANGED."

COMICAL POSTCARDS

Actual size black & white postcard.

Color print of actual size postcard. Copyright 1909.

COMICAL POSTCARDS

Man kissing women barber color postcard. Other details of postcard unknown.

"We cut your hair while you wait?" Colorized postcard is actual size.

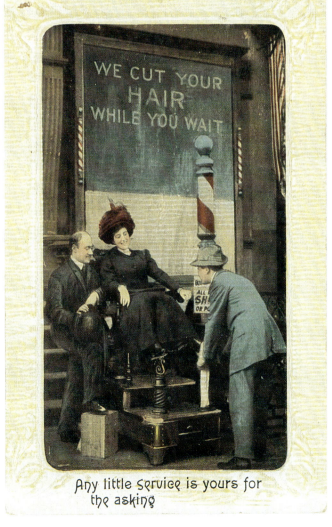

MWM© Color-Litho Postcard. Aurora, MO.

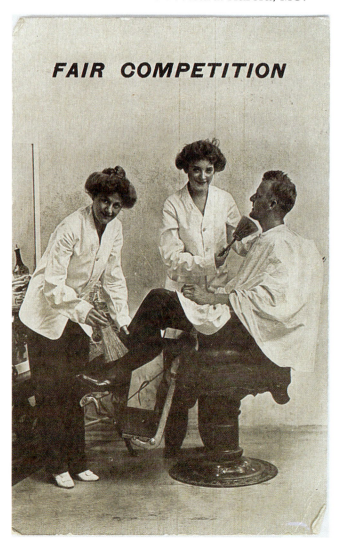

Black & White interior photo shown actual size.

COMICAL POSTCARDS

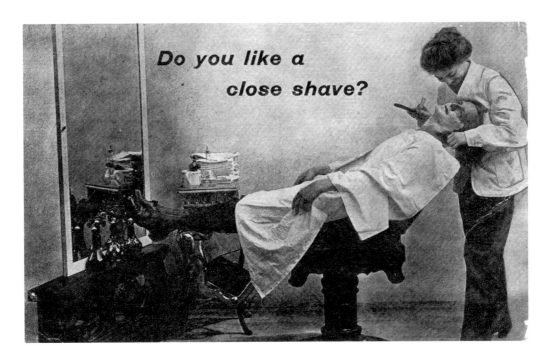

Interior photo of actual size postcard. (Circa. 1900's)

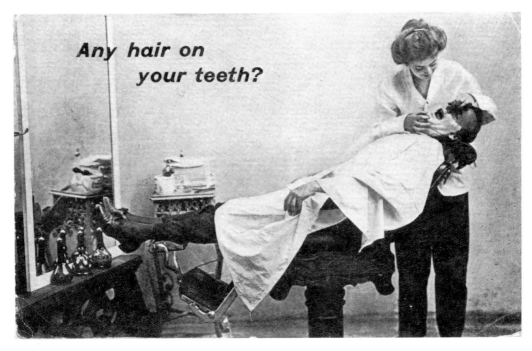

Interior photo of actual size postcard. (Circa. 1900's)

COMICAL POSTCARDS

Interior photo of actual sized postcard. (Circa. 1900's)

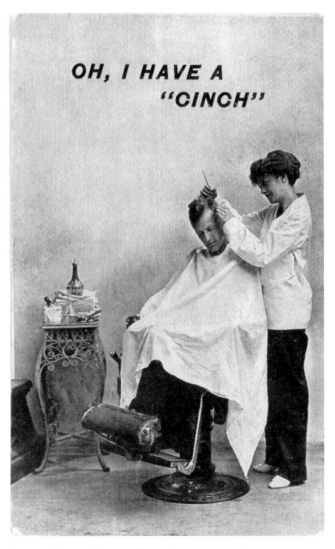

Interior photo of actual sized postcard. (Circa. 1900's)

PHOTOGRAPHS

Large interior photo of four chaired barber shop.

PHOTOGRAPHS

1928 Rosecart Building, Muncie, IN. The barber by chair No. 3 is Jake Richards.

PHOTOGRAPHS

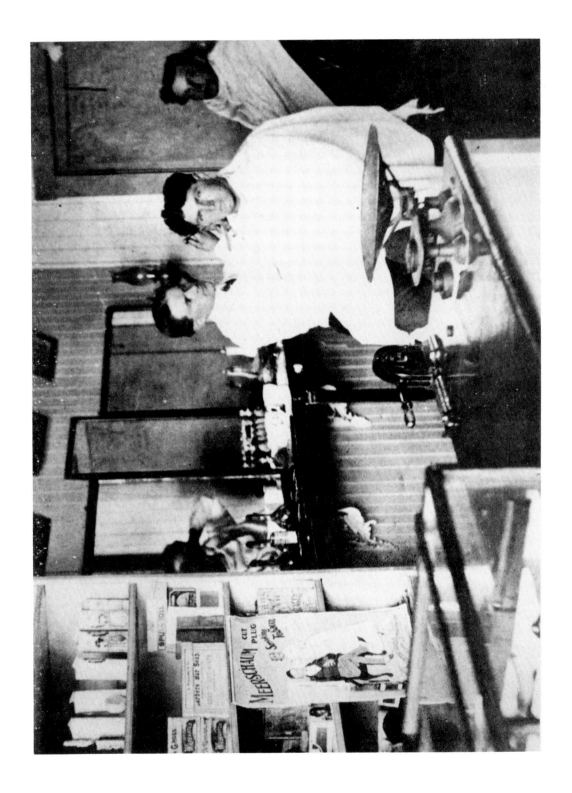

Large interior picture commonly available today.

PHOTOGRAPHS

This interior photo was taken from an early glass slide.

PHOTOGRAPHS

1912 interior photo of a barbershop.

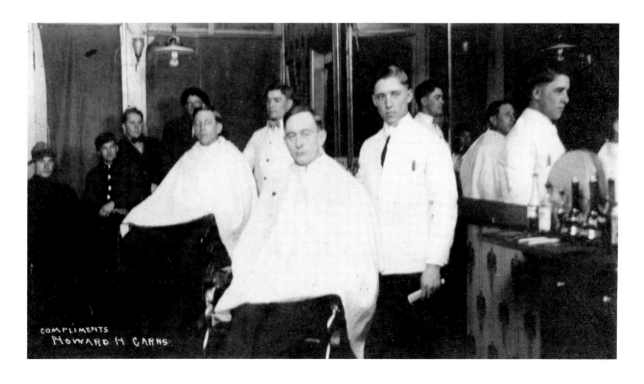

Interior photo of barber shop.

PHOTOGRAPHS

Exterior photo of Sylvester B. Buffington's barber shop in Van Buren, IN.
The person on the left is Sylvester Buffington and on the right is his son, Guy Buffington.

PHOTOGRAPHS

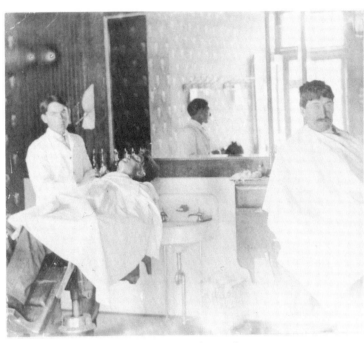
Interior barber shop photo.

Photo showing barber chair & mugs.

1922 exterior photo of some young men standing outside a barber shop in Gas City, IN.

Interior photo of man in barber chair.

385

PHOTOGRAPHS

Studio photo on cardboard.

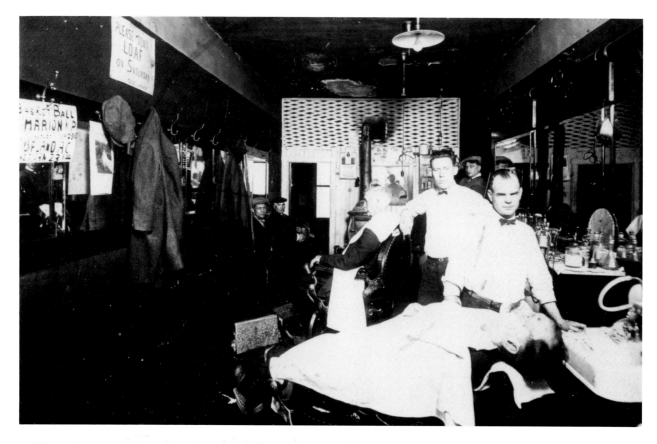

This photo was donated by Gary Felton who is barbering in Upland IN. where this photo was taken. Here are some of the names to the faces in this picture. Barber chair #1: Jerry Shafer. Barber chair #2: Al Horner. Barber #1: V.H. Trout, Barber #2: Jack Stewart, Shoe shine chair: Fred Bronio. The two men sitting against wall are unknown. (Mid 1930's)

PHOTOGRAPHS

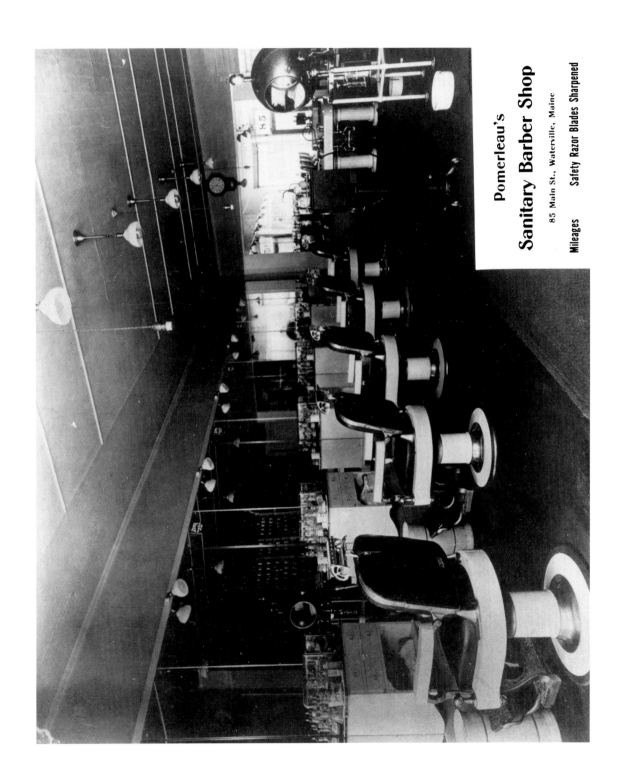

Very nice detailed photo showing various barber shop collectibles.

BARBER CATALOGS & MAGAZINES

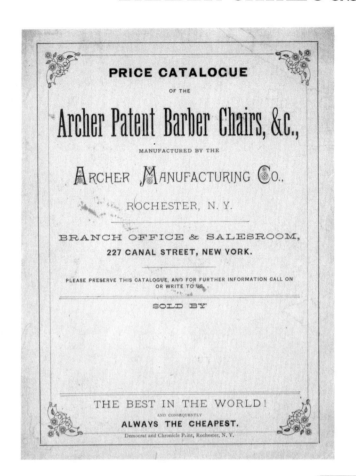

1880 catalog 6" X 8" 22 pages.

1882 catalog 6 1/4" x 7 1/2" 48 pages.

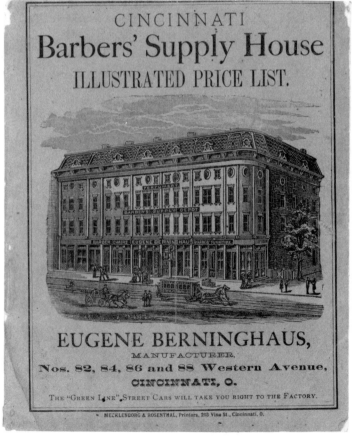

BARBER CATALOGS & MAGAZINES

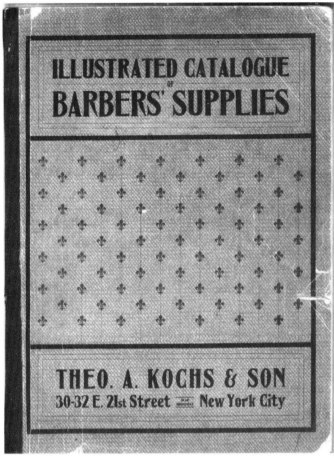

1898 catalog 9" x 12" 116 pages.

1903 catalog 8 1/2" x 11 5/8" 156 pages.

BARBER CATALOGS & MAGAZINES

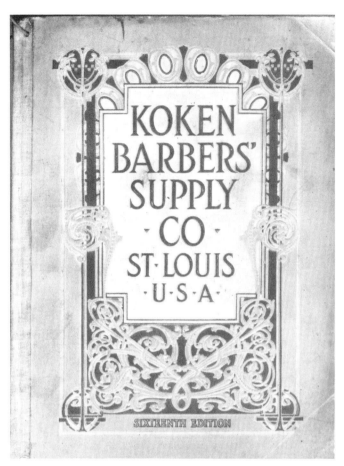

1904 catalog 9" x 12" 172 pages.

1910 catalog 9" x 12" 241 pages.

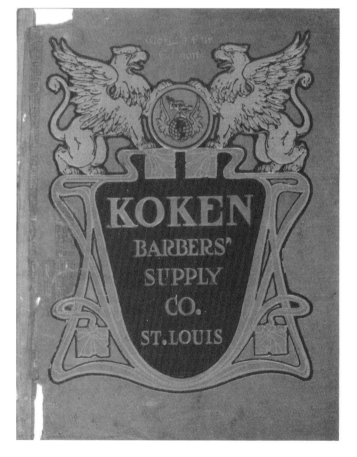

BARBER CATALOGS & MAGAZINES

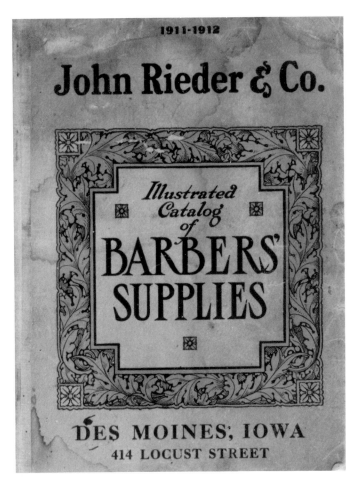

1912 catalog 9" x 12" 156 pages.

1924 catalog 8" x 10 3/4" 90 pages.

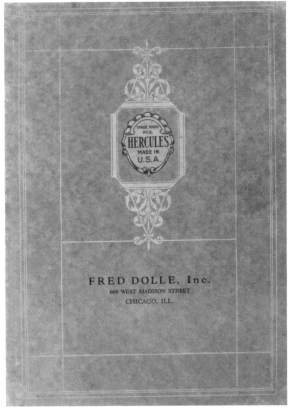

BARBER CATALOGS & MAGAZINES

1925 catalog 13" x 10 1/4" 60 pages.

1932 catalog 12" x 10" 20 pages.

BARBER CATALOGS & MAGAZINES

1936 magazine 8 1/2" x 12" 20 pages.

PRICE GUIDE

PRICING NOTE: The values of items on the next few pages are based on near mint or restored condition and should only be used as a guide. They are not intended to set prices. Auction prices as well as dealer prices vary greatly from one section of the country to another. Neither the publisher nor the contributors assume responsibility for any losses or gains that might be incurred as a result of consulting this guide.

PAGE #7: All Three Chairs Are $1500+
PAGE #8: "Garden City" Chair - $2000+
   "Keystone" Chair - $2200+
PAGE #9: "Archer's No. 2" - $2500+ "Archer's No. 3" $2000+
PAGE #10: "Archer's No. 4" - $1500+ "Archer's No. 5" $2000+
PAGE #11: "Archer's No. 6" - $1500+ "Archer's No. 7" $1500+
PAGE #12: "Archer's No. 8" - $1500+ "Archer's No. 9" $1500+
PAGE #13: "Archer's No. 10" - $2000+ "Barber chair No. 0" - $1500+ "Child's Chair" - $500+
PAGE #14: All Three Chairs Are $2000+
PAGE #15: "Novelty" - $2500+ "Lady Gay" - $2200+
PAGE #16: "Phoenix" - $2000+ "Paragon" - $2200+
PAGE #17: "Beauty" - $2000+ "Favorite" - $2200+
PAGE #18: All Three Chairs Are $2000+
PAGE #19: "Chair No. 514-B" - $750+
PAGE #20: "Chair No. 528-B" - $750+
PAGE #21: "Chair No. 560-B" - $750+
PAGE #22: "Kochs' Chair No. 21" - $2000+ "Kochs' Chair No. 36" - $2500+
PAGE #23: "Grand Prize No. 2" - $1500+
PAGE #24: "Grand Prize No. 3" - $1500+
PAGE #25: "Columbia No. 4" - $2200+
PAGE #26: "Grand Prize No. 6" - $1500+
PAGE #27: "Grand Prize No. 10" - $1500+
PAGE #28: "Columbia No. 12" - $2000+
PAGE #29: "Columbia No. 14" - $2000+
PAGE #30: "Columbia No. 15" - $2000+
PAGE #31: "Columbia No. 16" - $1500+
PAGE #32: "Columbia No. 17" - $1500+
PAGE #33: "Columbia No. 19" - $2000+
PAGE #34: "Gold Medal No. 21" - $2000+
PAGE #35: "Grand Prize No. 21" - $1500+
PAGE #36: "Gold Medal No. 23" - $1500+
PAGE #37: "Gold Medal No. 24" - $1800+
PAGE #38: "Gold Medal No. 25" - $2000+
PAGE #39: "Gold Medal No. 26" - $1500+
PAGE #40: "Gold Medal No. 27" - $1500+
PAGE #41: "Gold Medal No. 28" - $1500+
PAGE #42: "Columbia No. 34" - $1500+
PAGE #43: "Columbia No. 35" - $1500+
PAGE #44: "Columbia No. 36" - $1500+
PAGE #45: "Columbia No. 37" - $2000+
PAGE #46: "Columbia No. 47" - $1800+
PAGE #47: "Grand Prize No. 50" - $1500+
PAGE #48: "Columbia No. 53" - $1800+
PAGE #49: "Columbia No. 54" - $1800+
PAGE #50: "Columbia No. 58" - $1800+
PAGE #51: "Columbia No. 59" - $2000+
PAGE #52: "Grand Prize No. 60" - $2000+
PAGE #53: "Columbia No. 61" - $1800+
PAGE #54: "Columbia No. 62" - $1800+
PAGE #55: "Columbia No. 63" - $2000+
PAGE #56: "Columbia No. 64" - $2000+
PAGE #57: "Columbia No. 65" - $1500+
PAGE #58: "Hydraulic No. 71" - $1800+
PAGE #59: "Hydraulic No. 72" - $2000+
PAGE #60: "Hydraulic No. 73" - $1800+
PAGE #61: "Hydraulic No. 75" - $1800+
PAGE #62: "Hydraulic No. 76" - $1800+
PAGE #63: "Gold Medal No. 79" - $1500+
PAGE #64: "Grand Prize No. 80" - $2000+
PAGE #65: "Gold Medal No. 83" - $1800+
PAGE #66: "Gold Medal No. 85" - $1500+
PAGE #67: "Gold Medal No. 86" - $1800+
PAGE #68: "Gold Medal No. 87" - $1800+
PAGE #69: "Grand Prize No. 88" - $1500+
PAGE #70: "Gold Medal No. 89" - $1800+
PAGE #71: "Grand Prize No. 90" - $1500+
PAGE #72: "Hydraulic No. 92" - $2000+
PAGE #73: "Hydraulic No. 93" - $2000+
PAGE #74: "Hydraulic No. 94" - $2000+
PAGE #75: "Hydraulic No. 95" - $2200+
PAGE #76: "Hydraulic No. 97" - $2100+
PAGE #77: "Hydraulic No. 98" - $2000+
PAGE #78: "Hydraulic No. 99" - $2000+
PAGE #79: "Columbia No. 100" - $1500+
PAGE #80: "Hydraulic No. 102" - $1800+
PAGE #81: "Hydraulic No. 103" - $1500+
PAGE #82: "Columbia No. 105" - $1200+
PAGE #83: "Hydraulic No. 107" - $1500+
PAGE #84: "Hydraulic No. 108" - $1500+
PAGE #85: "Hydraulic No. 109" - $1500+
PAGE #86: "One-Lever No. 135" - $1800+
PAGE #87: "One-Lever No. 152" - $1500+
PAGE #88: "One-Lever No. 160" - $1500+
PAGE #89: "Vulcan No. 165" - $1000+
PAGE #90: "One-Lever No. 168" - $1200+
PAGE #91: "Vulcan No. 171" - $1000+
PAGE #92: "Gold Medal No. 302" - $1500+
PAGE #93: "Grand Prize No. 331" - $1800+
PAGE #94: "Gold Medal No. 340" - $1500+
PAGE #95: "Grand Prize No. 345" - $1800+
PAGE #96: "Congress No. 111" - $1200+
PAGE #97: "Congress No. 126" - $1200+
PAGE #98: "Congress No. 130" - $1500+
PAGE #99: "Congress No. 134" - $1500+
PAGE #100: "Congress No. 135" - $1500+
PAGE #101: "Congress No. 138" - $1800+
PAGE #102: "Congress No. 139" - $1800+
PAGE #103: "Congress No. 140" - $1800+
PAGE #104: "Congress No. 141" - $1500+
PAGE #105: "Congress No. 142" - $1500+
PAGE #106: "Congress No. 143" - $1500+
PAGE #107: "Congress No. 144" - $1000+

PAGE #108: "Congress No. 145" - $500+
PAGE #109: "Congress No. 146" - $1500+
PAGE #110: "Congress No. 147" -$1500+
PAGE #111: "Congress No. 149" -$1800+
PAGE #112: "Congress No. 150"- $1500+
PAGE #113: "Congress No. 151"- $1500+
PAGE #114: "Congress No. 152" - $1800+
PAGE #115: "Congress No. 157" - $1800+
PAGE #116: "Congress No. 159" - $150+
PAGE #117: "Congress No. 161" - $180+
PAGE #118: "Congress No. 164" - $100+
PAGE #119: "Congress No. 165" - $1500+
PAGE #120: "Congress No. 166" - $1500+
PAGE #121: "Congress No. 167" - $1500+
PAGE #122: "Congress No. 168" - $1500+
PAGE #123: "Congress No. 169" - $1500+
PAGE #124: "Congress No. 170" - $1500+
PAGE #125: "Congress No. 210" - $1000+
PAGE #126: "Congress No. 225" - $750+
PAGE #127: "Congress No. 250" - $750+
PAGE #128: "Congress No. 500" - $1000+
PAGE #129: "Paidar No. 319" - $750+
PAGE #130: "Paidar No. 322" - $600+
PAGE #131: "Paidar No. 409" - $750+
PAGE #132: "Paidar No. 549" - $1200+
PAGE #133: "Paidar No. 821-C. E." - $1200+
PAGE #134: "Paidar No. 822-C. E." - $1200+
PAGE #135: Both chairs on page - $1500+
PAGE #136: Both chairs on page - $1500+
PAGE #137: All chairs on page - $700+
PAGE #138: "Chrometal Model 1936" - $700+
PAGE #139: "Summer seats" - $75+ "Children's chair" $250+
PAGE #140: "Child's auto chair No. 108" - $1750+ "Child's chair No. 70" - $1000+
PAGE #141: "Child's horse chair No. 160" - $2500+ "Child's horse chair No. 107" - $2000+
PAGE #142: Both children seats No. 17 and No. 20 are - $75+ "Hair cutting chair No. 500" - $125+
PAGE #143: "Child's chair No. 2" - $200+ "Child's chair No. 466" - $125+ "Child's chair No. 9" $150+ "Child's seat No.8" - $50+ Folding chair No.1" $550+
PAGE #144: "Waiting chair No. 167" - $125+ "Stool" - $75+ "Child's chair No. 18" - $200+ Child's chair No. 17" - $150+
PAGE #145: "Chair No. 80" - $125+ "Chair No. 85" - $75+ "Chair No. 75" - $125+ "Chair No. 90" - $100+ "Chair No. 465" - $50+ "Chair No. 71" - $225+ "Stool No. 121" - $75+ "Stool No. 464" - $50+ "Stool No. 16" $75+
PAGE #146: "No. 275" - $100+ "No. 65" - $125+ "No. 1488" - $100+ "No. 1405" - $125+ "No. 41" - $100+ "No. 31" - $100+ "No. 1135" - $100+ "Foot rest No.69" $75+ "No. 15" - $55+ "No. 14" - $50+ "No. 121" - $50+ "Polishing horse" - $100+
PAGE #147: "No. 1077" - $800+ "No. 2" - $150+ "No. 1104" - $150+ "No. 1131" - $400+ "No. 1" - $850+
PAGE #148: "Mirror case No. 375" - $7500+
PAGE #149: "Mirror case No. 138" - $10000+

PAGE #150: "Mirror case No. 225" - $7500+
PAGE #151: "Mirror case No. 267" - $7500+
PAGE #152: "Case No. 429" - $800+ "Fixture No. 436" - $750+ "Rack" No. 427" - $700+ "Case No. 430" $850+
PAGE #153: "Mirror case No. 380" - $10000+
PAGE #154: "Mirror case No. 439" - $7500+
PAGE #155: "Mirror case No. 136" - $10000+
PAGE #156: "Mirror case No. 348" - $10000+
PAGE #157: "Mirror case No. 394" - $7500+
PAGE #158: "Mirror case No. 173" - $7500+
PAGE #159: "Mirror case No. 168" - $10000+
PAGE #160: "Mirror case No. 183" - $7500+
PAGE #161: "Mirror case No. 171" - $7500+
PAGE #162: "Mirror case No. 249" - $10000+
PAGE #163: "Mirror case No. 990" - $6000+
PAGE #164: "Mirror case No. 2222" - $8000+
PAGE #165: "Mirror case No. 4443" - $10000+
PAGE #166: "Mirror case No. 3650" - $7500+
PAGE #167: "Mirror case No. 1942" - $7500+
PAGE #168: "Mirror case No. 1963" - $7500+
PAGE #169: "Mirror case No. 4230" - $7500+
PAGE #170: "Mirror case No. 2942" - $7500+
PAGE #171: "Mirror case No. 3044" - $6000+
PAGE #172: "Mirror case No. 4254" - $4000+
PAGE #173: "Mirror case No. 358" - $4500+
PAGE #174: "Mirror case No. 2048" - $7500+
PAGE #175: Both lavatories on page are $300+
PAGE #176: "Washstand No. 5" - $1000+ "Washstand No. 4" - $700+ "Washstand No. 3" - $500+ "Washstand No. 6" - $300+ "Washstand No. 323" - $600+
PAGE #177: "Lavatory No. 4772 C. E. & No. 1921 C. E." are $250+ "Pedestal No.'s 4780 C. E., 4781 C. E., 4765 C. E., and 4764 C. E." are $400+
PAGE #178: All lavatories on page $300+
PAGE #179: "Fixture No. 208" - $3500+
PAGE #180: "Dressing case No. 12" - $5000+
PAGE #181: "Marble shelf" - $75+ "Shelf No. 2" - $75+ "Dressing case" - $850+ "Cup case No. 1 & 2" - $350+
PAGE #182: "Combination fixture No. 209" - $4000+
PAGE #183: "Mug case No. 635" - $1800+ "Mug case No. 644" - $2500+ "Mug case No. 638" - $1500+
PAGE #184: "Hat & coat rack No. 517" - $70+ "Costumer No. 34" - $125+ "Costumer No. 38" - $200+ "Costumer No. 40" - $100+
PAGE #185: "Hat & coat rack No. 518" - $400+ "Costumer No. 519" - $125 "Costumer No. 520" - $100+ "Costumer No. 521" - $200+
PAGE #186: "Hat & coat hook No. 27" - $50+ "Costumer No. 55" - $500+ "Hat & coat hook No. 537" - $30+ "Hat & coat hook No. 101" - $10+ "Hat & coat hook No. 389" - $3+
PAGE #187: "Shoeshine stand No. 561" - $1200+ "Shoeshine stand No. 563" - $2300+ "Shoeshine stand No. 562" - $1500+ "Shoeshine chair No. 546" - $2000+

PAGE #188: "Boot-blacking chair No. 428" - $300+ "Boot-blacking chair No. 421" - $200+ "Boot-blacking stand No. 427" - $600+

PAGE #189: "Shoeshine stand No. 538" - $200+ "Shoeshine stand No. 534" - $200+ "Shoeshine stand No. 549" - $450+ "Shoeshine stand No. 523" - 175+

PAGE #190: "Footrest No. 234" - $15+ "Handy stand" - $25+ "Anchor holder" - $40+ "Shining stand No. 493" - $55+ "Shining stand No. 501" - $75+ "Shining stand No. 501" - $75+ "Shining stand No. 550" - $60+

PAGE #191: "Footrest No. 51" - $15+ "Footrest No. 53" - $15+ "Footrest No. 55" - $20+ "Footrest No. 50" - $45+ "Footrest No. 52" - $15+ "Footrest No. 54" - $25+

PAGE #192: "Cabinet & sterilizer No. 1506" - $200+ "Sterilizer No 769" - $75+ "Manicure attachment No. 428" - $10+ "Sterilizer No. 1503" - $100+

PAGE #193: "Sterilizer No. 35" - $350+ "Sterilizer No. 37" - $500+ "Sterilizer No. 36" - $400+

PAGE #194: "Sterilizer No. 30" - $60+ "Heater & sterilizer No. 31" - $350+ "Sterilizer No. 33" - $800+ "Sterilizer No. 34" - $650+

PAGE #195: "Atomizer No. 9" - $30+ "Atomizer No. 11" - $30+ "Atomizer No. 501" - $40+ "Talcum No. 500" - $40+ "Talcum No. 401" - $25+ "Talcum No. 400" - $35+ "Talcum No. 536" - $75+

PAGE #196: "Razor sterilizer" - $35+ "Daisy sterilizer" - $80+ "Cabinet sterilizer" - $65+ "Hot-water urn" - $85+ "Vapor lamp" - $10+ "Monitor cash register" - $300+ "Gas burners" - $10+ "Copper boiler" - $75+ "Cash drawer" - $35+

PAGE #197: "Buffalo sterilizer with stand" - $750+ "Buffalo sterilizer" - $700+ "Cabinet sterilizer" - $850+

PAGE #198: "Puck atomizer" - $100+ "Oriental atomizer" - $100+ "Tetlow's pistol atomizer" - $175+ "Florence atomizer" - $25+ "Goodyear's atomizer" - $20+

PAGE #199: "Leyden enameled ware spittoon and cuspidor" - $40+ each. "Brown enameled ware spittoon" - $30+ "Brass cuspidors" - $75+ each. "Sanitary two piece" - $25+ "Cuspidor mat" - $5+ "Cuspidor with floral design" - $55+ "Flat bottom cuspidor" - $50+

PAGE #200: "Cuspidor No. 889" - $60+ "Cuspidor No. 888" - $100+ "Cuspidor No. 886" - $75+ "Cuspidor No. 891" - $35+ "Cuspidor No. 880" - $35+ "Wood fiber" - $35+ "Paper box" - $35+ "Cuspidor No. 890" - $100+ "Shaving paper holder" - $20+ "Waste baskets" $30+"

PAGE #201: "Cuspidor No. 705" - $35+ "No. 703" - $55+ "No. 702" - $55+ "No.534" - $55+ "No. 710" - $75+ "No. 708" - $80+ "No. 701" - $80+ "No. 700" - $100+ "No. 535" - $85+

PAGE #202: Everything on page is - $35+
PAGE #203: Everything on page is - $25+
PAGE #204: Everything on page is - $30+
PAGE #205: Everything on page is - $30+
PAGE #206: Everything on page is - $10+
PAGE #207: Everything on page is - $10+
PAGE #208: Everything on page is - $10+
PAGE #209: Everything on page is - $15+
PAGE #210: "Feather dusters are all - $10+ "Shoe polishers and daubers - $5+ "Whisk brooms - $15+
PAGE #211: All brushes - $25+
PAGE #212: All hand brushes are - $10+ "Rotary brush - $30+
PAGE #213: All lather brushes are - $15+
PAGE #214: All lather brushes are - $15+
PAGE #215: All horn combs are - $8+
PAGE #216: All combs are - $10+
PAGE #217: All jackets are - $80+ "Oversleeves" are - $30+
PAGE #218: All coats are - $80+
PAGE #219: All garments are - $75+
PAGE #220: All vests and coats - $75+

PAGE #222: "Pole No. 1" - $550+ "Pole No. 2" - $750+ "Pole No. 3" - $2500+ "Pole No. 4" - $2500+ "Pole No. 5" - $3000+ "Pole No. 6" - $3500+ "Pole No. 7" - $3500+ "Index hand" - $80+

PAGE #223: "Index hand No. 381" - $50+ "Sign No. 467" - $45+ "Pole No. 561" - $1500+ "Pole No. 605" - $550+ "Pole No. 562" - $2500+ "Pole No. 604" - $250+ "Pole No. 563" - $1500+

PAGE #224: "Poles No. 627 & 628" - $250+ "Pole No. 4" - $2000+ "Pole No. 5" - $2000+ "Pole No. 3" - $1500+

PAGE #225: "Bath sign No. 468" - $55+ "Index hand No. 381" - $50+ "Barber shop sign No. 636" - $200+ "Pole No. 586" - $1500+ "Pole No. 608" - $350+ "Pole No. 607" - $350+ "Pole No. 582" - $1500+

PAGE #226: "Pole No.'s 27,21, & 24" - $1700+ "Pole No. 28" - $2000+

PAGE #227: "Pole No. 31" - $1500+ "Pole No. 45" - $1000+ "Pole No. 30" - $2000+ "Pole No. 46" - $850+ "Pole No. 32" - $1500+

PAGE #228: All poles on page are - $2000+
PAGE #229: "Pole No. 29" - $250+ "Pole No. 23" - $300+ "Pole No. 22" - $350+ "Pole No. 45" - $550+ "Pole No. 37" - $2000+ "Pole No. 36" - $550+

PAGE #230: "Pole No. 50" - $1500+ "Pole No. 59" - $2000+ "Pole No. 38" - $2500+ "Pole No. 48" - $2000+ "Pole No. 51" - $1500+

PAGE #231: "Pole No. 67" - $2000+ "Pole No. 71" - $1000+ "Pole No. 69" - $1500+ "Pole No. 72" - $850+ "Pole No. 68" - $2000+

PAGE #232: All poles on page are - $1500+
PAGE #233: "Pole No. 15" - $3500+ "Pole No. 17" - $2500+ "Pole No. 8" - $3000+ "Pole No. A" - $3500+ "Pole No. 16" - $3500+

PAGE #234: "Lantern No 13" - $450+ "Tool brackets" $500+ "Bath sign" - $60+ "Eagle" - $150+ "Man head on tin sign" - $1000+

PAGE #235: "Translucent sign" - $55+ "No.S 536 & 537" - $350+ "No. 521" - $650+ "Sign No. 468" - $55+ "Index hand No. 381" - $55+ "Sign No. 469" - $100+ "Glass sign No. 450" - $80+ "Rotary sign" - $85+

PAGE #236: "No. 484" - $700+ "Pole No. 9" - $1000+ "Pole No. 14" - $900+ "Pole No. 15" - $800+ "Pole No. 12" - $500+ "Pole No. 13" - $500+ "Pole No. 5" - $600+

PAGE #237: "Corner sign No. 486" - $200+ "Sign No. 487" - $125+ "Pole No. 480" - $500+ "Globes" - $100+

PAGE #238: "Pole No. 1211" - $1000+ "Pole No. 1212" $1000+ "Pole No. 30" - $700+ "Pole No. 31" - $700+ "Pole No. 54" - $1000+

PAGE #239: "Pole No. 23" - $600+ "Pole No. 25" - $500+ "Pole No. 26" - $900+ "Sign No. 84" - $175+ "Sign No. 94" - $100+ "Sign No. 74" - $225+

PAGE #240: "Pole No. 7" - $350+ "Pole No. 10" - $1000+ "Pole No. 277" - $300+ "Pole No. 9" - $300+ "Pole No. 742" - $300+

PAGE #241: "Pole No. 376" - $1000+ "Pole No. 377" - $1000+ "Pole No. 378" - $1000+ "Pole No. 379" - $1200+

PAGE # 242: "Pole No. 371" - $1000+ "Pole No. 372" - $800+ "Pole No. 373" - $800+ "Pole No. 374" - $800+

PAGE #245: "Swift razor" - $20+

PAGE #246: "Damascus" - $30+ "Diamond" - $20+ "Henry Martin" - $20+ "Bessemer" - $20+ "Silver king" $20+

PAGE #247: "Wizard" - $40+ "Jupiter" - $60+ "Lucifer" - $30+

PAGE #248: "Kabiesco" - $25+ "Apollo" - $30+ "New charmer" - $25+

PAGE #249: "No. 315" - $40+ "No. 475" - $20+ "No. 575" - $35+ "No. 585" - $35+

PAGE #250: "No. 128" - $50+ "No. 127" - $25 "No. 112" - $20+ "No. 221" - $35+

PAGE #251: "Moor" - $35+ "Oxford" - $25+ "New congress" - $40+

PAGE #252: "Harvard" - $25+ "Gazelle" - $30+ "Kosmo" - $30+

PAGE #253: "Royal" - $40+ "Special" - $20+ "White celluloid Simmons" - $20+ "Rubber handle Simmons" $20+ "Bay state" - $20+ "No. K88" - $40+ "No. K14" $40+ "No. K17" - $40+ "No. K44" - $30+ "No. 421" - $25+ "No. 321" - $25+

PAGE #254: "Castle" - $35+ "Falconette" - $40+ "Ensign" - $35+

PAGE #255: "Lucifer" - $30+ "Wizard" - $40+ "Bessemer" - $20+

PAGE #256: "Autocrat" - $45+ "Attila" - $25+ "Monte Carlo" - $50+

PAGE #257: All strops on page are - $30+

PAGE #258: All strops on page are - $20+

PAGE #259: "No. 39" - $25+ "No. 45" - $25+ "No. 43" $20+ "No. 53" - $15+

PAGE #260: Everything on page is - $35+

PAGE #261: "Kanyamba" - $15+ "Koenigstein" - $20+ "Double Diamond" - $20+ "Ideal" - $25+ "Harrington" $15+ "Escher's light green" - $20+ "Escher's yellow green" - $20+ "Swaty" - $25+

PAGE #262: "Moor" - $30+ "Risco" - $15+ "Cosmos" - $20+ "Royal blue" - $20+

PAGE #264: "No. 6433" - $125+ "No. 5489" - $100+ "No. 8001" - $50+ "No. 5488" - $50+ "No. 8000" - $50+ "No. 5490" - $50+ "No. 5487" - $75+ "No. 6437" $50+ "No. 6435" - $125+

PAGE #265: All mug sets on page are - $50+ "Razor strop" - $20+

PAGE #266: All mug sets on page are - $55+ "Shaving stand" - $65+

PAGE #267: All mug sets on page are - $50+ "Shaving strop" - $35+ "Shaving stand" - $40+

PAGE #268: "No. 7200" - $150+ "No. 7201" - $80+ "No. 7202" - $100+ "No. 7206" - $30+ "No. 7207" - $35+ "No. 7203" - $40+ "No. 7204" - $50+ "No. 7205" $50+

PAGE #272: "No. 129" - $150+ "No. 118" - $200+ "No. 112" - $150+ "No. 115" - $225+

PAGE #273: "No. 90" - $75+ "No. 139" - $250+ "No. 123" - $75+ "No. 140" - $300+

PAGE #274: "No. 91" - $125+ "No. 132" - $300+ "No. 124" - $125+ "No. 133" - $500+

PAGE #275: "No. 145" - $300+ "No. 146" - $350+ "No. 95" - $375+ "No. 147" - $300+

PAGE #276: "No. 137" - $400+ "No. 117" - $300+ "No. 138" - $350+ "No. 136" - $400+

PAGE #277: "No. 127" - $100+ "No. 134" - $400+ "No. 126" - $75+ "No. 96" - $350+

PAGE #278: "No. 125" - $100+ "No. 141" - $350+ "No. 113" - $150+ "No. 142" - $300+

PAGE #279: "No. 143" - $300+ "No. 120" - $75+ "No. 144" - $350+ "No. 122" - $75+

PAGE #280: "No. 121" - $75+ "No. 130" - $300+ "No. 110" - $75+ "No. 131" - $450+

PAGE #281: "No. 135" - $350+ "No. 128" - $75+ "No. 116" - $250+ "No. 111" - $75+

PAGE #282: "No. 431" - $80+ "No. 322" - $100+ "No. 301" - $160+ "No. 571" - $100+ "No. 321" - $100+

PAGE #283: "No. 592" - $90+ "No. 831" - $400+ "No. 621" - $200+ "No. 652" - $70+ "No. 572" - $70+

PAGE #284: "No. 942" - $40+ "No. 941" - $40+ "No. 944" - $40+ "No. 943" - $40+ "No. 923" - $100+

PAGE #285: All on page are - $40+

PAGE #286: "No. 951" - $100+ "No. 952" - $75+ "No. 953" - $50+ "No. 954" - $40+ "No. 955" - $40+ "No. 956" - $40+

PAGE #287: "No. 911" - $40+ "No. 912" - $100+ "No. 913" - $40+ "No. 914" - $40+ "No. 915" - $40+ "No. 916" - $125+ "No. 917" - $40+ "No. 918" - $40+ "No. 919" - $100+

PAGE #288: "No. 920" - $40+ "No. 922" - $40+ "No. 921" - $40+ "No. 923" - $100+ "No. 924" - $50+ "No. 929" - $75+ "No. 931" - $100+ "No. 933" - $40+ "No. 936" - $400+

PAGE #289: "No. 937" - $40+ "No. 938" - $225+ "No. 932" - $40+ "No. 935" - $40+ "No. 926" - $40+ "No. 939" - $40+ "No. 925" - $50+ "No. 934" - $100+ "No. 940" - $50+

PAGE #291: "No. 973" - $40+ "No. 621" - $200+ "No. 975" - $40+ "No. 974" - $40+

PAGE #292: "No. 977" - $40+ "No. 976" - $40+ "No. 979" - $45+ "No. 978" - $45+

PAGE #293: "No. 986" - $40+ "No. 987" - $200+ "No. 988" - $50+ "No. 989" - $50+ "No. 990" - $100+ "No. 991" - $75+

PAGE #294: "No. 980" - $100+ "No. 981" - $75+ "No. 982" - $75+ "No. 983" - $50+ "No. 984" - $50+ "No. 985" - $50+

PAGE #295: "No. 733" - $100+ "No. 746" - $50+ "No. 737" - $40+ "No. 734" - $400+ "No. 739" - $40+

PAGE #296: "No. 672" - $100+ "No. 725" - $40+ "No. 728" - $40+ "No. 727" - $40+ "No. 730" - $40+ "No. 731" - $40+

PAGE #297: "No. 749" - $75+ "No. 750" - $75+ "No. 751" - $200+ "No. 752" - $225+ "No. 753" - $75+ "No. 754" - $125+

PAGE #298: "No. 618" - $75+ "No. 701" - $50+ "No. 676" - $300+ "No. 637" - $250+ "No. 664" - $50+ "No. 674" - $50+

PAGE #299: "No. 136" - $40+ "No. 23" - $100+ "No. 198" - $60+ "No. 156" - $60+ "No. 200" - $40+ "No. 199" - $300+

PAGE #300: "No. 204" - $75+ "No. 202" - $40+ "No. 211" - $40+ "No. 208" - $40+ "No. 213" - $50+ "No. 212" - $50+

PAGE #301: "No. 796" - $175+ "No. 755" - $250+ "No. 798" - $50+ "No. 797" - $45+ "No. 928" - $40+ "No. 799" - $275+

PAGE #302: "No. 977" - $75+ "No. 955" - $45+ "No. 983" - $40+ "No. 978" - $40+ "No. 990" - $125+ "No. 984" - $40+

PAGE #303: "No. 209" - $40+ "No. 973" - $35+ "No. 203" - $75+ "No. 207" - $75+ "No. 206" - $50+ "No. 201" - $100+

PAGE #304: "No. 806" - $40+ "No. 805" - $200+ "No. 807" - $40+ "No. 757" - $75+ "No. 804" - $45+

PAGE #305: "No. 800" - $250+ "No. 801" - $40+ "No. 773" - $40+ "No. 802" - $40+ "No. 803" - $325+ "No. 784" - $275+

PAGE #306: "No. 792" - $40+ "No. 793" - $40+ "No. 794" - $40+ "No. 763" - $40+ "No. 795" - $75+ "No. 740" - $350+

PAGE #307: "No. 214" - $40+ "No. 205" - $300+ "No. 219" - $50+ "No. 217" - $40+ "No. 220" - $300+

PAGE #308: "No. 255" - $45 "No. 256" - $45+ "No. 252" - $40+ "No. 253" - $300+

PAGE #309: "No. 310" - $400+ "No. 258" - $50+ "No. 780" - $400+ "No. 336" - $400+

PAGE #310: "3 engraved bottles" - $100+ "Celtic" - $125+ "Elson cut" - $200+ "Catalpa" - $100+

PAGE #311: All on page are - $30+

PAGE #312: All on page are - $30+

PAGE #313: All on page are - $150+

PAGE #314: All on page are - $150+

PAGE #315: "Standard No. 2 bottles" - $150+ "Keystone bottles" - $200+

PAGE #316: All on page are - $125+

PAGE #317: "Bowls" - $100+ each. "Bottles" - $125+ each.

PAGE #318: All on page are - $125+

PAGE #319: "Bowl" - $75+ "Stand bottle" - $150+ "Pomade jar" - $100+ "Small bottle" - $150+ "Stand bottle" - $150+ "Paper vase" - $400+ "Stand bottle (green)" - $150+

PAGE #320: "3 Stand bottles" - $125+ each. "Paper vase" - $450+ "Small bottle" - $100+ "Bowl" - $100+ "Pomade jar" - $75+

PAGE #321: "Bottle No.'s 591, 592, & 593" - $150+ "Bowl No. 593" - $100+ "Bottles No. 374" - $75+ each. "Bowl No. 734" - $50+

PAGE #322: Top 3 bottles - $150+ Bottom 3 bottles - $200+

PAGE #323: "No. 2" - $125+ "No.4" - $150+ "No. 3" - $125+ "No. 12" - $125+ "No. 8" - $125+ "No. 6" - $175+

PAGE #324: "No. 9 bottles" - $100+ "No. 14 bottles" - $150+

PAGE #325: "No. 240" - $250+ "No. 241" - $175+ "No. 242" - $150+ "No. 243" - $150+ "244" - $200+ "No. 245" - $150+ "No. 1 sifter" - $200+ "No. 1 bottle" - $150+ "No. 2 sifter" - $250+ "No. 2 bottle" - $150+ "No. 3 sifter" - $200+ "No. 160" - $75+ "No. 161" - $75+ "No. 50" - $75+ "No. 162" - $75+ "No. 163" - $75+

PAGE #326: All bowls - $40+ All bottles - $150+

PAGE #327: "No.'s 8, 12, & 24" - $150+ "No. 16" - $175+ "No. 785" - $350+ "No. 16" - $175+

PAGE #328: Shaving paper vases - $350+ each. "Stand bottles" - $175+ each.

PAGE #329: All three bowls are - $100+ "No. 45" - $150+ "No. 37" - $100+ "No. 7" - $200+ "No. 26" - $100+ "No. 17" - $100+ "No. 4" - $75+

PAGE #330: "Stand bottles" - $225+ "Bowl" - $300+ "Paper vase" - $400+

PAGE #331: All bottles on page - $175+

PAGE #332: "No. 241" - $125+ "No. 265" - $175+ "No. 266" - $125+ "No. 256" - $100+ "No. 170" - $60+ "No. 171" - $75+ "No. 172" - $60+ "No. 267" - $125+ "No. 268" - $150+ "No. 269" - $175+ "No. 270" - $150+

PAGE #333: "No. 271 bottles" - $175+ each. "No. 272 bottles" - $175+ each.

PAGE #334: "No. 20" - $250+ "No. 7" - $200+ "No. 35" $125+ "No. 524" - $375+ "No. 31" - $350+

PAGE #335: All bottles on page - $250+

PAGE #336: "No. 27 bottles" - $100+ each. "Bay rum & Hair tonic" - $150+ "No. 8 bowl" - $100+ "No. 24 bowl" - $100+

PAGE #337: "Florida" - $30+ "Rose" - $15+ "Mandroline" - $20+ "Talcum" - $25+ "Face" - $20+ "Cold" - $15+ "Laureline" - $25+

PAGE #338: "Egg" - $20+ "Rose in box" - $100+ "Military" - $35+ "Castle" - $20+ "Spanish" - $15+ "Athenian" - $25+ "Vegetal" - $35+ "Quinine" - $25+ "Lilac hazel" - $25+ "Toilet" - $35+ "Lavender hazel" - $25+ "Shaving soap" - $100+ full case.

PAGE #339: "Camphor" - $15+ "No. 798 talcum" - $25+ "Cold" - $15+ "Arctic cream" - $25+ "Cream la mint" - $20+ "Cream for face" - $20+ "Quinine jelly" - $20+ "Emmoline" - $20+ "Pine tar" - $20+ "Egg shampoos" - $20+ each. "Bay rum" - $25+ "No. 797 talcum" - $25+ "Pomade" - $35+ "Humoline" - $20+

"Shaving soap" - $65+ full case.

PAGE #340: All bottles on page - $35+

PAGE #341: "Lavender" - $25+ "Rosaline" - $35+ "Romero" - $30+ "Rum & Quinine" - $35+ "Violet" - $35+ "Lilac" - $35+ "Quinine" - $20+ "Shampoo liquor" - $20+

PAGE #342: "Violet" - $25+ "Heather bloom" - $35+ "Ruby quinine" - $35+ "Kobarco" - $40+ "Dandruff" - $25+

PAGE #343: All items on page. - $25+

PAGE #344: "Lilac" - $10+ "Special" - $10+ "Military" - $15+ "Exquisite" - $10+ "Mustache" - $8+ "Hungarian mustache" - $12+ "Spanish" - $10+ "Williams" - $5+ "Colgate's soap" - $5+ "Colgate's powder" - $8+ "Quality soap" - $8+ "Colgate soap in box" - $55+ full case. "Sea foam" - $5+ "Coconut" - $45+ full case. "Williams soap in box" - $45+ full case.

PAGE #345: "Nobby" - $75+ "Powder bowl" - $60+ "Powdered stand" - $100+

PAGE #346: "No. 3 jar" - $125+ "No. 3 bottle" - $200+ "No. 3 bowl" - $75+ "No. 2 bowl" - $75+ "No. 15 bowl" - $300+ "No. 785 vase" - $300+ "No. 8 bowl" - $60+ "No. 2 vase" - $200+ "No. 762" - $350+ "No. 4 bottle" - $150+ "No. 4 jar" - $125+ "No. 4 bowl" - $75+ "No. 5" - $75+ "No. 6 bowl" - $100+ "No. 6 vase" - $300+

PAGE #347: All on page are - $300+

PAGE #348: All on page are - $200+

PAGE #349: All on page are - $300+

PAGE #350: All on page are - $200+

PAGE #351: All on page are - $250+

PAGE #352: All on page are - $300+

PAGE #353: "No. 61 bowl" - $75+ "No. 53 vase" - $350+ "No. 25 bowl" - $60+ "No. 37 sifter" - $150+ "No. 26 jar" - $125+ "No. 4 jar" - $125+ "No. 17 bottle" - $150+ "No. 61 vase" - $200+ "No. 53 bowl" - $200+ "No. 25 vase" - $200+

PAGE #354: All on page are - $300+

PAGE #355: "Top picture" - $15 "Bottom picture" - $35+

PAGE #356: "Woolson Spice Co. - $10+ "Tebbetts & Ladd" - $5+

PAGE #357: "R.W. Bell" - $15+ "L. Cook & Co." - $10+ "C.D. Torr" - $40+

PAGE #358: "D.E. Taylor" - $25+ "Elmer Ackley" - $25+

PAGE #359: "Lion coffee" - $20+ per full set of four.

PAGE #360: "Vegederma" - $350+

PAGE #361: "Turkish shop" - $35+ "Happy New Year" - $35+

PAGE #362: "Market street" - $10+ "Blackstone" - $5+

PAGE #363: "George Herold" - $40+ "Hollenden" - $35+

PAGE #364: "Three chaired" - $60+ "Tri-city" - $40+

PAGE #365: "Urn/vase on counter" - $100+ "Lathered head man" - $65+

PAGE #366: "Hello Frank" - $50+ "Barber shop/electric $45+

PAGE #367: "Man reading paper in chair" - $35+ "Mortimer" - $40+

PAGE #368: "May, 1916 calender" - $85+ "Man holding razor" - $50+

PAGE #369: "Coat rack" - $70+ "Lumberman" - $40+

PAGE #370: Top card - $35+ Bottom card - $40+

PAGE #371: Top card - $10+ Bottom card - $10+

PAGE #372: Top card - $30+ Bottom card - $5+

PAGE #373: Top card - $40+ Bottom card - $30+

PAGE #374: Top card - $30+ Bottom card - $30+

PAGE #375: Top card - $20+ Bottom card - $20+

PAGE #376: Top card - $10+ Bottom card - $60+

PAGE #377: Top card - $60+ Bottom card - $60+

PAGE #378: Top card - $60+ Bottom card - $60+

PAGE #379: "4 chaired shop" - $40+

PAGE #380: "Little girl in chair" - $80+

PAGE #381: "Meerschaum cut plug tin" - $10+

PAGE #382: "Early glass slide" - $100+

PAGE #383: "Women & Man barbers" - $80+ "Compliments of Howard H. Carns" - $50+

PAGE #384: "Slyvester Buffington" - $30+

PAGE #385: "Barber chair & mugs" - $10+ "Man sitting in chair" - $40+ "Interior photo" - $70+ "1922 exterior" - $20+

PAGE #386: Both photos on page - $65+

PAGE #387: "Pomerleau's shop" - $50+

PAGE #388: "1882" - $150+ "1885" - $150+

PAGE #389: "1903" - $325+ "1899" - $350+

PAGE #390: "1905" - $325+ "1910" - $350+

PAGE #391: "1912" - $350+ "1924" - $200+

PAGE #392: "1925" - $300+ "1932" - $225+

PAGE #393: "Barber's Journal" - $5+